From Eagle to Chicken and Back

Mark P. Schowalter

Edited by
Kellene Maddox,
Debbra Manly,
and Jeannie Douglas

authorHOUSE®

AuthorHouse™
1663 Liberty Drive, Suite 200
Bloomington, IN 47403
www.authorhouse.com
Phone: 1-800-839-8640

This book is a work of non-fiction. Unless otherwise noted, the author and the publisher make no explicit guarantees as to the accuracy of the information contained in this book and in some cases, names of people and places have been altered to protect their privacy.

First published by AuthorHouse   2/18/2008

ISBN: 978-1-4259-6151-0 (sc)

Printed in the United States of America
Bloomington, Indiana

This book is printed on acid-free paper.

FORWARD:
"EAGLES IN A STORM"

Did you know that an eagle knows when a storm is approaching long before it breaks? The eagle will fly to some high spot and wait for the winds to come. When the storm hits, it sets its wings so that the wind will pick it up and lift it above the storm. While the storm rages below, the eagle is soaring above it. The eagle does not escape the storm. It simply uses the storm to lift it higher. It rises on the winds that bring the storm.

When the storms of life come upon us, and all of us will experience them, we can rise above them by setting our minds and our belief toward God. The storms do not have to overcome us. We can allow God's power to lift us above them. God enables us to ride the winds of the storm that bring sickness, tragedy, failure and disappointment in our lives. We can soar above the storm. Remember, it is not the burdens of life that weigh us down; it is how we handle them. The Bible says, "Those who hope in the Lord will renew their strength. They will soar on wings like eagles." (Isaiah 40:31)

Simply say a small prayer for the person who told you about this book, then tell someone else about it. Then sit back and watch the power of God work in your life for doing the thing that you know He loves.

ACKNOWLEDGEMENTS

God gives each person the ability to choose how we experience life. We can either begin each day by saying "good morning Lord" or "good Lord, its morning". It took a near drowning experience along with several other life changing events for me to realize the fullness of God's grace that brings goodness into my life. For that I give thanks to God and for the opportunity to write this book.

There are many deserving of thanks and appreciation for their help in writing, collecting, proofing, and publishing this book. I begin by dedicating the publication of this book to my loving wife Sue. She has been my inspiration, encouragement, and strength to get it accomplished. Without her support and sacrifice I believe it would have never happened. Close behind my wife are my parents George and Joyce along with my four siblings LouAnn, Karen, John, and Joel and their families. They have been inspirational, encouraging, and supportive.

I owe much to the following friends who have been very instrumental and inspirational to the publication of this collection. My thanks go out to Kellene, Debbra, and Jeannie for their dedicated work and time spent at proofing and being honest with me about this publication. Several others including Barb, Jeannie, Phyllis, Ellen, and Eileen who have laughed and cried with me, shared constructive advice, and who have been critical in helping me to write in such a way to truly communicate my thoughts and feelings. My son Jason and good friend Jeff have lent their artistic talents in drawing and sketching the illustrations while John helped in making the illustrations happen through the computer. To these folks as well as many others I owe much for this publication of short stories, reflections, and experiences.

Mark P. Schowalter

TABLE OF CONTENTS

THE BEGINNING:
FROM EAGLE TO CHICKEN

Since my twenty-third birthday I have been totally blind. I have been learning how to live as an independent blind person. Sometimes I come face to face with my blindness and realize there are things that I cannot do. Other times I know that my blindness makes me capable of doing much that people with vision cannot. I am constantly learning there are definite limitations that cannot be changed. Other times I know my blindness gives me a definite advantage in being able to see beyond and experience that which lives within. Sometimes I feel my blindness and my diabetes are frustrating losses. Other times I choose to make these disabilities a unique gift given to me as tools for my life. I choose to call them a gift. The gift is I am able to use my disabilities as an insight to see beyond the first impressions that people present and discover the real person that lives within.

I am a blind diabetic. I am blind because of my diabetes. Since the age of seven I have learned how to live with my diabetes. Sometimes I would test my own limitations and fail miserably. Other times I discovered how to create effective new habits that helped me.

This collection of short stories, reflections, and thoughts are about these experiences.

When I first lost my sight I started spending lots of time journalizing my thoughts, reflections, and memories on an old manual typewriter that had gotten me through college. It was something to do while I waited. I was spending a lot of time waiting, wondering, and searching for questions and answers why these two disabling diseases were happening in me. The stories became one of the ways I could deal with all of the changes taking place within an extremely short period of time. Some close friends had the opportunity to experience me through my journal as they now began reading the many entries back to me. These friends encouraged me to continue writing and to think about perhaps sharing my journal with others.

As you will find English and grammar are not my strong suits but the seed was planted and the idea grew. In the early stages of writing I retired not only my college manual typewriter but a second used manual and a third small electric typewriter before receiving a beautiful commercial style electric that would assist me through my seminary career and my long excessive journaling moods. Then I graduated to a talking computer and suddenly my journal comes to life! The idea of organizing my journal into a book to share with others blossomed into a real concept. The concept of this book continued to grow yet it lacked a purpose, a reason for wanting to share my story with others. My journal was a loose-leaf notebook. Some of the entries were clipped into the binder while others were stuffed into the pocket flaps.

I struggled with finding a purpose for this book. Then I shared an experience leading a workshop for over two hundred youth at the 1984 National Youth Event of the United Church of Christ. When I agreed to do the two workshops I was told that I would have about twenty-five participants in each session. The first session had over one hundred and twenty-five! I thought I was in the wrong room. The second session was about the same number. The participants were identifying me and my guide dog Babe as someone who was dealing with difficulties in life and being successful.

The topic for the workshop was dealing with relationships. There was a connection between the way we participate in our relationships, be it between ourselves with ourselves, with other people, and with God. They were dealing with handicaps and disabilities just as I was. Through many countless hours of dialogue after the workshops the purpose for this book was clear. If perhaps by chance I could help even just one other person experience their own successes and frustrations as a part of the relational circle of life by sharing my story then this collection of stories, reflections, and thoughts would be well worth the effort of organizing them into book form.

As I began to organize and re-write some of the entries I found my story filled with laughter, humor, and celebration. This is the optimistic part of me. At other times I found myself crying and filled with sorrow as I experienced and remembered the pain which sometimes happens in life. I kept discovering a familiar fraternal value, "I am only as strong as I am when I am at my weakest moment." My story is complex yet simple. There is much that I have accomplished and still more that I dream of accomplishing. Sometimes I think that I have not done any great things noteworthy of anyone remembering. Other times I discover that I have survived! A surprise in and of itself and I have done marvelous things. I am constantly aware that I am a unique person, the likes of which will never ever be seen again in this world, as we know it. I have dreams and failures, successes and frustrations, and all in all, I am constantly in forward gear working through one relationship after another. Just like you!

As my story begins to take shape and form through these pages I find by looking backwards I am able to see more clearly where I am going. I am in a constant state of motion focusing on the moment realizing that all of my dreams for tomorrow are in direct relationship with the experiences from my past. My struggles in life come when I do not understand myself or the relationship I am currently in; be it a relationship with myself, with someone else, or with God. I am always in a struggle attempting to define and understand where I am going and how it fits into the call to life which I must respond to. There is a small voice deep within calling me to continue forward, dealing with the struggles, and making celebrations of the successes which take place. The failures become learning moments and keep me participating in the forward relationship. This book's purpose is to help others look at their life's journey, identify and listen to their small voice that calls from within, and attempt to understand their own relationship with themselves, others, and the Holy Spirit.

Music is an important part of my understanding of who I am. Music often times is able to express some of the feelings found within. The familiar words from the gospel hymn Amazing Grace reads so beautifully: "Amazing grace, how sweet the sound, that saved someone like me. I once was lost, but now I'm found, was blind, and now I see." These words became ever so important to me as I learned to look beyond myself through my blindness and discover so much more. Please do not misunderstand what I am saying. Being blind is not easy! There are many times when I hurt, feel trapped by my blindness, and find myself discriminated against because I am different. Because I do know the profound depth of my disability, its pain and sorrow, I am also able to laugh at myself, share my joys and celebration, and enjoy the abilities and skills that I do have. Because I can understand these limitations I am able to work through and around them making them gifts. This is something I choose to do, making my experiences whether they are good or bad a part of the gifts which I am given. This is what my story is about.

This book is my story about my experiences and how each one interacts with the other. My greatest discovery in my life is realizing all of my experiences work in relationship with each other. Each experience has something that will help me in a different situation. What a tremendous gift to be able to grow by learning from our mistakes, celebrating our successes, and sharing our experiences with others. There is never a moment when the humor does not mix with the pain, celebrations with failures, laughter with tears. I was well into my experiences with my blindness and feeling all of the different emotions of being blind when I began to see the much larger picture of what my story might do for someone else. As I reflected over many of the entries, the things I had gained from each experience and the importance each story held for me, I began applying the K.I.S.S. theory of "keep it simple stupid." This became my guide and philosophy for sharing with you parts of my story. The hope is that you will find your gifts within your experiences by sharing your story with someone else. Remembering not to get too complicated and attempting to apply the K.I.S.S. theory will hopefully make you stronger in your relationships with yourself, others, and your understanding of the Holy Spirit.

This part of my story begins on the morning prior to my twenty-third birthday. I had already been seduced for surgery by a yahoo harpoon in my posterior regions! Feeling no pain and confined to a gurney in the pre-op staging area, my parents and I waited for my turn. The doctors would attempt to rebuild the inside of my right eye hoping to stop the massive scarring that accompanies diabetic retinopathy. I had already undergone laser surgery in both eyes to stop the hemorrhaging which had been taking place for the past nine months. Now prepped for surgery and waiting in the pre-op staging area, my parents and I were scared about what lay ahead. We had lots of questions but no answers. Our strength came in the faith and trust we had with the doctors and other medical staff which had been so wonderful.

Our wait grew longer than expected as another retinal emergency was taken care of. It became a special time for the three of us as we prepared for a long day ahead.

I had the easy part, as I would be sound asleep. They had the hard part waiting and hoping to hear from the surgeon that all had gone well. We held hands feeling a wonderful spiritual bonding. We found comfort in our family's faith. My dad shared these words from Isaiah's prophecy as we prayed and waited. --

[Isaiah 40:28-31] "Do you not know? Have you not heard? The LORD is the everlasting God, the Creator of the ends of the earth. He will not grow tired or weary, and his understanding no one can fathom. He gives strength to the weary and increases the power of the weak. Even youths grow tired and weary, and young men stumble and fall; but those who hope in the LORD will renew their strength. They will soar on wings like eagles; they will run and not grow weary, they will walk and not be faint."

The last thing I remember seeing was a large wall clock facing the operating table. The clock read 10:30 a.m. The discovery of my blindness would not be known for another twelve hours. Yet something inside of me already knew and was preparing me for this discovery. I was scared! Frightened! And confused! In the midst of my struggles, frustrations, and despair there was a small voice speaking to me, guiding me, helping me to see things differently? I questioned my abilities and capabilities. I doubted myself and the small voice calling from within. I had no idea of what lay ahead. I felt that my restlessness to move ahead was being inspired by the image of the eagle rising on its wings from Isaiah's prophecy. It started to give me strength to look forward.

I underwent eight hours of surgery in hopes of retaining some usable vision. I had only myself to blame for not accepting my illness sooner. I had lost vision in my left eye three months earlier in another surgery. The doorway to a different lifestyle was open before me. I stood on the threshold fighting back my tears and fears of losing my vision. All of my hopes for being able to see like any other person were rapidly dwindling as I anxiously awaited the results. I was restless!

My parents were waiting with me in my hospital room for the doctor's arrival. I had undergone surgery the day before with the hopes of retaining perhaps 90% of workable vision. My parents were with me then also. We prayed and comforted each other as we waited just as we had done the day before. The familiar words of Isaiah's prophecy sang through my mind as I laid in darkness with bandages over my eye. My parents held my hand. There was a tremendous feeling of strength in the support and love they provided. The doctor joined us in the room and shared in our prayers. Then he removed the bandages. Oops! The surgery had not worked as planned. I was now totally blind.

As my parents and I waited for the doctor I was reminded of the many special friends I had who were quietly praying and supporting me and my family. This is an important part of my celebration and success in dealing with my disability. I have many friends who try to understand what I am going through, who struggle with me and my blindness, who also know the grace of God in being able to look forward even when the end of the tunnel is dark and unseen. There were four special friends in Peter, Jeff, Neil, and Carl who spent the entire day with my parents while I was in surgery. These friends would also become important spiritual brothers as I began to spread my new wings and attempt to soar once again like the eagle in Isaiah's prophecy. I began to stumble forward, blind, yet determined!

There is no beginning and no ending to this book. I believe that all things are relational and continue in a circle around us. As there is a beginning to life, birth, and an ending, death, this story is about what happens in between. You may start anywhere you like. I decided to write each chapter as its own part of the story. I do this with the thought that you might be in a unique and different place when you want to read. I believe everything is relational. Each chapter somehow ties in with the one before, the one after, the beginning, and the end. This is also where my idea for a title got started. There are chapters of humor, laughter, celebration, and joy. They will make us feel good. There are also chapters of pain, sorrow, hurt, loss, and despair and we will cry for obviously different reasons. Sometimes you will sense the eagle rising and other times you will feel the chicken running. All in all it is part of the magical mystical dance that I feel apart of within yet not contained within.

There are several important images for me found in Isaiah 40:28-31 which I wish to share with you. These images are an important part of my story and will hopefully assist you in seeing where I am coming from and where I am going. I feel these images draw an important parallel picture between the people of Israel and some of my experiences with blindness. When I picture the people of Israel being held in captivity I can easily see a parallel to my own captive bonds of blindness. I can begin to understand their frustrations as Isaiah told them better days were ahead if only they remained faithful. "Faithful to what," they asked? Faithful to a

God whom they believed had forsaken them? After all, if this great God was so good to them then how come they were being held in captivity? I sense that they were asking, "Who is this God anyway?"

I felt a similar captivity by my blindness. In the early stages of my darkened reality I felt a unique bonding parallel with the people of Israel. I felt like a prisoner in my blindness unable to move as freely as I once had. I was struggling with my identity, faith, and participation in relationships. It appeared easier to give up rather than be patient, faithful, and wait. I too, was questioning the existence of a God who was seemingly absent or at least not paying attention to my struggles. Who is this God that could let something this bad happen to me? And I was supposed to be faithful? What is faith if I could not use it to find the answers to questions I somehow could not ask? In many ways I became like the people of Israel, ready to accept my captivity, a comfortably known limited destiny. Somehow this did not feel right for me.

As time moved forward and I began to better understand myself as visually impaired person Isaiah's words spoke louder and became clearer. My faith became stronger as I started to experience and struggle with everyday events as a blind person.

My own identity began to take on a new image. I learned to feel good about myself. I was learning to understand how God was becoming more important in my daily life. I started to understand my roles in different relationships with God, others, and myself. As my mentor, my guide, and my friend I discovered new relationships with the power of the Holy Spirit. Isaiah's words of prophecy, hope, and faith became my liberation, comfort, and strength. I began to see my blindness as a gift. And my story began "to rise like on the wings of eagles..."

My first discovery in blindness was I was not alone. Those precious few moments my parents and I shared before surgery began a new understanding of my relationship between parent and child. For the first time I would see my parents through an inward sight showing me just how special they both were. My lesson was that for so many years I had taken this relationship for granted, not being able to remember if or when I had ever said "Thanks!" for all they had given me. This new insight was comforting and strengthening. It gave me the courage to continue onward and forward with my life, my expectations, and my dreams. I understood deep inside myself they would be there to support, comfort, and love me regardless of the events which lay ahead. They would also be there to challenge and encourage me to stand on my own feet despite my disabilities and handicaps. This was another important parallel relationship of liberation through Isaiah's prophecy.

As the first day of my blindness continued and I struggled to understand the darkness surrounding me I felt my spirit begin to dance. Like the image of the eagle rising on strong powerful wings I could feel myself beginning a new magical mystical dance. With a whole lot of support of family, friends, and professional people I took my first steps in this new dance. I was not alone. There were many partners. I would make mistakes, stumble, and even fail at tasks set before me yet I discovered I could lean on my partners for support. The dance went on. I discovered how to celebrate in the midst of adversities. The doorway to a new world was opening. I only needed to step forward into it. Did I want it?

I began reaching out to friends with a new understanding of relationships. Sometimes difficult for them to understand the different vision I was experiencing we were able to redefine our roles within our relationships. They started to see a different me emerging while I continued to struggle with another lesson from my mistakes of taking some of them for granted. We began to experience our new relationships as unique and exciting gifts. A new experience began, as I was able to feel vulnerable with my friends. I was able to cry with them as I shared my fears. I was able to express myself better through tears of joy and celebration. The presence of a renewed and rising spirit added to the magical mystical dance in relationship to those around me. The small voice deep within continued calling me out and away from isolation. There was a dance to be danced called life and I felt compelled to participate by soaring like the eagle on strengthening wings.

The dance slowed as we waited for surgery on that December morning. We cried as we prayed. The tears were mixed with those of fear and comfort. There was confusion yet new understanding. Inwardly my family's faith was bonding closer. Our assurance was that our faith was firm and secure. We could face and adapt to whatever lay ahead. Things would be okay.

Diabetes and I began our unique relationship early in the second grade. I struggled with two difficult concepts: learning the disciplines of piano practicing and learning how to stick myself with an insulin syringe. Neither was on my list of favorite things to do. The next fifteen years would be spent learning to accept my diabetes and taking piano lessons. There were many trials and errors in an attempt to convince myself I was just like any other kid; non-diabetic. That was the tough part! I started learning my limitations through many trials and errors. When I made major mistakes I ended up in the hospital. When I discovered how to accept my diabetes and live within my limitations I felt good, both physically and emotionally.

I suppose somewhere in the beginning of my battle with diabetes there was mentioned the possibility of losing my sight if I did not learn all the limitations. I continued struggling with accepting my diabetes and still practicing piano. When the opportunity came to move from my parent's home to college I readily packed all that I owned. Again I refused to be seen as different and quickly established poor health routines and habits not permitted within my diabetic limitations. I would pay a severe price for my own stubbornness and foolishness. By the time I was given the first indication and diagnosis by a doctor that I had a serious vision problem it was too late. The news shook my world!

It was a tremendous shock when the doctors told me severe diabetic retinopathy could and might cause total loss of sight. The possibilities of retaining some useable sight looked probable. It would mean extensive treatments, different surgeries with some being experimental, and definite changes in my diabetic management program. This was extremely frustrating. Once again it was making me different. I hated being different. I would struggle through many major changes in nine short months including graduating from college, attempting several different forms of employment, and eventually losing total sight. Just when I thought I had the routines of my life established everything started to change. It changed fast!

I believe all of us develop routines which we are comfortable with. Sometimes these routines become habits, perhaps even ruts. If we become too comfortable in our daily ruts it is difficult to change. The night before my big surgery was spent wondering what would happen next. I found myself getting angry at God. It was easier to blame the fast uncomfortable changes in my routines and ruts on God whom I felt I could keep at arms length. I tried hard for my own survival to push God into a convenient position. Somewhere in the confusion I started to hear this tiny little voice deep within speak to me. I began feeling different but did not understand. It would be much later before I realized it was God attempting to speak to me in words I could hear.

The story continues nine months after that surgery as I entered seminary to grow and train as an ordained clergy. The same voice which I had heard through the chaos and confusion while losing my sight had continued to grow stronger. It was calling me onward into the new patterns and routines which were taking place. The voice kept repeating the words of Isaiah's prophecy "those who hope in the Lord shall have their faith renewed; they shall rise as on the wings of eagles..." When I was able to focus my attention on the direction I felt it was calling me it became the loudest and clearest inside me. There was a burning desire to share my experiences, celebrations and frustrations, accomplishments and failures with others. The same voice which had comforted me the night before surgery now challenged and pushed me to do something with what I had learned through my experiences of losing sight. The still small voice deep within me was no longer still or small. It leaped and danced in celebration, full of expectation for what lay ahead.

Seminary was tough. There were little if any resources in adaptive media for the blind. There was a lot of reading required. Papers would be many and hard. In my weakest moments of frustration the small voice within would speak the words "those who hope in the Lord..." and I would be able to push on. I somehow found the necessary ingredient to keep moving on. My family, some old friends, and many new friends became my support network. I was not alone. I was never alone! The voice called me onward. I followed.

One of my biggest stumbling blocks in my seminary journey was passing the first half of my required Old Testament course. I failed this section three times. I needed the course to graduate. With prayerful and careful consideration my Old Testament Professor, my advisor and I worked out an agreement whereby I was offered the opportunity to study another Old Testament course under a different professor. If I passed this elective Old Testament course and could demonstrate good disciplines in biblical interpretation I would receive credit for the required Old Testament course. Much to my delight Isaiah appeared on the course schedule. The familiar words of Isaiah's prophecy became my center of attention. This passage would become my graduating paper. When I was down and out and in need, Isaiah's words of strength, comfort, and hope came alive!

One month after graduating from seminary and still feeling like a rookie as a blind person I was ordained into the Christian ministry. It was Pentecost Sunday, June 10, 1984. It was a day of celebration. My family and friends gathered in a crowded sanctuary to participate in a magical mystical dance of affirmation of faith. I would prayerfully take my vows to be a teacher of the Words of God accepting the cost and joy of discipleship, and responding to the call of that still small voice deep within. These familiar words from Isaiah's prophecy were my chosen passage for the day.

My wings were still wet with new growth. I was eager to rise with my experiences and soar with new wings. My spiritual wings beat steadily as I was rising confidently to answer the voice deep within. There were new directions, new support networks, new challenges, and new frustrations. I felt ready to face the new path my journey was taking. Fully aware every moment of life is filled with blessings and excitement there is strength in acknowledgement and celebration. There is comfort in recognition and acceptance of limitations and parameters. There is challenge in knowing no matter who I am, what I have, and even what I do not have, I always have something to offer, something that gives me self-worth. I stretch my wings out as far as I can, rise on the updrafts of successes, and soar gracefully through my failures and shortcomings.

I am constantly learning how to understand my own disabilities. I grow stronger with every adaptive success and understand more fully through every failure. I am able to experience the profound depths of my own character the more I am willing to face the adversities set before me. My strongest abilities are when I am at my weakest moments. When I learn to convert failures into successes, disappointments into celebrations I discover another new step in the magical mystical dance of my faith. I continue to "rise like on the wings of an eagle…"

As I continue to write of my experiences I know my spiritual wings as a person are not yet dry. I continue to find myself rising to new and exciting heights as I explore the world around me. I am in an ongoing concert with my faith and my understanding of what God is calling me to do. As my understanding of God expands my faith strengthens. I am always learning who I am. Although not always sure, often times restless and uncomfortable, I am reminded life is a journey. I know what has passed and where I have been. My dreams drive me forward to discover what still lies ahead. The journey is a gift and I must treat it as such. I cannot take the gift for granted but must respond in such a way which makes every moment uniquely special and different from the moment before.

One of the hardest lessons I needed to learn in the process of losing my sight is people are gifts. Relationships with people are important and a necessary part of our journeys. Relationships are experiences. The more relationships we experience the greater our wealth of resources become and the more we have to draw upon when we are in need. These experiences become the foundations upon which our`` faith in the one God are built. We are in a relationship with God, the one who has created us, who continues to create within and through us, and the same God who goes before us creating. Each of our relationships with God is a unique individual experience. These experiences are important for us to share with one another so we might learn from each other.

There are those among us who find it necessary to challenge the existence of God based upon bad and adverse experiences. They attempt in whatever way possible to separate themselves from their relationship with God and with others. I believe separating ourselves from others is a sin against God. If we use people in relationships we are attempting to separate ourselves from our relationship with God. When we treat relationships with others as a matter of convenience we respond the same way to our faith and relationship with God.

To some is given the gift of thinking, enjoying the process of thinking about the ways things are and/or what they might be. To others is given the gift of doing; being able to work through their hands with skills and talents to create effective moments of teaching to share with others. Both are necessary. If we have the gift of thinking about the way things are we must work perhaps at being more of a doer. If we are blessed with the gift of doing I feel it is necessary we work at being more of a thinker, sometimes working through the process in our mind before acting. This process of journaling and then organizing the entries into a collection became both the thought and the action. I had to think about the process. I had to study the cause and effect of the different ways I do things. It became important to be both a thinker and a doer. The important function was to write in the journal the things I felt and then re-read the entry to seek the true meanings and understandings of who I am, what I am becoming, and where I have been.

The pages that follow are but a small part of my story and experience. It is a gift for me to be able to share my story to perhaps help someone to begin to understand the complexities of their own situation. Perhaps someone will find a way to learn from their experience within their relationships. Perhaps someone else will learn how to laugh at themselves despite the shadows of despair and frustration lingering ever too close. It is a gift to be able to look at ourselves as we participate in the magical mystical dance called life. Although I lost my sight through complications with my diabetes I have gained a better understanding of myself because I can smile at adversity and laugh at my despair. My faith enables me to continue forward. When I had every reason to quit I found the resources of my experiences, my stories helped me to continue in that ongoing journey. There is never a dull moment for I have learned to become my own best friend. I can challenge myself, comfort myself, laugh at myself, and criticize myself. More importantly, I can share myself with others. In writing this book I now am able to share with you my experiences of learning to become my own best friend.

Each chapter in this collection can be read by itself. You can start anywhere you like. Each piece is a unique part of me, my experience, and hopefully something that you can relate to. When we are able to relate we begin a new relationship, a new experience, and a new understanding of both ourselves and someone else. Sometimes the new relationship is perhaps a way we react in a given situation. Sometimes it is with a new person we have yet to meet. Other times it is simply beginning another new piece of our own life. The excitement is there is always an adventure unfolding right before our eyes and we have the opportunity to participate!

When I first started writing this book I was scared. The task seemed too big, too unreal, impossible for me to accomplish. As words became sentences, then paragraphs, pages, and chapters I began discovering new things about myself and a new drive to accomplish the project. In as much as I hope and pray my experiences and stories will help you to a better understanding, the writing has also been therapeutic for me. I have enjoyed countless hours reliving the memories of the stories as I attempted to capture the right moment in a static line of words. I discovered I still have much to learn about myself and how I interact with the world around me. So even though the book might have a front and a back, the story continues far beyond the page could ever hold.

As I live moment to moment, experience to experience, three main ingredients stand firm a foundation for my life's experiences. My faith in God remains strong, unchanged, supportive, and active. I am always in concert with my relationship with God through Jesus Christ to understand what it is that God intends for me. My fraternity's motto in college was "I Seek to Serve." When I am able to serve others I find my rewards great. This is my intended purpose, to serve others.

My family is my support network. When I find myself stumbling from moment to moment it is my family, both blood-relative and extended family that is there to support me. They might disagree with me and even tell me so. I have learned to accept unconditionally their love and support knowing there will be times when I return the favor.

Be open to new experiences, new relationships, and new stories. We are constantly bombarded by new opportunities. Take full advantage of the situation and experience each moment to its fullest. Some will say one should treat life's little moments as if they were your last. I believe this only to a point. My difference is be sure when treating a moment, an experience, a new story that you also continue to dream about what lies ahead. Dreamers are necessary for they create the next opportunity, the next moment, and the next new experience to happen. This will never make a dull moment! Rather, I think you will find you will be able to rise on the wing like a great soaring eagle, to run and not grow weary, to walk and not faint.

Allow yourself the opportunities to be filled with new experiences in life. Be adventuresome in your seeking new relationships while celebrating the gifts of present ones. Be strong in your faith and what you believe. Never be afraid to dream and to pursue those dreams. Make those dreams larger than life and as big as you can for it will increase your commitment to pursuing and making them real. Discover new ways of sharing your experiences with others so both learn from the success as well as the failure. Learn to journal your thoughts so you always have a starting point to which you can return and from which you can constantly grow as you learn and understand who you are. Follow the voice deep within that calls you forth "...to rise like on the wings of eagles, to run and not grow weary, to walk and not faint."

CHAPTER ONE:
I AM THE EAGLE

Life is full of dreams; things we desire to have, people we desire to be, places we hope to visit, and people we hope to meet. I have always been a dreamer, one who dreams about tomorrow. In my dreams there are many things I want to encounter, accomplish, and discover. Many of these change as I travel through my life. Many of my journeys have happened because I dare to dream.

Many have been attempted; some have been successful. Some have failed. I enjoy dreaming. I find tremendous reward and satisfaction in helping others experience and realize their dreams. Dreams are important to me.

A soaring eagle has always been the image representing my dreams and holds me a captive audience in awe of their creation. The graceful wings powerfully beating the winds and updrafts, gracefully lifting them high above the hills, rocky cliffs, and treelines brings comfort, inspiration, and reverence. Watching an eagle soar high above the land brings hours of fascination, respect, and dreaming.

Growing up along the Mississippi River in central Wisconsin frequently provided sightings of the magnificent eagles. Yearly summer vacations and trips to a church camp in northern Wisconsin provided the same. For the past twenty-three years plus of attending the same campsite I have been aware of the eagle at least once during the week. Sailing the Great Lakes, especially the Apostle islands off northern Wisconsin is another favorite location for spotting the soaring eagles. There are several islands designated as refuge and protective habitation for the graceful birds.

The eagle is an image of strength, a vision of grace, and an understanding of power to me. John Denver wrote in one of his folksong ballads of the 1970's: "I am the eagle; I live in high places, the lofty cathedrals that reach to the sky..." Being a John Denver fan the words and music blended into a piece of my tapestry, a common thread that began to run through the fabric of my life. When I hear the song or even just the words I can vision the eagle. When I picture an eagle I hear the words and the music. I dream of soaring like the eagle; I vision the grace of the eagle's motion; I desire the freedom that for me the eagle represents. I find myself connecting with the eagle which becomes one thread woven into my story.

There is another eagle that connects with my story. It is an eagle that started as a dream and became reality. Soaring much higher than a feathered winged creature, traveling into space has been a dream. When Neil Armstrong and the crew of the Apollo 9 moon mission landed on the moon's surface it was as if I were there. I can distinctly remember hearing as Houston Control listened and responded to "roger Houston, the eagle has landed." There was a moment of silence around the world as viewers watched in awe and reverence. Then there was an explosion of applause as the dream was realized... the first manned landing on the moon. Even we sixth graders applauded and cheered. Inside I always visualized someday being one who would soar far beyond the earth's atmosphere. I still hold the dream as NASA now launches its space shuttle. I have attempted not to miss a launch and to keep close track of the progress of the mission. Perhaps, someday.

My friend, the feathered eagle does not always have it so easy. For many years eagles were scarce here in Wisconsin having been chased away by the "progress of man." Their habitation invaded, their source of food exploited, and their environment changing faster than they were allowed to adapt, moved the eagles farther away from civilization where they were harder to sight. I felt an emptiness tugging inside not being able to spot the eagles as often. Hope prevailed though and slowly the eagles have returned. Many groups have supported the re-induction of the eagles back into their natural habitats. Once again it is possible to watch their powerful wings beat the winds, lifting them gracefully upward as they soar. Their existence marks the presence of the Holy Spirit. All of God's creation has the ability to adapt if given the proper time. This is the significance and connection between the eagle, the dream, and me. For me the message is God's grace, mercy, and love inspires hope. If hope is the essence of my life, then like the eagle I can eventually adapt to an ever-changing environment and continue to pursue my own dreams. The transition has become an ongoing inward and spiritual journey continuing to bring me to a new understanding of self. The outward and physical change was going from having excellent sight to total blindness. What follows in these pages are stories of the inward and spiritual journey.

When my problem with diabetic retinopathy was discovered I was a senior in college, I was engaged to be married, and I was looking forward to getting a job to support my wife-to-be while she completed her education. I had a master plan. After her graduation from college I would enter into seminary and pursue my calling to be an ordained minister. The dream of being a minister dates way back. It was also more than a dream; it was a nagging voice deep within that was only quiet and satisfied when I was on track to realizing the dream. When the retinopathy appeared life changed drastically. I would illustrate my feelings by describing a person standing on the threshold in a doorway. The room ahead was dark and full of uncertainties. The familiar and known behind me was quickly being taken away and I could not return. I had only one direction to go, to step across the threshold into the unknown. My step forward was difficult and painful for I felt I was losing everything. I suddenly had no master plan; just one day, one moment at a time.

As time moved from March toward December, things happened quickly and changed drastically. It appeared that many little things were being patched together, quilted so to speak, to keep me going. I graduated from college, found some part-time employment, and entered the dark and mysterious world of medical science in dealing with my retinopathy. My marital engagement became postponed and soon after ended. I desperately clung to some precious experiences. I attended church camps, struggled through laser treatments for the retinopathy, experienced the joy of a new relationship, and participated in the celebration of some close friends' wedding. Although there seemed to be much happening, it felt as though for every step forward something pushed me back. I began feeling my wings of freedom had been clipped and I could no longer soar like an eagle. I found myself becoming frustrated, angry, and depressed. I saw my visions of tomorrow dissolving and felt I could no longer dream. When I would dream, the dreams were painful reminders of a disappearing past.

Before things would start to get better they seemed to get worse. Shortly after participating in the wedding of my friends Norm and Joan I was to begin a new job as Youth Coordinator for a church in Milwaukee. The good people of Faith United Church of Christ knew of my situation yet they were excited about having me. I was excited, too since this would be putting me back on track toward seminary and serving in a ministry I felt called to do. But on the first morning of my job when I was suppose to be in the office I was lying in the hospital waiting for my turn in the operating room. More complications with the diabetic retinopathy were occurring and emergency surgery to relieve some rapidly building destructive pressure was necessary. During this surgery some blood vessels in my left eye would hemorrhage and I would lose my vision in that eye. Another attempt at the same surgery a week later to correct the loss of sight was also not successful. I was now partially blind having lost total sight in my left eye. My right eye was doing as well as expected but there were signs of deterioration. I was more concerned I would lose my job. But the good people of Faith Church were not giving up on me and waited with faithful anticipation.

I started my new job as Youth Coordinator two weeks later than expected. The youth responded tremendously. Youth started returning to church, participating in different programs, and got excited about being part of the community of faith. I started feeling a rebuilding of my own spiritual foundations and maybe perhaps even a glimpse now and then of a vision about tomorrow. But then another complication would set in and I would slide backwards. About two weeks into my new job I attempted suicide. Fortunately I failed. My silent scream for help was heard and my family became my refuge and support network. Several other close friends joined in as well. The youth and folks at Faith Church remained supportive and would not let me quit. "We" pushed on.

In mid October my sister got married. At first I was frustrated, depressed, and angry. This was my younger sister getting married and not me. I was supposed to have gotten married earlier that summer but saw my engagement dissolve. Now she was getting married and I was upset to say the least. I attempted to avoid the issue. It caught me from behind and tortured me internally. Then God's grace appeared and I began to understand myself. My sister asked me to read scripture for her wedding service. I reluctantly accepted fearful the instability of my right eye, my only functioning eye, might take me out of the ball game. So contingency plans were made and I prepared to read scriptures. I copied the words of the passage onto separate pages writing in big block print. Then I practiced and practiced. I wanted it to be perfect for my sister. On the day of the wedding when it was my turn to read I headed for the lectern. In route, I suffered a major hemorrhage and my vision became blurred. I attempted to gather my wits about me hoping my vision would clear. As I looked out into the congregation I only saw a massive blur of colors, no details, no faces, no print on the pages before me. I hesitated, and then panicked! But somewhere in the chaos God's grace took over and I began to recite my passage from memory. Later I would learn from my friend as she had followed in her Bible and I had not missed a word. There was a mixed sense of fear and reverent awe.

About two weeks later another setback would happen. This time I was headed into Milwaukee on a Sunday morning to go to work. Just a few miles from home my right eye hemorrhaged again. I was alone, driving my car, and suddenly everything went to a blurred red. I managed to pull the car off the main highway onto a side street and safely pull to a stop alongside the curb. I sat in quiet fear and panic for several long moments waiting for my vision to clear. This time it would not. Eventually I felt in control enough to leave my car and started to walk back home. I could just barely see the gray ribbon of sidewalk in front of me. It took me well over an hour to walk the two miles back to my home church. I felt relieved to be back in a safe place yet mighty scared of what was happening. I felt I had no control of tomorrow or my destiny. I began to feel what I would assume an eagle must feel when it is locked in a cage. Shortly after this experience, when I had to turn in my car keys and my independence, the eye specialists informed me my only hope for retaining any usable sight was to undergo a radical surgical procedure known as a vitrectomy. I reluctantly agreed and was enrolled in a governmental study which would pay most of the medical expense. In a unique way God's grace was once again taking over.

The end of the old chapter of my story and the beginning of my new journey started during the week of my twenty-third birthday. I was struggling. I was fighting my fear my eyesight was gone in my left eye and my right was not doing much better. I had many feelings of anger, frustrations, and disappointments. I saw most everything negatively. I was facing a long difficult experimental surgery to attempt to rebuild my right eye. I was preparing myself for the worse, which made me an unpleasant person to be around. Just ask my family!

With autumn changing to winter, football season changing to basketball, and my vision getting less and less I began preparing myself for the darkness which lay ahead. My youngest brother Joel was in training for basketball. He was doing a lot of running. I started training for my surgery by running with him. We used a bathtowel held tightly between us as we ran together in the evenings. My night vision was gone and with my right eye failing it was just a blur passing rapidly by. My brother and I became closer friends as we learned to communicate by telling me things to look out for; when to jump a curb or avoid an obstacle as well as supplying a running commentary of what he saw. The exercise felt good and my physical condition improved. With all things considered my physical and mental condition was getting ready for the long surgery and recovery period which lay ahead.

My diabetes was improving thanks to a new management program a close family friend had found. She was a nurse and involved in diabetic education. When she learned of my situation with the diabetic retinopathy developing she put me in touch with an excellent progressive diabetic center. I started changing my diabetic management in hopes of making myself healthier. The two programs, the diabetic center and eye institute, worked in concert to help me. I developed many new support networks for my situation although the new diabetic management program was unfortunately too late. However, as I prepared for the pending surgery I at least felt confident my diabetes would stay stable. The still small spiritual voice inside of me encouraged and challenged me to work myself into a better physical and mental place in preparation for the surgery. At the time, the surgery was scheduled for early February so I thought I had plenty of time. When my right eye hemorrhaged that morning on my way to work the doctors informed me I would need the surgery much earlier. Training soon ended as our makeshift running track around the park became snow-covered. I got ready to enter the hospital.

The week before my rescheduled surgery was a perfect week, all things considered. A special female friend and significant spiritual partner came to visit for the weekend. We spent much time Christmas shopping. It was becoming a new experience for me to be dependent upon her to drive and lead me through the many stores and shops we visited. It was a new experience to be learning things by feeling them as many things were becoming obscure blurs. We attended my fraternity's pledge banquet of which one of my closest friends was being received into the brotherhood. We were very close friends having counseled camps together and shared an apartment for a brief time after my college graduation. Jeff would also be a strong supporter of my family and me when the day of surgery would arrive. His induction into the same fraternity I had been so very active in became another important connection between us. Escorting my beautiful friend Barb to the banquet brought many compliments of how good we appeared together. They were happy for us and pledged their continued support of my endeavors. The banquet became very important to me as I found myself studying every detail of my lovely special friend and my fraternity brothers for this would be the last times I would see them. It became a special memory I can still see in my mind so many years later. It was a clue to what lay ahead which I was not yet ready to accept.

The next week following was anxiously filled with several eye exams and a conclusion my surgery would be in one week. The patchwork quilt of things happening got faster and time seemed to be slipping away. The surgery was scheduled for a Wednesday morning, the day before my twenty-third birthday and I had one week to prepare. I got scared! Real scared! I spent much of my time silently praying and crying. I feared the end of my eyesight was near and I was not as prepared for blindness as I thought. I spent much time on the telephone talking with my spiritual friend attempting to avoid the fears and issues at hand. In many ways I was trying to somehow stop the process and return to my master plan, the ways I thought things should be. But the day of my surgery drew closer.

My mother and I sang in a local choral group and our Christmas concert was the Sunday evening preceding my scheduled surgery. My grandparents came earlier in the day to visit and would attend the concert after supper. We spent the afternoon visiting and decorating the family Christmas tree. This became a difficult situation. Christmas tree decorating had some traditional roles. Father put the lights on, we kids would hang the ornaments, and while we slept Mother would add the final touch of tinsel. This particular year we would hang paper stars which we as a family had made. These had become a Christmas tradition. These folded paper stars had sixteen points constructed by folding four narrow strips of paper and then dipping them in wax to seal the edges. Each star got its own unique touch of different color patterns and glitter sprinkles. As Father completed the placement of the light sockets I began to insert the colored light bulbs. To my frustrating dismay I suddenly discovered with my failing sight and lack of depth perception I could not insert the light bulbs. In fact, many times I had a hard time grasping the tree branch threatening the welfare of the Christmas tree. Shortly thereafter I retreated from the process and took a seat nearby to watch. It was a painful, frustrating, and anger- building realization. I was learning the hard way there were going to be things I could and could not do.

The concert that evening was equally as difficult. It was exciting and fun to sing many of the favorite Christmas songs both sacred and secular. However, because of my failing vision I could barely see the conductor, needed to hang onto the person standing next to me to get on and off stage, and only saw a massive blur of colors out in the audience. I began to accept I would soon not be able to see any of this even though the doctors felt with surgery I would maintain some usable sight. They kept saying ninety percent! Ninety percent! I was experiencing the ten percent. I was afraid the only thing left for me would be to work in a sheltered workshop for the blind punching out aluminum ashtrays. The concert was an exciting success, but the dreams were fading fast. I entered the hospital the next day and got ready for the surgery.

The first two days in the hospital were anxious moments going through many tests and examinations in preparation for the surgery. All of the different elements to the procedure were explained. Although it sounded fascinating in what they planned to do and how they could do it, I was climbing the walls with fear! All I could see was this doorway into a dark unknown future. I was scared! More scared than I had ever experienced before! I tried to be strong, to laugh with myself, and tried to hide behind a protective mask. Inside I was scared, crying, and afraid of being blind. I felt helpless for there was nothing I could do but wait for the surgery to happen.

On the night before my surgery I was visiting with my spiritual partner on the telephone and looking out the window. The lights of the city in the dark of night were colored blurs. I could see very little when something caught my eye on the window ledge. It was a big pile of bird dropping, the biggest pile I had ever seen. It was pretty obvious the local pigeons which frequent my windowsill had left. Yet through my blurred vision the massive pile looked like something an eagle would have left. Being in a strange place emotionally and under much stress something caused me to describe this disgusting and obnoxious scene to my friend. We started laughing. I started cracking up. Sometimes humor is the best medicine and suddenly it felt good to be laughing uncontrollably. My fears were not quite as bad. My friend was able to see through my protective mask. I felt good about my relationship with my spiritual partner and felt there was nothing I could not share with her. At times we cried together in our conversation for she understood my pain and fear. Most importantly, we laughed long and hard at times getting so loud the nurses came in and told me to keep it a little quieter. I felt better after the telephone conversation and I prepared to sleep for the night. But sleep would not happen.

When I tried to close my eyes to sleep my mind would race through many things. I knew when the morning came it would be busy getting ready and going to surgery. My parents would be there with me to spend some precious moments of support. This would be the last time I would see them. I knew this internally yet tried to ignore it, push it out of my way, and convince myself I would have sight after the operation. But the nagging voice inside of me was telling me differently. At other times during the night I was filled with many fond memories of friends, places I remembered seeing, and things I would have liked to accomplish but required sight. These things would bring long moments of tears as I feared the morning and felt the end coming fast. I began to tape a letter to my parents, family, and friends on my cassette recorder. A friend had lent me a guitar and the tape began with my rendition of J. Denver's "I Am the Eagle." Through the remainder of the long dark night I painfully attempted to explain what and how I was feeling inside. The voice and spirit within was telling me I would be blind after surgery. My struggle within was I still wanted to ignore the whole situation hoping that this was just a bad dream and in the morning I would wake up and go home with good vision.

The night seemed endless. I tried many times to fall asleep only to be kept awake by my wandering mind. I struggled with my feelings and with waiting. The more I waited, the more I struggled. The more I struggled, the more I waited. The good feeling of laughing with my friend on the telephone seemed countless hours past and at times perhaps it had never happened. I watched the clock and waited. I waited and watched the clock. Time seemed to stand still and I was rapidly becoming overwhelmed by my fears, frustrations. As morning drew near those fears and frustrations had worked themselves into anger. My adrenaline was pumping hard and fast. I was being swallowed by my fears as they turned into anger. I could feel this enormous spring winding tight in my chest. The hospital room became a blur, then became clear, and then became a blur again. I could have easily been a classic case for the funny farm as I continued to work myself into frenzy. I felt like I was losing the battle and felt myself being consumed by my own anger and despair.

A nurse appeared in my doorway with towels and told me I could shower. Morning had arrived and things would begin to happen quickly now. It was still dark outside when I went into the shower. I remember taking one last look out of my window at the darkness and thinking to myself; "so this is what it will be like." While I was in the bathroom showering the staff evoked the hospital's "no clothes for surgery" policy. When I got done with my shower I had no clothes! There were no clothes to be found anywhere in my room. I only had the couple of bath towels, which they had given me for my shower. Having some modesty left and figuring I could not spend the day in the bathroom I wrapped one around my waist. I returned back out into my room to my bedside nearest the window. The anger was still present and getting stronger! I could feel this tension spring winding up in my chest. My heart rate increased rapidly as every muscle in my body got tense with anger. I felt like I was going to explode!

By now the darkness of night was rapidly passing. My room faced the west. I was looking out of the window and discovered a huge pumpkin orange moon settling towards the horizon. The sky surrounding it was a deep rich royal blue. I found myself stepping back from the window and looking at the picture framed before me. The anger exploded deep inside and suddenly I was screaming out loud! I think I called God just about every name I could think of! I blamed God for my retinopathy! For my diabetes! For my messed up master plan! For all the problems in the world! And for anything else that came to mind!

Why was this happening to me? What had I done to cause such a tremendous effect on my life which now was causing my blindness? Strange things floated in and out of my mind. I remembered a Bible passage about a blind man who was reported to have been blind since birth because of something his parents had done. Was that my situation? I knew better for my parents were strong in their faith. There had to be something else. Had I missed something along the way, which was now haunting me? The questions, comments, editorial phrases, and curses spilled forth. The nurses came running. I was burning out of control and blaming everything on God through the huge moon still patiently and silently settling onto the horizon.

The moment the nurses entered my room because of the loud commotion something else happened inside. All of the anger which had built up inside me toward God was gone, suddenly replaced by this quiet still voice calming and comforting me. God's grace, mercy, and love were present silently taking over my anger. I felt embarrassed standing naked in front of the window with the nurses behind me. I felt a different presence within, the presence of the Holy Spirit pushing the anger out and allowing me to once again spread my wings and soar like an eagle. The nurses said nothing and quietly watched, sensing something happening. The anger spring which had gotten so very tense inside of me was gone. I felt comfort, peace, and a new sense of strength filling my deflated person. I remember looking at the nurses both in confusion yet understanding. I felt embarrassed to be standing there with only a towel girding my waist. I remember telling them as I spoke into my tape recorder; "I am going to be blind after this surgery."

All through the process of preparing for surgery there had been an overwhelming presence of optimism. The doctors were constant in giving me a ninety percent chance of retaining usable sight. There was even talk that with corrective lenses I would probably be able to get my driver's license back. Internally I was discovering a new source of understanding and as I watched the moon changing from the pumpkin orange to a yellowish white I was no longer afraid of the blindness which lay ahead. I studied the picture of the setting moon framed by the window and committed it to memory. This lasting image would become an important vision in my struggles and journey forward as things were changing. In my blurred vision I was even able to imagine I could see the American flag planted on the moon by the astronauts as well as some of the lunar junk they had left on its surface. In the next few moments as the huge moon slipped through the slot where the sky and horizon meet I found myself getting tired yet ready for the rest of the morning, especially the surgery. If the doctors could retain some usable sight it would be great! If not, I was ready to face the unknown. I said, "I'm ready." As the words verbally left my mouth and the room grew silent through my failing blurred vision I believe I saw an eagle soar gracefully across the moon and the brightening morning sky. I was touched! I could feel the presence of God surrounding me and giving me strength. Although I had not yet heard the words of Isaiah's prophecy there was a connection between the vision of the rising eagle and the feeling within. I would discover the connection and a new understanding of how strong my faith was. Standing naked before God and the world, watching the moon disappear, I felt stripped of my fear and was made humble to accept what tomorrow would bring. I was ready.

I was still standing before the window watching the last little piece of the moon slip away and watching the brightness of a beautiful sunny day beginning when I felt a soft hand on my shoulder. One of the nurses had returned to make sure I was okay. All things considered I smiled with tears starting to roll down my face and nodded affirmatively. Then she delivered the bad news; she had the "yahoo!" harpoon for my backside. I hate these shots and worse yet hate getting them in the posterior regions. I attempted to argue my case but soon found myself lying on my bed on my stomach and my backside hurting. The room began to spin and I knew I had been hit! I was able to glance out the window realizing the fullness of a new day had arrived. The words said "thanks, you did this to me!" but the thoughts were more "I'm ready now, ready to accept that which lies ahead." Things started to happen quickly now.

My parents arrived to find me floating. Actually, I was bed-bound and pretty sedated. I felt like a human puddle poured between the sheets. Still having nothing to wear and having surrendered the towel, the blankets on my hospital bed were warming and comforting. There wasn't much I could do but talk as the muscle relaxers continued to circulate through my body. It was interesting. I felt as if I could fly, could take a trip around the room, even out into the hallway, and perhaps far beyond, yet never have left the comforting confines of my bed. I was floating! I felt like I was soaring with the eagles.

My brain does strange things when I get hit in the hindquarters with a harpoon. First, my body knows no matter what the source of pain or injury or type of surgery, and I have had a few, it will take longer to recover from the harpoon hit in the backside! Second, the experience of feeling the muscle relaxers taking effect and leaving me totally helpless is almost exciting. I feel as if though, no matter what anyone wanted to do to me, with me, or without me, I didn't care. I just smiled a lot, attempted to laugh, and thought the whole world was pretty groovy from my perspective. This is why I call it the "human puddle" experience. Third, my brain started to play with memories which seemed to flash by. I started laughing uncontrollably thinking about the pile of bird droppings outside the window from the night before. I remembered seeing how beautiful my special friend had looked the weekend previous. I remember seeing the wedding party which I had participated in as bestman some four months earlier standing playfully trying to pose for pictures. There were flashbacks to a trip with my special friend to a nearby amusement park spending the day on all the rides, several sailboat races from earlier in the summer, and my college graduation. In between all of the memory flashes I remember my parents asking me questions, the medical staff getting me ready, and my spiritual partner calling to wish me luck. Inside I could hear my spiritual voice comforting and strengthening me in preparation to face surgery. I was becoming more and more familiar with a realization I would be blind after the surgery although the medical staff was still holding to their ninety percent optimism.

When the gurney arrived to take me to surgery I made a big mistake. They had the gurney in position and realized they were missing something. The nurse left the room and while she was gone I got out of bed and onto the gurney. She returned, surprised to find me on the gurney, and questioned how I did this. I showed her by getting off the gurney, back into bed, and then back on the gurney again. She left the room only to return moments later with another yahoo harpoon! I suffered another hit in the hindquarters! Ouch! That smarts! Fortunately for her the first injection was partially in effect and I really didn't care what they did to me. I would feel it later.

The time came and I changed locations riding the gurney from my room to surgery. My parents were allowed to stay with me during the pre-operation wait. It was a frightening and anxious yet precious time together. I know it was difficult for my parents to observe everything which was happening and feel totally helpless. From the time I first got diabetes, through the many different setbacks and crisis, it had been difficult. Now it was a complication with the diabetes and we were all still helpless while the fears increased. But the time we had together was precious and special. I could feel their faith in a healing and protecting God pouring out into me through our physical touching. We held each other's hands and I could feel a new, stronger connection in relationship with them. I felt like a small child wanting to crawl into the security of my protecting parents' laps to keep me from the dangers and my fears. My father began to pray out loud opening with the words from Isaiah's prophecy: "Do you not know? Have you not heard? The LORD is the everlasting God, the Creator of the ends of the earth. He will not grow tired or weary, and his understanding no one can fathom. He gives strength to the weary and increases the power of the weak. Even youths grow tired and weary, and young men stumble and fall; but those who hope in the LORD will renew their strength. They will soar on wings like eagles; they will run and not grow weary, they will walk and not be faint." [Isaiah 40:28-31]

When I heard the part using the image of the eagle I made the connection with my vision which I had seen earlier in the morning with the moon. After Father's prayer and feeling much more comfortable about what was to happen I asked if they had seen the moon that morning? They had and we shared a common memory of how huge it appeared and its fullness in color. I shared with them my vision of the eagle. Suddenly the words of God spoken through Isaiah were speaking to me and they continued to roll through me over and over again. I told them about the tape which I had left for them to listen to while I was in surgery. It was difficult but I told them I had this feeling, this experience I would be blind after the surgery. Many tears were shed.

For me the rest of the day was easy. I slept. I remember waking up once during surgery hearing someone says "he's coming to." The next thing I remember was waking up in the recovery room. I was hungry. I wanted steak and potatoes. I got neither. I came to pretty fast and soon I was back in my room with my parents. Four close friends from college were also there. They had been there for the day spending time supporting, laughing, and sharing jokes with my parents to pass the time. I was still hungry for the steak and potatoes. I was told I would get some Deserta just as soon as I went to the bathroom. This would be impossible since I had consumed nothing for over eighteen hours. Then I realized I had been out for over eight hours. My eye was bandaged and I saw nothing. We would have to wait.

There was much laughing in the room, many of the jokes shared earlier now being shared with me. The laughing felt good for it made me cough which got the anesthesia out of my system. There was a lot of touching happening, as we all were comforted with apparent good results of the surgery. That was the doctors' feeling at that point. But we would need to wait another twelve hours until the next morning for any direct results. As things began to settle in my room my mind once again was swarmed with different images of the eagle soaring and my vision of the setting moon from earlier in the morning. Soon I would accomplish the bathroom routine, get something to eat and drink, and then lazily fall back to sleep.

Two weeks after my surgery was Christmas. Christmas that year was strange. I was struggling through my new reality of blindness. In the same time period a relative was killed in a car accident and another relative's dairy barn burned. Shortly after Christmas I received word a former college roommate was killed in a car accident. God's grace continued to make its presence known in good things, too. First, my sisters and brothers coordinated the purchase of a Hammond organ entertainment center as a gift from my extended family. It had many of the bells and whistles of electronic organs and provided countless hours of music to pass the time. During the Christmas Eve worship service of my home church the words of

Isaiah's prophecy were read. Immediately I could see the huge moon setting on the horizon in my mind's eye from the morning of my surgery. Very distinctly I saw once again the eagle soaring across the morning skies as the words resounded through the sanctuary. I was able to recognize the pain and anger which had consumed me before surgery and let it go. My spirit was now filled with comfort and strength with God's grace. In the celebration of Christmas I found a new relationship with the Holy Spirit. It was exciting to feel this new understanding of God's grace present in the gift of the Christ-child. It was almost overwhelming. Even in my darkened world of blindness there was new light!

If you can picture a young fledgling eagle just coming out of the nest for the first time and not yet ready to fly you can get a pretty good feeling of how I felt. There were many struggles with my blindness but there were many positive feelings, too. The biggest thing for me was I felt closer to my family. I was suddenly thrust into total dependency upon them for everything as it took me time to begin learning how to adapt. They were adapting, too. One of the big items was making sure chairs were pushed into the table after meals. If you stop and think for a moment you will get the idea of what can happen to a blind person finding a chair sticking out of place! My family's love for each other grew in many new ways. We even found ways to playfully tease and make jokes about my blindness, which is a necessary part of our faith. In God's presence and experiencing of grace, humor is a necessary and important part. When we made mistakes, and we all made mistakes, we were able to laugh about them. I got left many times standing next to the car in a parking lot wondering where my guide had gone. It was an important connection which wove us closer together.

A month after my total loss of sight I found myself back in the hospital for a repeat vitrectomy. Since it was my second such surgery in a month my body had a more difficult time recovering. I was bedridden longer. I had much more time to think about things. I clung dearly to the words of Isaiah's prophecy and to the love and support from my family and friends. The foundations of my family's faith remained strong. I started to dream again redeveloping a vision of self and purpose. The physical eyesight was gone. A new insight vision was taking shape. My dreams became mixtures of things from my past blended with the present headed to visions of the future. I was excited, fascinated, and anxious. I was also scared and afraid.

The first part of my healing process after losing total sight was to rebuild my sense of humor. I believe humor is a direct result of having hope. Hope is the ability to look beyond the immediate to the long range, to see visions of tomorrow based on what we know today and where we have come from. My humor came back and got stronger. It did not take me long to rekindle my sense of humor finding plenty of "blind" jokes to share with others. With the dreams returning and my ability to once again hope about tomorrow it was fairly easy to laugh at myself and find my own humor from within.

The second part of the healing process was listening to my inner self struggling for a new sense of independence while re-establishing the new relationships with my family. My inner self was crying out for independence, which through my family I would learn it was more of inter-dependence. Through our spiritual and family bonds we need each other for survival and growth. I started researching and discovering reference points of others which were blind, who had gone before me. This voice also kept reminding me of the vision of the eagle soaring across that last morning sky. The vision of the eagle was the necessary hope and determination that I needed for the struggle ahead. That same voice also kept reminding me of the love and support of my family and friends. When I started to get down on myself and felt like inter-dependence was not possible the memories and visions of their images spoke to me and encouraged me on.

I realized there was much I could still do. At home I started washing dishes enjoying the quiet time for meditative thought, reflection, and thinking. It felt good to help around the house. I took a trip on a Greyhound bus to see my spiritual partner and other friends. It was the bus driver's first trip on the route, a familiar route I had driven many times. He got lost. Yet I knew where he was and with a few verbal descriptions of intersections and landmarks I guided him into the bus depot. He was appreciative for my assistance and also teased me about really being blind. I smiled and let my sense of humor keep him wondering. I was discovering there were many components to fit together. The participation in my healing was going to be putting those components together.

The third piece to the healing process was returning to my goals and ambitions to be an ordained minister. There were new obstacles in the way. I returned to the words of Isaiah's prophecy. There was much to hear and understand. I could not ignore the voice within which called me out. I found myself dreaming about tomorrow and the voice was only satisfied when I agreed to pursue my career in the ministry. It was the opening sentences of the prophecy which spoke first that caught my attention: "Have you not heard? Do you not know? The Lord is the everlasting God, the maker of the heavens and earth, and God never grows weary nor sleeps." There is an everlasting God who is always watching out for me. Not just me, but for me. No matter what I do, what happens to me, or how far away I might wander from the truth, there is a God who loves me, watches over me, protects me, and helps me. With that kind of support network pushing me from behind I had no other choice. The voice from deep within would not let me alone nor be satisfied until I returned to my goals and dreams of being an ordained minister. With a God like this creating and renewing inside of me I just had to spread the news. The best way was to become an ordained minister and find unique and positive ways of sharing the good news. So I prepared for seminary.

I believe at some time or another each one of us has experienced the presence of the Holy Spirit speaking to us. Although many times we hear the voices we perhaps do not fully understand. Often times we ignore the small voice deep within afraid the cause and effect relationship of which it speaks will take us into places we would much rather not go. Yet I have learned to believe and trust in that voice for direction.

I have spent many hours challenging God to prove to me why I should be faithful. Before the loss of my sight God was always something on the fringe, someone or something for my convenience sake. God was there when I needed, not when God needed me. I was becoming a captive hostage in myself, trapped within a sightless body losing self-esteem real fast. My world existed around me. I was the center. I was the reason for the cause and effect relationships of my life. I was in control and not willing to let anyone tell me different.

I believe there is a God because of the cause and effect relationship within our experiences. The cause and effect begins when we are but a twinkling in our parent's eyes. In our baptism our parents, families, and sponsors vow to teach us the ways of truth and justice, to walk in the ways of Jesus Christ, and to struggle with the Holy Spirit such as Abraham did so we learn by cause and effect in our relationships there is a presence which watches over us. I recall a familiar childhood prayer I said every night before going to sleep: "Now I lay me down to sleep, I pray the Lord my soul to keep, if I should die before I wake, I pray the Lord my soul to take." Although simplistic in its understanding and theology it was a cause and effect relationship to be experienced.

Somewhere along the way we have our own hands-on experience and God becomes real to us. It happens in a cause and effect situation, an environment where we exist but have very little or no control. It happens when we least expect it and when we are not looking for it. We might attempt to become comfortable and familiar with our experience and understanding of which God is to us only to find it changing. There is so much of God to attempt to understand. I believe this is the magical mystical dance of life which makes us so wonderfully human.

When Isaiah was in captivity with the people of Israel he knew his cause and effect relationship with God was dependent upon his patience and his ability to see the larger picture. The people of Israel doubted this God to whom they were supposed to be faithful. They felt as if they had been abandoned. They figured they knew everything there was to know about God. Israel could only see themselves and not the larger picture. Being held in captivity was sort of like having the jigsaw puzzle scattered. Isaiah could see the larger picture and as a mouthpiece for God took the responsibility of keeping Israel together while in captivity until all could see the larger picture. The words of his teachings and prophecy were words of comfort and challenge. The comfort was God had not abandoned them. God was still there never slumbering or sleeping. The challenge was to be faithful, to look at the larger picture, to see the cause and effect of their captivity and how it would make them a stronger people.

I began working at the little pieces of me trying to understand the new direction my life was taking. From birth to death, from beginning to end I began working and struggling trying to put the larger picture of myself together. When pieces started to fit together I could feel the eagle beginning to soar gracefully across a blue sky. When frustrations and disappointments happened I would struggle to find endings and to start new beginnings. I experienced celebrations and disappointments, successes and failures, joy and sorrow.

Like the people of Israel I would often times feel me held in captive bondage by my adversities? I believe there is a cause and effect relationship to everything which happens to me. By experiencing these adversities and working at fitting them into the larger picture I experienced growth and understanding in myself relationship to God. The harder I struggled with myself the stronger I became. The stronger I became the better I felt. Soon the captive bonds were lifted and I felt the eagle soar. As I spread my wings encouraged by the words of Isaiah I felt much like Neil Armstrong as he stepped into the lunar dust from the Eagle's ladder proclaiming: "That's one small step for man, one giant step for mankind."

CHAPTER TWO:
HANDICAPS AND
DISABILITIES

My greatest summer pleasure and recreation is sailing. My favorite getaway is the Apostle Islands off the north shores of Wisconsin in Lake Superior. Lake Michigan has provided many adventures, too. I first began when I joined the Explorers Scouts of the Boy Scouts of America whose focus was sailing. We were known as Ship 50-Sea Scouts sponsored by the local yacht club. I started learning how to sail by racing 19 ft. Lightning and smaller 11 ft. Penguin class sailboats. Teamwork was essential for crewing aboard these two types. My interest quickly helped me to learn the art and technique.

I completed the Sea Scouts program and my adventure continued when I was invited to crew aboard a 32-ft. yacht called the "Carcayne." I learned how to handle all the sail changes on the foredeck required for racing large yachts, including how to fly a spinnaker. The spinnaker is the most colorful of sails and the most dangerous to handle. It is also the most exciting.

When I started having problems with my eyesight one my growing fears was not being able to sail. I dreaded the thought of being reduced to just a passenger; I would rather not sail at all. There is a tremendous sense of freedom I feel and enjoy when I work the many integral parts of a sailboat. I was scared I would never sail again. But not so mate!

Although there are many things I cannot do because of my blindness, sailing is one thing I can do. I have lots of experiences in different sailing adventures. Spend a little time with me and you will hear many stories, from a night-crossing of Lake Superior in a bad storm to an exciting sun-drenched summer cruise off the Apostle Islands. Each adventure represents another example of my ability to use a gift and skill despite my loss of sight. My sense of freedom enables me to become one with the boat, water, and wind; to sail as if I can really see what I am doing. It allows me to defy my own handicaps and disabilities. There is nothing better than to share these experiences of liberation with others. Being open and sincere helps me to understand my own situation. In sharing my story someone else shares theirs and we both learn something new.

Your mind is filled with many wonderful treasurers which tell part of your personal story. Each knickknack, every book, all the wall hangings, etc. share parts of the bigger picture which makes you who you are. My home has many things related to sailing. I have working navigational charts on the wall; blueprints of a sailboat hanging like wallpaper, pictures, and models, all somehow significant to the art and experiences I have had. They are pieces of my story, reaching out far beyond to include friends who have shared in them. Working through my own handicaps and disabilities involves my story being interpreted by the others. The process of dialoguing with them and their understanding of my story helps me understand myself better.

My greatest sense of freedom is finding the balance between wind, water, boat, and self. This is achieved when all things are working together in "close trim" and the boat seems to sing through the water. Smooth sailing ahead. The same sense of freedom comes when I find the balance between my handicaps, disabilities and me. "Close trim" while sailing requires using the necessary equipment aboard the boat. Likewise, life requires using all the gifts, talents, and skills which one has been given.

Sometimes sailing encounters rough waters, storms, and other difficulties, which deter the boat from moving forward in a true course. Sometimes life encounters adversities which limit and threaten our journeys and accomplishments. I believe it is possible for us to work through our handicaps and disabilities. It is through a sailing illustration I wish to tell another part of my story.

My father shared an early morning daily devotion he was reading. We were vacationing together on the coast of Maine. It was exciting to be with my parents. I had missed many family vacations due to summer employment, educational requirements, and personal conflicts. The devotion drew a parallel between a sailboat and our spiritual life. Listening to my father read created a moment of reflection about how I navigate and work through my handicaps and disabilities. There are many parallels between my sailing skills and the way I handle life. Being able to adapt to my many adversities is demonstrated by how I embrace my spiritual life. My sailboat is my faith. I must trim the sails, steer the rudder, and find the balance of my faith in order to function and adapt to the many obstacles which stand before me.

The early morning was quietly bathed in sunshine with a slight hint of a breeze off the bay. My father read the devotion about the similarity of a sailing vessel and our spiritual life while we sipped our morning coffee. These were precious moments to me. Most of my ministry is fashioned in my father's footsteps. He read the devotion with affection and dedication to his own faith and to me as a son, a friend, a parishioner, and a colleague. Not many sons can boast about the unique relationship which I experience with my father. Here's how I remember that morning's devotion...

Sunrise on a quiet protective marina is a perfect picture of serenity. Boats lie quietly at anchor, sea gulls drift lazily; lighthouses stand erect, weathered, and dark. Most of us have seen such a picture, or perhaps experienced it when visiting a coastal community. There is a quiet peaceful presence about the lazy harbor. There is also a uniqueness about each harbor at sunrise. Each vessel has its own distinct appearance; from different colored hulls and sailcovers, to sleek racing sloops and sturdy cruising yachts. Each vessel has basically the same equipment yet each sails different from the other, a unique individual characteristic. This is the first parallel between sailboats and people. We all have the same basic equipment wrapped in a unique individual package which makes us so wonderfully human.

We share many similarities because we are all created equal. We are also uniquely different from each other, like the picture of a sleeping harbor. We are given the basic equipment necessary to function plus a spiritual gift driving us forward on our journey. In our own way each one is created in the image of God, given the opportunity to learn and grow, and the ability to develop into the individual person who we are. We are alike in that we are human, sailing vessels on the sea of life. We are also unique in that each one of us is slightly different in appearance. There are no two of us alike. We are unique individuals the likes of which have never been nor will ever be seen again in all of history.

A sailboat needs several important things to function: a hull, mast, sail, and rudder. Each has a significant role in making the sailboat move forward through the water. Each is important yet their design and location might differ slightly from vessel to vessel. Each piece of equipment is necessary and cannot really function without the other. The hull is needed to stay afloat. The mast is needed to carry the sail. The sail is needed to catch the wind. The rudder is needed to steer a course. In order to sail forward all things must work together. There are and will be forces which might hinder movement. Without the proper balance the boat flounders, loses the wind, and becomes stagnant in the water resulting in no forward progress.

As we develop our physical attributes we learn how to stand (hoist the sail), walk (forward progress), and navigate (use our rudders). We have the ability to find our balance so we can negotiate forces which might push against our forward progress. We all have and experience different types of physical limitations. Our forward progress creates new opportunities to help us navigate so we can find a balance in our lives. We also have the unique human quality of having a spiritual presence which gives us our determination.

In our spiritual lives we cannot be complacent. We must have forward progress in order to create opportunities for growth and understanding.

Complacency creates stagnation and no forward progress. Stagnation means we do not use the gifts, talents, or skills we have. Failure to use these gifts means we do not care about our spiritual lives, leaving us vulnerable. Some would consider this type of vulnerability as a threshold to evil. I believe evil is separation from God, which for me is sin. I also believe because we are human we can navigate around sin, away from evil, and continue working on the balance in our life necessary to be successful at whatever we desire. Like sailboats, we all have the basic equipment. We just need to do something with it. So too with our spiritual life, we have the necessary parts, we just have to put the pieces together.

"God gives strength to the weary and increases the power of the weak." [Is. 40:29]

As my story continues I would like to reflect upon this particular verse of Isaiah's prophecy. I believe no matter what our situation, it is ultimately the presence of the Holy Spirit which gives us the ability to move forward. It is God who gives us strength. It is God who gives us life. It is God who gives us our body as a vessel for our spiritual journey. It is in God and through God we are able to experience all we encounter including our handicaps and disabilities. I believe we are only as strong as we can be when we are at our weakest place. If we ignore we are human, filled with all sorts of weaknesses, and disappointments, then we can never enjoy the "smooth sailing" of a well balanced vessel.

I believe Isaiah was trying to tell the desperate people of Israel not to give up in despair so easily but to trust in their faith and God-given strength. They had to first recognize their weakness in order to experience the kind of inner strength which comes from God. I believe we, God's people today, must do the same. The people of Israel had allowed themselves to become comfortable with the routines of captivity. They were floundering in their despair and losing hope. In a sense they were afraid to be weak and in their complacency they could not experience the opportunities created by forward progress. The people of Israel were ready to give up and simply become a non-identity. Isaiah was speaking with the authority of God to encourage the people of Israel to seek a balance. This created forward progress thus giving them options as well as steering them clear of the obstacles of evil. Isaiah put it in very distinct words; "God gives strength."

God gives us strength by the presence of the Holy Spirit working within and through our spirit. We are given the determination to succeed. We are given the ability to develop and use our talents and skills to make something of our lives. Regardless of what we do, what we feel we can do, and perhaps what we think we should be doing, all of us have value in God's creation. We all have a reason to exist. We all have the forward progress to make something happen which creates the opportunities for other things to happen. God gives us the inner strength to keep on going especially when things get rough.

No sailing adventure is completely free of some struggle, storm or obstacle which must be navigated. Our personal journeys are filled with struggles, rough places, and obstacles, too. We must choose how we will interact and respond with these obstacles. We must take the helm of our journey and work at finding the balance which can and will provide smooth sailing. Our handicaps and disabilities can define some of these obstacles.

I believe all of us have some sort of handicap and/or disability. I believe there is an important difference between them. Handicaps are things we decide or desire not to admit to in our lives. Handicaps are things we *do not* want to do. Disabilities are physical limitations which we *cannot do*. A good example is blindness is a disability: I cannot see. I will never be able to get my sight back. Ignoring the fact I am blind or refusing to accept my blindness would be a handicap. Each one of us has certain things which we cannot do and things we do not want to do. This makes us wonderfully human. It also gives us the ability to work through and adapt to our handicaps and disabilities in very unique ways. What works for me might not work for you and vice versa?

I believe this unique individuality is a gift given to us through creation. Even identical twins will develop tastes which are different from each other. We might purchase and wear the same brand and style of jeans but each one of us will look different in them. Picture a classroom full of students and with a little imagination you can see the same picture of the sleepy harbor. Nothing appears the same yet there are many similarities. Allow me to consider the similarities and differences as a way of sharing and working through the ways we can deal with our handicaps and disabilities. I believe it is possible through this process to identify our handicaps and disabilities and then take the liabilities and turn them into assets. These assets can and will allow for smooth sailing and the opportunity to find a balance within our personal and spiritual lives.

Each one of us has certain physical and mental barriers which might stop us from doing things. An experience of falling off something will produce the handicap of a fear of heights. Going blind becomes a physical disability of not being able to see where I am going or read a navigational chart. The handicap becomes something I *do not* want to do whereas the disability is something I *cannot do*. Both are real. Both will alter how we do or not do something. The handicap is a mental block against outside stimuli. The disability is the physical limitation prohibiting us from accomplishing our ultimate goal. Each of us experiences handicaps and disabilities in different ways. What blindness is to me in total darkness might be some limited vision for another. Both are blind yet different in how they perceive blindness. A hearing impaired person cannot hear. A quadriplegic cannot use their arms or legs. On the other hand, someone who does not accept their disability is burdened with a handicap because they do not wish to accept the physical limitations they have. Someone who avoids doing the dishes because they do not want to has a handicap.

That morning my father read and shared the devotion with me we sat in silence and reflected upon the images the words had created. After a short time we shared another cup of coffee and talked about some of our thoughts. The devotion had caused me to remember some of my first days without sight. I recalled my first journey from the hospital bed across the room to the bathroom. A simple trip for most yet an adventuresome journey for one newly blinded.

When the doctors removed the bandage from my right eye on the morning of my twenty-third birthday I had limited vision out of the far right corner. I could see a little bit of movement as I tried to look out the remaining peripheral vision. There was a massive black spot over most of my eye. This was the same place where the surgeons had made the incision during the operation. There were several tiny stitches in my eye causing irritation. As my eye started to tear heavily the darkness continued to fill my vision until I was without sight. This was my first moment of blindness. I felt lost, hurt, and stagnant. Then suddenly there was a different feeling within. I felt a new breeze starting to fill my sails and I started to move forward once again.

Now that I knew I was going to be blind, I was ready to trim the sails of my life and move forward. I could hear the still, small voice inside reminding me God gives strength. Ahead of me were new opportunities.

I began to think of a course of direction which I could and would go as a blind person. Up until that moment I was afraid I would be confined to some sheltered workshop punching out aluminum ashtrays or assembling ballpoint pens. But with my new discovery and the internal voice of my faith, I started to trim the sails and move on with my life. The surgery did not work! Ahead of me were new opportunities, and unseen horizons.

My first adventure outside the safe harbor of my hospital bed was a simple trip to the bathroom. The bathroom was on the opposite side of the room, a rude joke to a newly blinded person. I had enjoyed the window bed when I could see. It had given me something to do while I waited and prepared for surgery. But now I was faced with a new obstacle. The bathroom was fifteen feet away. How was I going to get there? The nursing staff was insistent I make the trip by myself since they would not always be available to assist me. I considered using the bedside urinal. In their own way of helping me learn, the nurses had removed it. I would have to make the trip.

I was struggling to find any sort of balance in my life with this human condition of needing to go to the bathroom. My bladder was full. There is a mystery after surgery of having to go to the bathroom before they give you anything to drink or eat. Somehow the process seems backwards. First they take away all intake twelve hours before surgery so you are all cleaned out. Then after surgery they want you to produce but there's nothing in there to produce. So where's the balance? It's backwards. But somehow in the mystery of the process the thought and idea suddenly induced the product and it was getting rather necessary to make the trip to the bathroom...soon!

I swung my legs over the side of the bed, shifted my weight, and stood up. I was a bit foggy at first from having spent so much time lying down. I steadied myself against the bed as the cobwebs cleared. With a new urgency being signaled by my bladder I took my first steps carefully following the edge of the bed. I clung to the safety of the bed for security. These were my first steps in over thirty-six hours. These were also my first steps as a blind person. Suddenly my thought process paused for a moment, forgetting what I was doing. I laughed out loud remembering the words of Neil Armstrong during his mission to the moon: "one small step for man, one giant leap for humankind." It was Armstrong's first steps on the moon all over again. This gave me new inspiration.

I knew soon I would have to let go of the security from the bed and step forward on my own. I tried to picture in my mind the course I needed to take. I remember thinking if I missed my turn and didn't hit the corner I could slip through the doorway and out into the hall. This could prove to be interesting. I hesitated, sighed, and made my first turn. The next thing I remember was this tremendous pain shooting through my right leg! I caught myself on the edge of the bed and held on as the pain crawled up through my knee into my hip. I had clobbered my shin on the easychair in the corner of the room forgetting it was there. I bent over to rub the subsiding pain from my shin and suddenly felt another sharp shooting pain in my forehead. In bending over to comfort my aching shin I forgot about the small dresser next to the chair and slammed my forehead hard against its corner! More pain! I could feel the goose egg rapidly forming on my forehead as I caught myself securely with the bed. I tried catching my breath amidst the throbbing pain.

This was not a good start. I remember wondering if Neil Armstrong perhaps tripped as he climbed off the lunar module onto the surface of the moon? The camera did not show him doing so but the thought crossed my mind. I took another step. I considered climbing back into the security of my bed and forgetting the whole thing. Then the growing pressure in my bladder reminded me of the task at hand. The next couple of steps went fairly well and I decided to let go of the bed. Wham-o! I tumbled into my roommate's bed holding my midsection, which I had clobbered on the corner of his bed. Curled into a fetal position moaning in pain my roommate laughingly pushed me off and back onto my feet. He had been instructed by the nurses not to assist me under the threat of not getting fed or worse yet, getting a hypo you know where. I could sense the conspiracy against me as I tried to focus on the task at hand. The bathroom was still on the other side of my roommate's bed. My bladder was increasingly warning of the necessity of completing my journey. My destination not yet achieved, I would have just as soon had an accident in my pajamas and call it quits. I could easily leave a puddle on the floor and crawl back into my own bed. I had two options. Decision time.

I could follow the edge around my roommate's bed to the bathroom. This meant working hard at my task and perhaps success. I could leave a puddle on the floor and crawl back into bed just a few inches away. That seemed too easy and would probably mean having to wear a hospital gown, since I had no spare pajamas. (I hate hospital gowns.) I could crawl back into bed, and admit defeat. That meant giving in to my blindness. I was stubborn enough; I hated losing. There was only one real option. I took another step!

I made the final turn for the bathroom and quietly stepped into the world of porcelain fixtures. As I felt the relief of having accomplished my task on my own, I was reminded of the difficulties by my throbbing shin and forehead. It had taken me almost ten minutes to get to this place. I was exhausted. It felt good to sit for a moment and rub my bruises. Trying to recover from my pain I decided it was as good a time as any to panic! I pulled hard on the emergency cord hanging next to the toilet. This rang the nurse's station down the hall. I felt a renewed sense of calmness overtaking me. I was even more relieved when a friendly voice responded over the intercom with "may I help you?" I explained my situation and need for assistance. They responded with "thank you" and the intercom when silent.

I waited for ten minutes in the bathroom. There was no knock on the door. I became confused. I tugged once again on the call chain and waited. Again a voice on the intercom said, "Can I help you?" I explained my request. "Thank you" and the intercom went silent. I waited. Still no knock on the door. I tugged on the call chain a third time. This time one of the nurses arrived at the door. I again requested assistance. She thanked me for calling and left without me! There I sat, still waiting to get back to my bed. I was beginning to believe there really was a conspiracy against me.

Have you ever experienced one of those moments when the light bulb goes on inside your head? Suddenly it all became clear. The nurses were helping me learn how to be mobile. Getting to the bathroom is one of those necessities in life all of us have. My adventure was only half-complete. I started to prepare myself for the return trip to the safety of my bed. I tried to make some mental notes of the mistakes which had caused my aches and pains on the way. Was I ready? I grasp the doorknob and stepped forth.

The return trip shouldn't be that difficult. In my mind I could hear a voice telling me to just retrace my previous steps and I would avoid all obstacles. With new confidence filling my luffing sails I took the first few steps toward my roommate's bed. I winced a bit as my shins clumsily found the edge of his bed. I recovered nicely, made my left turn to the foot of his bed, a right turn along the bottom, and came to a nice quiet stop at the corner. At this point I was faced with crossing open space without any kind of guidance. If I could make this short distance between our beds I was home free. I took a deep breath and a step forward. The bed wasn't there! I panicked! Time seemed to stop. Where was my bed? I reached out searching with a slow arching curve and to my surprise found the bed not too awfully far away. I was comforted and relieved.

I have always been an over-achieving, self-confident go-getter type of person. Being stricken with this type of self-determination, I could have and should have crawled into bed at that point. However, I decided to take my success one more step and return to the other side of the bed where I had started. I even felt good enough to attempt moving around the end of the bed without holding on. Dumb mistake!

When I took my first step away from the bed and started to turn the corner my left leg found the other easychair in the room. The sudden shooting pain ripped through my leg! I went to bend over and sooth my painful injury and suddenly had this sharp piercing pain in the left side of my forehead. I had forgotten about the corner of the dresser which had not move since my earlier passage. I felt myself falling and desperately grabbed for the bed for support. The momentum of my fall moved the bed and I ungraciously slid to the floor throbbing in pain! I heard one of the nurse's gasp from the doorway as I collapsed on the floor. I heard another snicker. With what little dignity I had left I somehow managed to crawl on all four back into the safe security of my bed with a bruised ego and throbbing "thumb's up" to the audience in the doorway. They applauded my first successful journey to the bathroom.

I slipped between the sheets rubbing the huge double goose eggs on my forehead and feeling the throbbing pains of my bruised shins. I was back in safe harbor from my adventure. I tried to convince myself bedpans and urinals were not all bad. I wasn't convinced. I knew I would be making the trip again and probably sooner than I would like. It couldn't get any worse could it? It had to get better. I sighed with relief, closed my eyes, and tried to forget the throbbing pain. Another light bulb went on in my head and I realized I was starting to accept my disability. My journey to the bathroom was a moment in teaching, and learning I could convert my liability into an asset. After all, I now knew I could find the bathroom with my eyes closed and the lights off.

Some of us have disabilities. All of us have handicaps. My blindness is a disability I cannot change. I cannot see or at least see the same way someone else can see. Blindness can be a liability if I were to allow it. My physical limitation does not have to keep me from doing things normally done by those with sight. For example, I can still sail any size sailboat, back my van and trailer into any spot, work with a large power tablesaw or chainsaw, and even read printed text with the help of a talking computer and scanner. There is always a way to adapt to any given situation to make one capable of moving forward. There are many ways to adjust to a disability thus turning the liability into an asset. When I made my first journey from the hospital bed to the bathroom I began learning how to adapt to my environment through my blindness. I eventually learned how to rely on my other senses for data input to help me become more mobile. I believe there is always a way to find options for adapting to any situation. Remember, when the lights are out I can still find the bathroom.

I believe all of us have handicaps. Handicaps are liabilities which are harder to convert into assets we can use. Handicaps have a nasty way of constantly haunting us because they are usually something we fear. Handicaps take more energy because the limitations are emotional, psychological, or spiritual. Handicaps can change and alter their appearance without any warning. I do believe it is possible to change the liability of a handicap into an asset. I believe turning these liabilities to assets requires a deepening faith that God does give strength.

I have discovered through my own experiences in spiritual journeys, faith is often times seen and felt as a handicap. So many times it is easier not to be involved in direct relationships with the Holy Spirit. Being true to one's faith is difficult. It means having to face conflicts, adversities, and obstacles. In order to turn the liability of our handicaps in our spiritual lives we have to be ready and willing to take the helm and steer a good course through the many temptations before us. Sometimes we have to face a painful truth and get a tighter grip on ourselves in order to make the necessary changes. The change is well worth the effort, which becomes the asset.

Another example of turning a liability into an asset occurs when I am out sailing on the Great Lakes. Through my years of experience I have learned how to trust the feel of the boat against the wind and waves. This gives me the ability to steer a straight course without the handicap of being glued to the compass with my eyes. I can perceive where the boat is and what the boat is doing without really looking, yet seeing everything. I can see the whole picture of sailing without looking. Sometimes I forget I am blind, which becomes a handicap to a certain point. Fortunately these times usually end in a humorous way. An example of this happened on one particular sailing trip on Lake Superior. I was at the helm of a fairly large sailboat heading into port through a narrow channel of very large rocks. Many were at least three times the size of our boat. I had strategically placed members of my crew at different points around the perimeter of the deck. Each one of them was feeding me information as we slowly worked our way through the narrow shallows of the channel. We easily brought the boat dockside and with little effort the crew secured the lines. We had completed the difficult navigation process with no problems. We started to get off the boat. Other sailboats with their crews were already tied to the dock and had seen our approach and entrance. They were somewhat amazed when I worked my way off the dock using a white cane for the blind. I could hear many whispered comments as I moved past the other boats. I had just demonstrated how it was possible to adapt to my disability by turning my liability into an asset. I was now known as an experienced sailor rather than the blind guy who likes to sail. However, the next day while leaving the dock I got disoriented. We were walking the boat away from our overnight berth. With a sudden splash and a roar from my crew I had taken one step too many and fell off the end of the pier. What a shock to my body, hitting the cold waters of Lake Superior!

We all handle our disabilities differently. I choose to look at things from a humorous perspective. I believe God has a sense of humor. I generally look at things which happen to me with the ability to laugh at myself. If I can laugh at myself then others laugh with me, not at me. When I allow myself to be overwhelmed by self-pity then folks feel uncomfortable around me and have a tendency not to understand me. People start doing things for me rather than asking how they might help me. Then we have a lot of handicaps to deal with. You would be surprised at the number of people who will turn on a bathroom light for me. Who needs the light? I'm trained by experience to go in the dark. It works both ways. When I feel uncomfortable or unsure then communications with them become difficult and strained. With a healthy sense of humor and the ability to laugh at myself people are more at ease with my blindness and we are able to do so much more. It becomes another way in which I can turn a liability into an asset. When this happens all of us learn something about ourselves and each other. How exciting!

I do believe we all have handicaps and disabilities. How we choose to work with them communicates to others how we feel and what we perceive about ourselves. When we are able to understand ourselves with our handicaps and disabilities the better we can communicate with others. This makes our relationships much stronger. If we can laugh at ourselves and our mistakes people laugh with us instead of at us. The words of an old song remind us when we are smiling the whole world smiles with us. However, when we are crying we cry alone. If we choose not to accept our handicaps and disabilities we allow them to be liabilities which limit our opportunities to move forward. It would be something like going sailing and never hoisting a sail. So why go sailing?

However, if we choose to turn our liabilities into assets I think we will be greatly surprised and amazed at the many different opportunities which become available. Folks will feel comfortable with us and relationships can begin and grow strong. We have to make the effort. Like sailing, we have to hoist the sails (self-determination and motivation), trim the sails against the wind (being open to new and other options), and a steady helm (the ability to steer away from evil temptations). If we choose to be overwhelmed by or not to deal with our handicaps and disabilities then we choose to allow ourselves to be stagnant, floundering aimlessly, and vulnerable to taking the easy, most often time, evil way out.

Many times people will ask me how I am able to do so much with my life despite my blindness. God gives me strength. I depend upon the presence of the Holy Spirit to give me the abilities to turn my liabilities into assets. When something bad happens to me I study the situation to find what I need to learn and make the necessary adjustments. Sometimes bad things simply happen to good people. Accidents are an adverse part of life. But with our ability to adapt to our environment we can learn to adust to any situation. We can take our handicaps and disabilities and make them work for us instead of against us. And God gives us the strength. Trust in the Lord and many opportunities will come your way for you will be strong.

CHAPTER THREE:
COPING WITH LIFE
WHILE MAKING
OMLETTES

"There's a monster in the closet and the ghosts are on the wall; So why you keep on telling me there's nothing there at all; I know they're there, it's clear to me, I see them every night; And all I want is when I'm scared to come and hold me tight". [T. Hunter]

This chorus of one of my favorite children's songs helps me work at keeping things in perspective. I enjoy children's songs because so many times they express the feelings and emotions we older folks have a tendency to block out, hide, or try to ignore. Children have a very distinct way of letting us know how they feel, what they feel and when they feel it. If only we could retain the innocence of a child as we grow. Whenever I am with my nephews and nieces they request this song of me. It is fun to sing for them as they are like sponges and absorb every word. They can sing the song with me and also enjoy it being sung to them. The connection between us is together we are expressing something we all feel or have felt.

Depression is an ugly monster I think all of us have experienced sometime or another. It attacks us when we least expect it. It is able to change its appearance so it is hard to recognize. Just when we think we might have a grasp on depression it changes its appearance and easily slips away from us only ready to attack again when we least expect it. All of us have struggled with the depression monster and know it is no picnic.

Life is a picnic. Picnics are food. Therefore life is food. Somehow this simplistic logic seems too easy to help uncover and understand what depression is and how it affects us. Can simple logic be used to understand the complexities of life? Just about the time you think you have it figured out, something screws up and things get complicated. However, if you really want to work at it you can grasp the complexities and celebrate life as a picnic! I believe if one works hard at understanding the many faces of depression we can celebrate ourselves and take our monster on a picnic. Now there's an interesting concept!

I celebrate life! I make life a picnic in which I enjoy myself and have fun. Despite my disability I can laugh at myself, learn from my mistakes, and work through my struggles with the depression monster. This is how I cope with life, learning as I go and celebrating all I have as gifts given to me. This is part of the uniqueness of my gift, I am able to cope with life and make a picnic of my complexities. When things get rough, when things seem to always go wrong, when it feels like I am not going to make it, I find something I enjoy doing and celebrate that I can do. One of my favorite things to do is cooking. I love omelets and when the depression monster makes its appearance I invite it to sit down and enjoy an omelet with me.

Until recently I never had a problem with weight. In fact, I had more of a problem putting weight on. For the longest time I weighed 137 pounds. I was a skinny hip-less wonder. If I did not wear a belt, my jeans were destined to fall. I wore the same size of clothes from my junior year in high school until I got married. It wasn't because I didn't eat! I was a big eater. Most people who observed the amount of food I consumed in order to stay healthy usually looked to see who else was coming to join me. I ate much and burned it off quickly meaning I had to also eat frequently. Some would even go so far as to say I was a real oinker! I wouldn't say that. I just required a lot of food. Fortunately I enjoyed (and still do) cooking.

My two favorite foods are omelets and Sheboygan styles bratwurst. When I am feeling depressed and know the depression monster is visiting there is nothing better for my enjoyment than a good three-egg omelet or a couple of double brats hot off the grill. Just the process of making either boosts my spirits and helps me cope. Then comes the exciting climax to my process of coping with depression, eating!

Coping with life is a process. I believe a way of coping with life is to find an activity you like to do. I believe that finding this activity has to be within our capability and must not harm or injure us. If one has a problem with weight, eating is not good. Purchasing things with a credit card while in a "shop 'til you drop" mode will cost you dearly at the end of the month when the payment is due, plus interest. If you cannot see, driving a car is not a good idea. There is however, something each one of us enjoys doing. Part of the process to a healthy spirit is to discover the activity and use it to help cope.

Life is not always a picnic. Sometimes it is tragic, filled with adversities, accidents, and unexplainable events which cause us pain and sorrow. These adversities make our lives complex, and vulnerable to a visit by the depression monster. We all have experienced some form of loss or tragedy, which reminds us life is a gift. We must treat it as a precious gift or suffer the consequences. When I started losing my sight the depression monster moved in and became my partner. The more I lost my usable vision the stronger this monster got a grip on me. I started to feel worthless and I was losing myself. I got to a time and point where suicide seemed the only way out. I was willing to escape as a coward and give up my understanding of life rather than working through the challenges.

The first stages of my visual problem did not appear to be all that serious. Doctors were working together and doing everything they knew to manage my diabetes and the diabetic retinopathy. Then I lost the sight in my left eye during a surgery to relieve an abnormal amount of pressure. Suddenly my world was in a tailspin. A knock on my spiritual door and in stepped the depression monster. I was frustrated, scared, and confused. I felt alone. It was not a good place to be. I felt like my friends had deserted me. Actually, I was deserting them. I felt like I couldn't do anything anymore. I decided to abandon myself by attempting suicide.

After losing the vision in my left eye I thought about suicide many times. Way too many times! I tried to make specific plans. Everything would have to work perfectly or it would not be successful. Not being successful would mean painful consequences, which is what I was trying to escape. The process became a vicious circle. I became a lost piece of the puzzle and fell deep into self-pity. I felt no hope. When I got into my car on the night I attempted suicide I was not myself. I was a zombie being controlled by the depression monster. All the plans were carefully laid out and in place. I was simply the mechanism to make the ticking timebomb function. I started the car engine and lit the fuse.

My left eye was useless. My right eye, although afflicted with retinopathy, was still usable. I had learned to compensate which enabled me to drive. I could still drive which is something I enjoyed. I left the house late at night and drove out into the country. I knew of several places where the road was curvy. The plan was simple: death by hitting a tree or rolling my car while driving too fast for conditions. I owned a 1971 American Motors Hornet SST which was my pride and joy. It was my second car and I worked hard for it. We were best pals. We spent many long hours together covering many miles. Driving was relaxation for me. Driving was also one of the ways I was able to employ myself and earn necessary income. I turned onto the road which was my planned demise.

I don't remember thinking about much as the car accelerated beneath me. I held the accelerator to the floor and gripped the steering wheel firmly. I enjoyed driving so much the steering wheel felt good in my hands and the car strong beneath me. I slipped through the first set of curves, sliding down along the inside of the turns, coming out high on the banks, and setting myself up for the next set of curves. Nothing happened, and quickly the road straighten out before me. I pulled to the side and stopped, gazing at the star-filled skies surrounding me, feeling very confused. The depression monster was riding next to me and still in control. I found a place to turn around and headed back through the same tight set of corners.

Like most teenagers, I started driving when I was sixteen. Driving was important to me. Driving meant independence. Driving meant power and control. I had an early start to my experiences because I had the fortunate advantage of having grandparents who lived on a farm. My grandfather had taught me how to drive a tractor and other farm machinery long before I started formal driver's education. Driving also became a form of employment as I got jobs as a delivery person and eventually a professional chauffeur. I paid many of my college bills by working as a chauffeur. Driving was a form of relaxation. The longer the distance to drive the more I relaxed and stayed alert to what was happening around me. Driving also gave me plenty of time to think. When I was tense I would drive. I could sort out many things while driving by myself. I was a good driver. I felt a tremendous sense of self-worth. I gained an important reputation for myself as a good driver. I enjoyed driving. Whether it was long distance or short hauls, driving was my life and my pleasure.

Back out on the quiet dark country road I once again felt the car accelerating towards the curves. The depression monster had control of the speed of the car and of me. I remember closing my eyes as I entered the first curve. I felt the wheels losing traction on the loose gravel of the narrow shoulder. I gripped the steering wheel tightly and waited. The car hit something hard and I hoped this would be the beginning of the end. I opened my eyes to watch. There were a lot of cornstalks and mud hitting the windshield. I couldn't see very far ahead. I continued to hold the steering wheel as tight as possible and closed my eyes again. The next thing I remember was my car stopped crossways on the road. I stepped out into the cool September night air and looked around. Behind me was a path of flattened crushed cornstalks and tire tracks through the field leading up to the back end of my car. I examined the front of my car. It was full of debris. I pulled many pieces off the grill, wiped the mud from the headlights, and got back in the car. I drove back into town to a self-help carwash and finished cleaning off the mud and debris before returning home. Boy was I feeling confused.

After returning home that night I had a lot more to think about. The ride off road was scary. Whenever I thought about my suicide attempt I got the chills and would shiver uncontrollably. The thought of my own mortality scared me. For about a week I was able to stay out of harms way. I felt I had successfully closed the door on the depression monster. Then things got sour again.

The second visit by the depression monster came silently late at night. I couldn't sleep. My mind kept me tossing and turning. The more I tried to relax the more tense I became. There were a lot of things on my mind. I seemed only to be able to look backward. I felt all of my dreams were gone, taken away by this stupid disease of diabetes and its complications with my eyesight. Whenever I looked forward all I could see was me losing my sight. I was terrified! I got out of bed and started writing a letter to my parents, family, and friends.

My suicide letter was filled with self-pity. Having major problems with my eyesight it was difficult to write. I sat in a rockingchair by a large picture window and wrote in big letters. I used to have neat penmanship. I would copy notes and notebooks in a very precise manuscript. I enjoyed writing longhand. I also knew how to work with calligraphy in composing and orchestrating music scores. Now in the darkness of my depression I had problems staying within the lines of the page. It only made me frustrated, having to deal with another effect of my problem. The depression monster was right there with me scattering the pages with great glee as I scratched my emotions and words onto the page. I remember thinking I needed to thank everybody I knew. I tried to apologize for causing so much trouble and being so dependent on them.

Somewhere in the process Mother Nature spoke to my father who got up and noticed the lights on in the living room. He came in to investigate. Discovering the many pages scattered across the floor he started gathering them together and organizing them for me. He began to realized something was seriously wrong. Parents have this unique ability to know what is going on without asking. They just have to look at any of their children and they know. They just simply know. My father looked at me starring back at him, and we began to talk. I don't remember exactly what we talked about but it helped. The depression monster slipped away from my presence realizing it no longer had sole ownership of my vulnerable state.

We talked early into the morning. My father listened as my story spilled from deep within. Together we cried and wrestled with the depression surrounding me. I know he was trying to understand what I was going through although he readily admitted he wasn't sure. His warm hugs and comforting touches let me know I was not alone. I started to gain back some of the self-confidence which was missing. Finally I felt exhausted and sleep was overwhelming me. He held me close in his strong fatherly arms and we prayed. In his own way he sang the "Monster Song" to me and I fell sound asleep.

Things started to change for a short time. My family made an effort to get me to participate in daily routines with increasing responsibilities. These gave me necessary internal hooks on which to hang some desperately needed self-confidence. I helped around the house doing what I could. My brother was training for his high school basketball season, so I started jogging with him in the evening. I was getting myself in shape for my impending surgery. I visited a training center for people with visual impairments where I saw others in much worse shape than me. An element of hope began to return for my future. I started writing letters to friends who were important to me. I could feel self-worth returning. I continued moving forward and new opportunities began to appear. I got part time jobs as a chef at a local pizza parlor and as a youth coordinator for a nearby church.

I hit another low point and the monster took over. This time I had gotten word I was going to be on a weight restriction. It signaled my sight was getting worse in my right eye. Since I already lost my sight in the left eye all the fears of going blind quickly accelerated deep inside. The depression monster feasted on these fears and I soon became overwhelmed. The burden of being blind was too heavy and I could feel myself starting to buckle under its weight.

I once again found myself sitting behind the steering wheel of my car contemplating the end to all of my concerns. It was fairly late in the evening. I sat there quietly for a short time rolling everything over and over inside my head. There just didn't seem to be any answers. There weren't any questions. It was all too complete. I could not see myself as a blind person. I could not handle the reality. I quietly convinced myself what to do. I turned the ignition key starting the engine and bringing both radios to life. I put the transmission into reverse and began backing out of the driveway. The CB crackled "breaker 1.9." I waited for the familiar response "goes breaker" but there was only silence. The radio crackled again. "Breaker 1.9. Anyone got their ears on?" I picked up the microphone and responded with a "go ahead breaker. This is Red Lead Foot" my CB radio name. I put the transmission into drive, pulled back onto the driveway, and continued the conversation.

Somewhere in the process of the radio conversation I turned off the ignition quieting the engine yet maintaining power to the radios. When the person on the other end of the broadcast connection started to fade because the distance between us was getting too great I turned off the radio and went back into the house. I felt different but did not quite know why. I went to bed. The next morning started like any other. I got up and went to work. What had taken place during the night still lingered in my mind without any reason or explanation. When I returned home from work I brought the mail into the house. My failing eye caught glimpse of one envelope which had no stamp or return address. It was addressed to me. It was not sealed. I pulled the envelope open and retracted its contents from within. Inside there was a plain piece of paper which had the words "God monitors 1-9" typed. There were no other markings to indicate who it was from.

I had some idea as to who was behind the note and it may have been the other person on the radio that night. The one whom I suspected has never admitted to being party to the activity. But that is not important. What became important was realizing I did not have to work through my vision problem by myself? There were plenty of people willing to help. There were good strong friends I could lean on when I couldn't bare the load by myself. I discovered new friends who were willing to help, too. I began learning how to face my difficulties as a challenge rather than an affliction. My sense of humor returned. With the help of my family my faith became a firm foundation upon which I could stand. I no longer felt sorry for myself and the depression monster started to fade away.

I love to cook. Breakfast is my favorite meal for it is my biggest and most important of each day. My diabetes requires I supply the necessary ingredients of proteins and carbohydrates. If I am to have a good day and feel good about myself I need to start with a good big breakfast. The better I treat myself to the important requirements for breakfast the better off I am for the rest of the day. Omelets became an excellent way for me to supply what my body needs. My omelets are not fancy. I would recommend since my omelets are created by a blind person, any guests not focus on how it appears on the plate but to trust it will and does taste great. My omelet specialty is called the "garbage omelet." What makes it unique is this omelet has an interesting parallel to life. Let me explain what I mean as I share my recipe for my "garbage omelet."

I find my best omelets are made with a good old fashioned cast-iron skillet. I like using my cast-iron skillet because it is dependable and solid on the stove. A good cast-iron skillet also requires a certain amount of upkeep, and if one is willing to take care of it then they are also willing to take care of themselves. I have had my cast-iron skillet for over ten years. It keeps getting better with age. I enjoy taking care of it and it provides me with good, delicious "garbage omelets." My cast-iron skillet is also versatile as it can be used on an electric range, gas range, open campfire, and on board a sailboat over a propane flame. A cast-iron skillet also comes in handy for self-defense purposes against attacking seagulls and other unwanted uninvited guests. I always say "carry a cast-iron frying pan with you wherever you go and nobody, including the depression monster will mess with you!"

My first parallel between preparing an omelet and looking at life is we need to use the proper tools. I believe if one uses the proper tools the project gets done quickly. Just as cast-iron skillets make the best omelets, with proper training the best tools for life can be found within.

The basic foundation for any good omelet is eggs, butter, and cheese. Without butter everything burns to the bottom of the skillet. Without eggs you have fried cheese. Yuck! Without cheese nothing sticks together. I always use three eggs for best results. Take the eggs and a little milk in a mixing bowl and beat the stuffing out of them. Put the butter (as much as you would like) in the skillet and wait for it to melt. As you wait for the butter to melt in the skillet slice a couple of pieces of your favorite cheese. Remember to share some with your favorite pet who most likely is waiting and watching close by. When the butter is melted, pour the eggs into the hot skillet and then let your pet lick the bowl. After all, they deserve a few treats in life once in awhile, too.

The second parallel is cooking is good therapy for whatever ails you. Half the fun of making the omelet is the expectation of how delicious it will taste when you are done. Half the fun of being successful in life is the process of putting all the effort into the task itself. Beating the stuffing out of the eggs is a good stress reliever. Finding something you enjoy doing, like cooking, is also a good stress reliever. When you enjoy doing what you like life works better, omelets taste better, and everything works for the good.

The next step in making a garbage omelet is the appropriate position. I find for best results, you should stand about three feet from the skillet so a slight arching toss of ingredients can be used. Ideally the best-planned kitchens will have the refrigerator located just about in the right spot in relationship to the skillet to make this toss perfect. Now open the refrigerator and begin looking for whatever strikes your fancy left on the shelves. This is where I believe the true fun begins.

I always like to start with something meaty: bacon, sliced ham, summer-sausage, left-over bratwurst, wieners, hamburgers, a piece of last night's meatloaf, or whatever your heart and taste-buds desire. If already sliced, diced, cut into proper chewing sizes just toss it over your shoulder into the hot and ready skillet. When you hear the familiar sizzle your garbage omelet is on its way! If you are brave and like taking big risks like me, continue searching through the refrigerator for other ingredients. Perhaps last night's leftover casserole looks appetizing. Mushrooms, onions, green peppers, red peppers, (if you like it hot) olives, broccoli, cauliflower, or any other fresh vegetables (depending upon taste) all flip back over the shoulder and into the hot sizzling skillet.

Having cleared the refrigerator of all the ingredients which are appealing to your taste buds it's time to hit the spice rack. Salt, pepper, Chile powder, Tabasco sauce, garlic, and/or anything else you find which looks, smells, and tastes good must also be included. Add these ingredients to your own personal liking (which comes with trial and error after making a few garbage omelets). Now find a long-handled wooden spoon so you don't get burned or splattered while stirring. Stir your omelet once or twice in a folding manner.

Another parallel between the garbage omelet and life is life is always giving us a strange mixture of events and experiences; some we like and some we don't. Sometimes we are in a particular mood for something most specific. Other times we sort of just roll with the flow and take what comes along. Our unique way of working through situations is like the sizzling skillet. If we allow situations to stick to us we get burned. If we keep ourselves lubricated with an open mind, a firm faith, and a healthy proportion of prayers, we can face any situation and find our way through.

As life continues and we gain more experiences we stir everything together in a folding manner and produce a well-rounded self. The final product will not only look delicious to us but to others, as well. Just think of the exciting relationships which are still to happen as you present your omelet to the world!

***Author's Note: I recommend teenagers not attempt this omelet unless supervised by an adult who has attempted it first. I also highly recommend any children or youth who have little or no cooking experience remain as far away from the kitchen as possible while these omelets are being designed and cooked. Rumor has it depending upon the emotional stability of the one making the omelet they might be included as a necessary ingredient. Good luck and delicious dining!

Having been in the clutches of severe depression and sure the depression monster had its icy grip on me I also have the experience of working through the difficulty back to a healthy place. I believe a person afflicted with depression cannot do it by themselves. I know I needed my family and friends close by to help. They believed in me when I felt I couldn't. They found ways of keeping me involved when I was looking for ways to escape. I could not have done it alone. I needed help.

In sharing my experience of depression and suicide with others in my many travels I have always found a common thread connecting each story. Depression is a serious illness often times overlooked. In today's society there are too many people locked into a self-centered "me first" frame of mind. They want everything and they want it now. They want it so bad they are willing to sacrifice just about anything, especially their personal relationships with their families and friends. This opens the door for the depression monster. We are people created by God to live in community. Just think about it. It takes two people to create a baby, a community. It takes two people to dialogue, a community. It takes two people to share, one giving and one needing, another community. We are created to live in community, not by ourselves. Jesus tells us, "wherever two or three are gathered in my name, there too shall I be." We need others in relationship so when the depression monster knocks at our spiritual door we do not have to face it alone.

The second part of avoiding the depression monster is to find an outlet, something we can do which keeps us participating so we do not start filling ourselves with self-pity. Perhaps cooking an omelet or grilling bratwurst is an activity which can be enjoyed without causing physical harm if you like to eat and don't have to worry about your weight or cholesterol. I know of someone who loves to cook and has a weight problem. They share their enjoyment with others. Important conversation takes place and the depression monster knows not to come calling. Some like to take long walks when they feel down. They have a special place to walk to, or a special route, and enjoy nothing more than to share the uniqueness of a place with another friend. Some like to write, read, or simply talk with friends they haven't seen for a long time. The important thing is they have discovered an activity they enjoy doing which helps them keep the door closed on the depression monster.

There is a passage in Romans, chapter 5 verses 4 & 5, "...rejoice in your sufferings. For sufferings produce endurance, endurance produces character, character produces hope, and in hope there is no despair." The Apostle Paul wrote these words. We theorize from biblical research Paul experienced a tremendous amount of guilt and depression after his conversion. When he realized how many Christians he had persecuted and sentenced to death before becoming a Christian himself he must have considered an easy escape to avoid the embarrassment of his actions. Yet we also find Paul turned around and worked through his predicament and made something of value and good to share. We can work through our situations and make something good.

Life is constantly changing around us. We have to be flexible and change, too. Sometimes things which might have worked for us previously are no longer effective due to circumstances beyond our control. I believe it is necessary to realize sometimes we have to change what we like doing best to discover a newer more appropriate activity. When I had sight I loved to drive when I felt the depression monster near. Driving through the quiet countryside listening to music on the radio always helped me relax and think. Now that I am blind I don't think it is a good idea for me to drive. So I changed my activity. I was fortunate to find working with my hands on very specific projects did the same thing as driving use to. Working on something very detailed with my hands helped me gain insight and perspective, keeping the depression monster at bay. I was fortunate to discover several different activities including cooking, sailing, woodworking, auto-mechanics, and music. Each activity has its unique therapy to assist my situation. Each activity also has the opportunity to share with someone else.

Finally, remember you and I are never alone. We always have a friend who will listen. The greatest of all friends is the one who created us, making us in the image God always sees. We can share every burden with God through prayer. When we pray God provides the necessary responses to us in the form of someone to talk to, who will listen, a soothing activity to do such as mentioned above, and sometimes simply a still quiet voice deep within us which helps us gain the necessary insight and perspective on who we are and what we are about. God doesn't make garbage, but God will help you create a garbage omelet. Think about it!

CHAPTER FOUR:
B.L.I.N.D.

I am able to accept my blindness as a gift. I use my blindness to help me understand myself better. I believe my blindness helps make me a stronger person. I believe God uses my blindness to help others "see" beyond themselves, beyond the physical attributes and masks we tend to hide behind. When I had sight I was guilty of hiding behind my own mask of recklessness, attempting to control all which was within my reality. Then I stepped into the world of darkness and discovered a new way to see. My blindness became my transformation to a place where I am able to "see" much more. Being BLIND began to mean "Beginning Life in New Dimensions."

Isaiah 40:31, "but those who hope in the LORD will renew their strength. They will soar on wings like eagles; they will run and not grow weary, they will walk and not be faint."

When I started to lose my sight I had to learn how to be patient. I was not a patient person. When things were not happening I made something happen. I was impatient, stubborn, short-fused and quickly angered, and pushy. If a group of people had difficulty making a decision I would take control and get things moving. Too many times it was more my decision than the group's decision. This caused separation among many friends. I was not patient. As my condition got worse and I spent more and more time waiting in clinics, doctor's offices, and hospitals I began to realize there was an advantage in being patient. The eagle inside me started to spread its wings in preparation for something new to begin.

In learning how to be patient I discovered ugliness is only skin deep while beauty goes through to the bone. I was guilty like most people of labeling things by how

I perceive things to appear rather than by experiencing them for their own beauty. I was passing judgement on something or someone based upon past experience rather than seeing the potential of a new relationship. I could not see beyond the masks and therefore made my decision simply by how I wanted the situation to go. I was not looking at the whole picture but only at the parts I wanted to see. Being able to use my blindness and my newfound patience as a gift with myself and with others required I see the beauty of the whole picture rather than just the components.

Beginning life in new dimensions requires much patience. Patience is something which is learned, not automatically assumed. Patience takes time to discover and nurture. Discovering and nurturing one's patience takes hope. Hope is an important element in one's journey through life. It is the foundation for ones faith, especially when we view our lives as a journey towards salvation, God's promise of eternal life. Hope is the energy which gives us the determination to reach for our dreams and aspirations. When we learn to hope in the Lord, our faith is renewed and we will sense something new and different happening inside. This is when the excitement begins.

My greatest experience of hope and patience happens when I am camping. Camping is one of my favorite hobbies especially when I can experience the gifts of the outdoors with special friends. Many of my best experiences have taken place at summer church camp. I try to spend at least one week in a church camp where I learn as much, if not more, about myself as I am able to teach others about hope and patience. Many of these camps vary in style from specialty programs such as music, arts, dance, and drama camps, to sailing camps, to family camps. I enjoy these different camps in the roles of director, counselor, and camper. These unique communities have helped me discover my greatest understandings of hope and patience. It is in these experiences I have discovered ugliness is only skin deep while beauty goes through to the bone. My experiences at camp have taught me to see past the outward and physical appearances into the inward and spiritual beauty each person has.

Being an experienced camper I have seen just about everything and anything imaginable. I have seen the beautiful serenity of a quiet sunset on a waveless lake to the power of a destructive raging tornado. Each experience had its own ugliness and its own unique beauty depending upon how I experienced them at the precise moment of their existence. I have seen the grace of an eagle drift silently from the sky, grab a fish from the lake, and then with its powerful wings carry its prey back to its nest. I have seen two friends reconcile their differences and enter into a deeper spiritual relationship. I have seen people come to the camp community lost and through new relationships and experiences find themselves. I have experienced one burdened with ugliness discover their own inward and spiritual beauty.

My camping experience is my place to find my faith renewed. Through the community of a camp environment I become most keenly aware my faith is my hope and hope is the energy to help me look forward to tomorrow. I find a sense of wholeness with myself, the Holy Spirit, and the world around me. I enjoy the serenity and challenges of new relationships. I find the inner strength which helps me face my adversities. I am able to see all that I am as a gift. I am able to "begin life in new dimensions." It is through these experiences I am able to see my hope rise like on the wings of an eagle.

My first summer of being a blind person came with an offer to be a counselor at a music, arts, dance, and drama camp. I was completing a program which taught independent living skills to the blind. I felt ready to face these new beginnings. Through my disabilities I was acquiring new skills of mobility, communications, and sensitivity to a new environment within yet not contained within. I was full of expectations and dreams as I had been accepted and enrolled to begin my seminary training later in the year and was excited to be invited to work with the campers. With no hesitation I accepted.

The camp had twenty-four junior high campers with five adult counselors. I was invited to be the specialist in the area of music having just recently received my Bachelor's degree in "broadfields liberal arts music" emphasizing piano, trumpet, orchestration, composing, and conducting. In other words, get a Master's degree if you want a job. I was headed for a Master's degree but not in music. Rather, music was only a part of my talents and skills which would make me a minister. I went to camp "loaded for bear" with everything in music I could find. I had tape players and cassettes, sheet music and musicbooks, staffpaper for writing original compositions and arranging old favorites. I took my guitar and trumpet. If there would have been enough space in my parent's station wagon I think I would have even packed the local symphonic orchestra. Thank God there wasn't room!

Due to rain, the first evening at camp was spent in front of a fireplace in the chapel. Suddenly I found myself the center of attention because of my blindness, a strange new experience. Many of the junior high females were developing "puppy-love" crushes on me. I was flattered and embarrassed. There were a lot of questions about my blindness, and I found myself admitting there were some answers I didn't know. The campers were also testing me to see what the perimeters for our relationship were going to be for the week ahead. This is found on page one of the camper's manual. Always find out how far campers can push the counselor before he/she snaps. Having lots of camping experience behind me I quickly identified this key issue and knew the rules of the game.

My first learning experience at this camp was to trust my hearing and intuition. Using my many experiences as a camper I quickly discovered I could stay one step in front of them and outsmart their playful little tricks. It did not take long for me to earn their respect. With some of the perimeters and ground rules defined we started to relax and enjoy our time together.

The second thing I learned at this camp was I was not as "blind" as I thought I was. The label of being handicapped was changing rapidly. The innocence of the campers saw beyond my disability and respected me for who I was. By the end of the first evening I had acquire the nickname of "Blink" which I accepted with a great deal of playfulness. The barriers which I had put up around myself were not necessary and very limiting. I was beginning life in new dimensions.

Each morning my special interest music group grew. With all the resources which I had brought along with me my surprise was the discovery the music was internal, not external. The countless pages of musical score meant nothing to the campers. They were more willing to learn by ear and experience music from within just like a blind person would. I had not thought of it in this way. I had eighteen years of formal training and music always came from the page. But the campers were right; the music was coming from within yet could not be contained within. We started to share what we could hear, not what we saw. Soon the M.A.D.D. Camp a Cappella Choir took form and voice. The choir this year had twenty-two females and two males. My role was quickly defined as one who could help interpret what another was hearing from within. We learned together to trust the inward music and to express it outwardly.

Throughout the day I would spend time with individuals and groups working on their technical skills and selections they had chosen to perform. Talented pianists, flutists, trumpeters, clarinetists, and drummers entered into relationships with my musical gifts. All of the campers participated in the A Cappella Choir. I was learning as much about myself as I felt I was teaching. I was discovering through the campers how to listen to the music within. I found myself starting to compose lyrics and music, a gift I had previously enjoyed but thought I had lost when I went blind. New creations were always shared with the community each evening as we gathered for vespers around the campfire. The once anticipated long week quickly passed and it was time to head home.

Each afternoon the camp would gather for some time to share different things which influence our daily lives. Pressures with school, family relationships, boy/girl relationships, and spiritual formations were all topics discussed, explored, and questioned. One afternoon the topic became handicaps and disability and I became the lead resource. There were many questions. How did it happen? What did it feel like? Was I afraid? What was I going to do? What could I do? Could the doctors do anything to correct it? Just to name a few. As our dialogue time began I remember having just as many questions about my blindness as they did. Perhaps together we would begin to find some answers.

I began my presentation by telling a story as we sat in a circle near the fireplace. I was reflecting about a particular night when I was a camper. The story took place in the same chapel in which we were now sitting. I shared with the group a vision I had experienced on Vesper Point not far from the chapel. I described to the campers my vision of seeing the image of Christ walk across the lake as a rainstorm developed. A special friend Kathy and I had been watching a thunderstorm far across the lake. We had learned much from each other during a similar week of camp and were celebrating a new understanding of our friendship. While we sat and talked the rain came across the lake and we started getting wet. It was in the quiet approach of the rain on the water I believe I saw Christ come and invite me to become a minister, a disciple, one of those chosen to serve in a unique relationship with Christ as an ordained minister.

In sharing this story with the campers I established a common place from which I was able to share some of my fears about being blind. My greatest fear was realizing I would never "see" my family again, which brought a tear to my vacant eyes. I shared some of the experiences of surgery which I had within the previous year. I shared some of my thoughts and feelings of the depression I experienced including the attempt of suicide. We began to dialogue how we all experienced different types of handicaps and disability. One of the campers shared a parallel which became very special to me in which we all experience some form of blindness, from physical loss of sight to a spiritual darkness. From this young unsuspecting theologian the issue was all a matter of relativity, how one looked at things and how one responded.

As the group continued to dialogue, sharing from their own experiences and asking questions of my experiences I could feel a new source of energy growing within. I remember imagining the strong powerful wings of the eagle lifting its prey from the water into graceful flight. I began to feel although there were many challenges yet before me, my faith would give me the strength to face them. I was discovering a new profound understanding of myself and my journey. There was still more to learn about being blind. The most important discovery and learning process was developing my communication skills so I could learn and "see" the world around me through the eyes of others. This would be difficult yet rewarding. This would be fear-producing yet comforting. The dialogue with the campers drew to a close. The ultimate experience thus far in my new dimension of blindness was about to unfold.

The staff had discussed the possibility of a simulation exercise in visual impairment when we planned this particular session. The campers were prepared, having brought blindfolds along. After everyone was blindfolded we spent some time laying out the ground rules and objectives for the exercise. We started the simulation by using our hands and fingers to braille each other's faces. Then I led them in an exercise of mobility using their sense of hearing and touching to move around the open vastness of the room. My imagination painted a delightful picture of the campers bumping and bouncing into each other enjoying themselves. Some felt a little uncomfortable at first but my co-counselors were always nearby to assist and make sure no one got hurt. We gathered back in the circle with our blindfolds still on to talk about how we felt. An interesting insight developed. The campers were not all so afraid of the exercise since inwardly they knew they could remove the blindfolds at anytime. I could not remove my blinding disability. That felt strange for there were still times when I thought perhaps at any given moment I would experience the darkness being taken away and I would see again. There was one more exercise to undertake as part of the simulation.

The final exercise of the day was going to be a trust walk. Most times a "trust walk" exercise involves one person wearing the blindfold and a partner who leads them. At a given time interval the partners change roles and continue. This trust walk was going to be different. The entire group would wear their blindfolds while I, using my trusty white cane, would lead them. Talk about the blind leading the blind. Our next activity was to be held in the basement of the main lodge about one hundred yards away. There was a narrow sidewalk following along the lakefront from the chapel to the lodge. This would be our desired course. I lined the campers in single file instructing them as to what each needed to do both in interpreting what the person in front of them would be communicating and what they needed to pass along to the person behind them. The other staff would be along watching to insure no one got hurt.

It was going to be absolutely necessary each participant remain directly in line and behind the person in front of them. The lead person would hold their left hand behind themselves approximately in the small of their back. The person following would hold onto the wrist of the person in front of them. If someone strayed from following directly behind the person in front of them or failed to do precisely as the person instructed, the consequences farther back in the line could be devastating. I informed the group they had the option to decline if they so desired. All volunteered to participate. I took my position at the front of the human train and we prepared to move out. I showed them how to use their right foot to locate changes in elevation. My co-staff took their places along the way. There was excitement and energy throughout the group as we stepped across the threshold, down a step, and turned to our right. The campers chattered amongst themselves, each communicating to the other precisely what they had been told and what they were experiencing. I invited them to become sensitized to the sounds and smells around them. Sharing my own experiences of learning how to use my other senses in my mobility skills I shared with them some of the things they could expect. I assured them I would have them experience a "talking tree" while enroute.

Carefully we moved out of the chapel. Each person shared the necessary information back through the line. Along the way I led the group directly past a tree. Many of them could "hear" the presence of the tree. Some of them also could "feel" the presence of the tree before they touched it. I invited them to braille the tree. While waiting to take their turn with the tree I invited them to listen to the raindrops falling from the leaves and to hear the quiet waves lapping at the nearby shore. We continued on along the path through the heavily shaded area and arrived at the doors into the basement of the lodge. All participants were safe and intact. No one had stepped off the sidewalk, which could have resulted in a sprain, no one had fallen on the steps, and everyone had communicated exactly what they had heard from the one in front of them. As they entered the room they removed their blindfolds.

As the campers found chairs to sit and let their eyes adjust to the light I faded back into the shadows to listen. I was exhausted. It had taken much more energy than I had expected to lead the group on the exercise. I presume I had been expanding my field of awareness to attempt to cover all of their movements. Impossible! I could not expect to cover all of their spaces in the chain. I was learning to trust my patience and hope perhaps they might learn through the experience a little piece of my world. The campers chattered with excitement of what they had experienced. As I listened to their shared stories I began to realize my own dimensions of my evolving reality. I could feel the new energy recharging inside.

The next morning camp came to a close. The campers, their parents and families, and a few friends gathered in the chapel for a performance sharing what they had learned and experienced during the week. The conclusion to the program was the camp's A Cappella Choir. The campers were excited. There was an electrical spark of energy flowing as they took their places on stage and I prepared to conduct. Their voices blended harmoniously filling the room. They were responding to the music within yet not contained within and sharing it with others around them. It was one of those rare moments when the music brought a tear to my eyes. They were tears of joy sensing the praises these young campers were singing. They harmonized the songs, too! I felt my heart rise like on the wings of an eagle.

Beginning life in new dimensions is an everyday process. Each new experience is filled with success stories, accomplishments, and sometimes failures. My hope is I will always find a way to face a new challenge and appropriate way to deal with that challenge. When I agreed to lead the trust walk I was not prepared for the wonderful consequences I would experience. The new sense of patience and hope I started experiencing began filling me with a new sense of confidence and purpose. I began experiencing my life with a new sense of hope in the Lord. I started to believe in myself. I started finding if I put my mind to any task chances are good I can accomplish the task. This newfound feeling of hope was also strength. I began discovering I had much more patience than I had ever dreamed. I began believing within my faith I could "March forward and not grow weary, I could walk and not faint."

Before I lost my sight I was a "do-it-myself" type person. There always seemed to be a hidden agenda if I did any project the reward would be all mine. Selfish! It seemed easier to do any task myself rather than ask for assistance. No risks involved and I only accepted tasks I assessed to be easy and within my realm of capabilities. I thought it made me a strong person but really it was making me very tired and alone. I felt I was a good hard worker. Set a task before me and I would accomplish the task as quickly as possible, by myself. I had misinterpreted an old familiar phrase; "when a job has once begun, never leave it till it's done: be the labor big or small, do it well or not at all." I thought it meant I had to do it by myself. Then, through that first camp experience as a blind counselor I started to learn I needed to work with others. There was a new developing sense of inter-dependence. I was discovering by working with others I was learning from others through others. Now this simple phrase reminds me once I enter into a relationship I must stick to it with all hope and patience and it will provide strength. This is how my batteries get charged.

Beginning life in new dimensions is learning I have new limitations because of my disability. Realizing and understanding these limitations has helped me to share my inner confidence with others. It has given me the ability to work better with others. I believe this ability to be a gift. A gift of being able to involve others, helping them to participate, to realize each has a unique gift of abilities, talents, and skills which can help others. When people participate in community all participating receive something for their effort.

Another story from a camping experience comes to mind to illustrate by example the gift of participating in community. As you know, I enjoy sailing. What I enjoy most about sailing is sharing a profound sense of community on board a tall-rigged sloop on the Great Lakes. Camping in this fashion induces participants into survival with each other because of close cramped living quarters and the necessity for everyone to participate in order to safely operate the boat. This is always a tremendous learning experience for everyone involved including me. I enjoy these experiences for I receive just as much as I give, sometimes more.

This particular adventure started in the small Lake Superior harbor of Bayfield, Wisconsin. Bayfield is the gateway into the Apostle Islands. The Apostle Islands are a series of islands of the northern shores off Wisconsin jutting out into Lake Superior. The water is crystal clear and cold. We have two definitions for the water temperature: solid ice! And melted ice! The summer winds of July and August are light and moderate as they warm across the mainland before heading out across the lake. The overall weather pattern for July and August is fairly quiet with hot summer days and cooler nights, variable winds, and perhaps an occasional thunderstorm. However, Lake Superior does have a reputation for getting mean and nasty rather quickly and one must always be prepared for the worse. That's another story in a different chapter.

Lake Superior will always tell you what is about to happen. The first rule I teach my friends is you can play on the lake, you can work on the lake, and you can survive on the lake but you will never beat the lake. This particular trip was no different.

On the third day of our adventure members of the crews were invited to either spend the day on the two smaller sloops exploring some shallow bays and coves, hiking some white sand beaches, or go with the two larger sloops headed for the open waters of Lake Superior to air out some damp sails and replenish fresh water tanks. The campers were to decide which adventure they would participate in. My First mate Bonnie and I accepted a crew of four; three females and one male. Daniel had become one of my favorite campers during the week. He reminded me of myself when I was his age. His innocence usually got him into awkward positions with other members of the camp yet always found a graceful way out. I could see many of the awkward situations during the week of sail camp hurt Daniel but he was also very forgiving, something I admired deeply. It was a pleasure to have him aboard our boat for the day. The two larger boats set sail and course due north for the open waters of Lake Superior.

In the protective waters of the islands the waves were hardly noticeable. As we headed into open waters the waves got much stronger and larger. Each of our young crew took turns at working the sails and steering the boat. The crew quickly discovered sailing the open waters was much harder than the protective places around the islands. Bonnie and I were always within an immediate reach of the tiller to assist in case there was any trouble. The boat felt good beneath me and I could sense it enjoyed the outing in the open waters.

The two boats easily put fifteen miles between them and the islands due north out into the lake. We spent a better part of the day chasing each other through many different tacks and points of sailing. The crew began to discover what real wave action can do to their stomachs and quickly found relief by eating crackers and bread. As the boats heeled to the wind it made it easy to fill the fresh water tanks with a bucket tied to a line over the side of the boat. Our tasks completed it was soon time to head back towards the islands. The trip back was the hardest for it was a close haul beating tack almost into the wind. The boat would raise high to meet a wave and then shudder as we split the crest of one wave and dove through the second. Water would run the length of the decks and pour of our transom. Bonnie and I enjoyed the tremendous strength of the lake and the graceful beauty of sailing it. The three female crew members took shelter down below in the main cabin. Daniel stayed faithful to the adventure and remained on deck in the cockpit learning the many different parts of the boat working in concert with each other. It was obvious he was enjoying the adventure.

As the boat tacked through a turn and began to settle onto its new course a large wave broke over the bow spraying the three of us with icy water. It was refreshing. It was also a shock! Daniel noticed another large wave approaching and asked if the boat was in any danger of tipping. I responded that the tall-rigged sloops were designed to cut through the water and the ratio of the ballast below would not let us tip. A short time later he asked again, this time wondering if six-foot waves would cause us to tip. I gave the helm to Bonnie and with my clipboard diagramed how a sloop's keel acted in the water the same as the sail did in the wind. The same windflow over a foil-shape which causes an airplane to lift skyward also drives a sailboat forward. There was a proportionate pressure applied to the water moving around the foil shape of the keel keeping us balanced. I also diagramed how we could control the balance by changing the trim of the sails or the direction of the boat. Bonnie and I demonstrated until we heard several cries of "uncle" from below. We returned to our fairly smooth tack slicing through the 5-7 foot swells. Our sister ship remained slightly ahead of us and off to our portside. We were on a starboard tack giving us a beautiful view of the other sloop under full sail. Moments passed as the three of us enjoyed sailing the boat together. Then Daniel asked me how the boat would handle in ten-foot swells? I began to wonder if he knew something I didn't. I asked Bonnie if she saw any storm clouds on the horizon, as we were only half way back to the islands. She replied in the negative and I sighed with relief. Again I explained the sloop was built in such a way that even if by accident we were to catch our sails in the water which would pull the boat over the sloop would stop its forward drive and the weight in the keel would effectively flip us back upright. I shared with him only a few stories I knew of sloops actually rolling completely over; "turtle" as we call it in sailing circles, yet the boat remained afloat and immediately returned to its proper upright position.

This confident answer seemed to fulfill his questioning inquiries. We sailed on.

As we sailed on back towards the islands it became a picturesque scene which you often see on paintings. Both boats were slightly heeled on their starboard sides driving through moderate waves and leaving a nice white churning wake behind them. The sky was a beautiful deep rich blue with large white puffy clouds. It was warm and friendly on deck. We tried to encourage the girls to come up from below but they were either napping or reading and quite content to stay within their safe secure environment. They knew not what they were missing. Then, clear out of the blue, Daniel asked Bonnie and me if it were okay if he prayed for ten-foot waves? Bonnie and I looked at each other in utter shock. Either this person had total confidence in us as a damn good crew or he was crazy? I wasn't sure? Attempting to shed the sense of shock which had overcome me I studied Daniel for some clue as to what he was looking for. I only saw his innocence and his eagerness to learn how to sail. I dug deep for an answer which might satisfy his curiosity and yet save the rest of the crew. "Perhaps some other day." Daniel was content with my answer and I could easily sense he trusted me and my decisions. It felt good trusting in our new relationship.

Later during the evening Daniel was the first of our crew to share his experiences of the day with other campers. With all four sloops lying quietly at anchor off one of the protective bays there were no signs of the large waves we had experienced earlier during the day. The camp was gathered around a campfire sharing their experiences of the day. Each told of how they had experienced the wind, the water, and in Daniel's case the waves. His three female counterparts refuted strongly remembering their upset stomachs. All in all the day had been good and each of us had learned something from the others. Bonnie and I felt good about his newfound ability to share his experience with others.

There are these words found in Romans 5:3 and following: "Not only so, but we also rejoice in our sufferings, because we know that suffering produces perseverance; perseverance, character; and character, hope. And hope does not disappoint us, because God has poured out his love into our hearts by the Holy Spirit, whom he has given us." Being able to look back in reflection of those experiences which build character is renewal for one's spirit. Even though some of the experiences were physically exhausting I also felt renewed inside. The harder I have to work at something, especially when it pertains to understanding me better, there is always a positive reward. I am able to rejoice in the situations which were perhaps a struggle to begin with yet produced a better me. Being able to rejoice in the sufferings is also being able to hope in the Lord.

"Those who hope in the Lord shall have their faith renewed, they shall rise like on the wings of eagles, they shall run and not grow weary, and they shall walk and not faint." Hope is everything. Hope is the ability to look forward and reach for the brass ring on the merry-go-round. Hope is the ability to make one's dreams larger than life so one becomes so determined to reach for their dream they will find the energy to succeed. Hope is believing in yourself and believing there is a God who walks with you, giving you strength, guiding you along the way. Hope is working, looking, and reaching forward to tomorrow. Patience is the ability to see hope come true.

Patience is the ability to keep ones cool in the face of adversity. We are all faced with adversity. Adversity is the unexpected which waits around the corner, hiding, and ready to become reality when we least expect it. Patience helps us to understand we have dreams.

Patience is being able to realize it takes time for dreams to come true. Patience means we have to work for our understandings in order to reach the fullest potential we can. In hope and in patience we "begin life in new dimensions."

CHAPTER FIVE:
BEING THE BEST YOU

Some people are born blind and others experience the loss of sight through accident or illness. Each person's blindness is different just as we are different from each other. Likewise there are no two people who will experience their blindness in exactly the same way. Many of us will encounter some form of visual impairment during our lifetime, from wearing corrective lenses or glasses to a world of total darkness. I have knowledge of both sides; I have seen more than most and now see nothing. There are also two kinds of blindness; physical and spiritual.

I have known all kinds of people with all kinds of disabilities. Some have chosen to make their disability a handicap. Others have accepted their disability and moved on. While those with handicaps remain in one place, in one frame of mind, in a world closed and limiting, others have gone on in pursuit of their wildest dreams. Handi-"capable" people know they have limitations, are able to assess and define those limitations, and are able to adapt so they can move on. Handi-capable people are always looking to grow, to learn, and to expand their world of experiences.

Often time's people who know me playfully accuse me of not being blind. Because of the many experiences I have had learning how to work with my disability, I believe I function better than most would expect. Blindness for me is an everyday occurrence. There is nothing I can do to change my situation. Just as any person with sight learns how to do something I have learned how to do it as a visually impaired person. I cook, wash dishes, clean the house, do laundry, and make my bed just like anyone else. I also found time for my hobbies of sailing, rebuilding sailboats, customizing a van, model railroading, and music. When I am in conversation with someone I have developed my sense of hearing so I face them straight on as though I were looking directly into their eyes. Just between you and me, I am looking in their eyes.

I have found some people with disabilities have a greater sense of self-confidence. They refuse to be left behind, labeled, or isolated because of their disability. They have an inward determination, a spirited drive to be successful. They have goals and dreams of what they can do with their lives. They are handi-capable. They have learned to work with their limitations and have found ways to adapt. They have also had a strong support network behind them. This network includes family, friends, and professionals who believe in them.

I want to draw a parallel between a young eagle and a person who makes themselves handi-capable. When a parent eagle knows a young fledgling is ready to fly the parent carries the young bird from the nest upon its back. The adult bird climbs to an appropriate altitude and drops the young eagle. It's either do or die! The young eagle immediately starts to flap its awkward wings as it plummets earthward. The parent is close by watching with hopeful expectations. If the fledgling does not recover and begin to fly on its own the parent is there to snatch the young before disaster strikes. The parent then climbs back to the appropriate altitude and the process begins again. It is called trial and error.

Working with my disabilities and learning to adapt to my limitations has been a process of trial and error. My family, friends, and professionals have been there to assist, to rescue me from impending disaster. Through my mistakes I am able to make the necessary adjustments so I can accomplish the task. Sometimes I have been awkward. Sometimes I and my support network have laughed long and hard. Other times we have cried in pain and sorrow. All are necessary and important parts of the learning process. Each experience has made me a stronger person capable at dealing with the challenges and adversities which lie in front of me. By the experience of trial and error with a strong support network I have become handi-capable. Like the eagle fledgling which eventually returns to the nest by its own wings I have gone forth with my own life.

I found it necessary to clearly define my limitations in order to understand my blindness. Disability is a physical limitation. A handicap is something I do not want to do. This is a very important difference to recognize. For example, I am visually impaired with total loss of sight. I cannot see. Unfortunately I will always be totally blind and I must accept the reality. I have a problem dealing with mice. I hate mice! I know mice are more afraid of me than I am of them, yet my handicap is in dealing with them.

Becoming a fully handi-capable person means taking risks. Risks are important for I believe they are the batteries which fuel our desire to grow. It is a risk for the young eagle to climb out of the nest and face a New World surrounding its once safe environment. It is a risk for us as humans to leave the safe security of our parent's home and go our own way. There are mistakes to be experienced. There will be trials and errors. It becomes a risk to venture out into the unknown in search of becoming what we want to be. As a newly blind person it was a risk for me to begin learning how to walk differently, how to take care of myself, and how to discover ways of adapting to the adversities I would encounter. Mom and Dad were not always going to be there to save me from crashing in the disasters of a mistake. Risks are an everyday part of life. We take a risk when we get out of bed in the morning, when we step into the shower, when we eat, when we cross the street, and when we tell some one we love them. There are high-risk takers who parachute out of airplanes just because they want to fly like a bird. There are low-risk takers who make every attempt to remain in the middle of the status quo. Everyone has to take a risk sooner or later. Handi-capable people know what risks are and know risks must be taken in order to improve one's self.

One of my adventures as a blind person was learning how to live on my own. I was a strong independent person before I lost my sight. I could and would do everything for myself, self-sufficient. The first days of my blindness were difficult. Slowly I began to discover little things I could do or adapt to doing. My batteries found new energy with each new adaptation to an old familiar process. With each success I got stronger. With each accomplished task under my belt I was ready to try more and more difficult activities. The horizon got larger and as it did I began to set my sights on once again pursuing my dreams. My family will testify to just how unique an individual I am! I was ready to place my signature on life with what I felt God was calling me to do.

I am always facing new interesting challenges which require me to discover ways of adapting to my environment with a great deal of uncertainty. There is a sense of excitement and sometimes a great amount of fear within facing many of these adversities. I understand there are certain things I cannot do and will never be able to do. I will not ever drive down any highway again, I will not read a book like people with vision do, and I will never be able to fill my own insulin syringes for my diabetes. These are known and understood. That's life.

There are many things I can do. Life is a challenge with a lot of fun and frustrations, accomplishments and failures. I have become handi-capable by being able to laugh at myself, believe in myself, and learning how to take risks which make me a better person. I learn from my mistakes, I celebrate my success. I share my rewards with those dear to me and I dream about a better tomorrow. My self-confidence and self-worth is established in my faith. My ability to continue comes from where I have been and who I am. My dreams for tomorrow drive me forward because there is still so much which I want to experience.

From a simple task of pouring a glass of milk to sailing across Lake Superior, becoming a handi-capable person has made me the best I can be. My humor has calmed panic in the face of danger; my faith has given me strength when hope was overwhelmed by despair.

I believe life becomes a more precious gift when we are able to encounter all it has to offer regardless of our disabilities and/or handicaps. I also believe life is not a gift simply given to those who wait around expecting it to be handed to them. I believe everyone must work for the fullness of God's promise by taking a risk and becoming involved with themselves, the Holy Spirit, and those around them. A disappointing handicap is one who isolates themselves and refuses to interact with their environment. Becoming the best you means becoming handi-capable, ceasing the moment, and using every experience you can to share in life. Being handi-capable is putting all of your cards on the table in front of you and giving it your best try. One has to risk, sometimes everything, if one is going to experience the fullness of the gift of life.

One of the first things I learned after losing my sight was how to pour myself a glass of milk. This is important in the process of independent living as a blind person because I love milk. The first time I was expected to pour a glass of milk for myself I forgot I was blind and simply took aim at where I thought the glass was. I missed, pouring milk all over the table. What a mess! The family dog thought it was great having a blind guy around for disasters in cooking and eating were usually profitable to his consumption of food. I was upset at first. Then I remembered I was blind and there would have to be a change in strategy for pouring milk. I quickly discovered that by hooking my index finger just inside the lip of the glass not only could I tell where the glass was and where I needed to pour the milk, I knew when it was full. Amazingly the little process worked and I stopped spilling milk on the table and floor. The family dog was disappointed. My process also worked for pouring coffee however it does get hot! But thanks to the nerve damage caused by my diabetes which took my sight, it also deadened some of the pain sensors in my fingers and even though it gets hot, it doesn't hurt, much. I continued learning.

The next step was learning how to find things on the table, especially at mealtime when locating food was a necessary ingredient for survival. I have countless experiences of knocking off a glass of milk, spilling hot soup, or starting a chain reaction, the domino effect, of condiments. This can be dangerous to one's health and safety not to mention embarrassing. I developed three ground rules for locating food. First, in my mind I divided the table into four sections. One section was my immediate place setting. The second section was the area immediately in front of my place setting.

Section three was to my right, and section four to my left. The second rule was I would place my fingers on the table at the edge near my plate and move slowly into any of the sections. At first sign of touching something carefully explore and identify its existence and make the necessary adjustments to compensate for its location. Finally, the third rule was never to reach across or beyond my own section for something I could not see. This meant I had to ask to have it passed, please. Disasters diminished. Meals became safer until I began noticing I could never find the butter dish at breakfast. I was getting frustrated until I heard the giggles of my family. They were teasingly moving the butter dish just so I would put my fingers in it! There were many other little things which happened which took time and practice to discover ways of getting through, around, or adapting to. I became rather proficient in the kitchen and even started learning how to cook for myself. This was going to be necessary if I was to leave the nest and establish a new home for myself. Cooking became a fun activity for me.

The next step in my process was learning mobility. Walking is easy. One step in front of the other. Wrong! Mobility as a blind person needs to replace the vision with something, some useful tool to recognize potential disastrous obstacles in the way. Picture if you will what could possibly happen to a blind person if someone leaves a chair pulled out from the kitchen table? It is rather painful and can be used as a crude form of birth control for the male species. So off I went to "blind school" to learn mobility. This is where I met "Spike" and "Rover." Spike was a fifty-four inch collapsible white cane while Rover appeared to be more like a modified curtain rod painted white with a golf grip and red plastic tip. Rover was rigid and quickly became my favorite cane for long distances. Spike was more the party-go'er since it could be collapsed and inserted into a pocket, inside my boot, or otherwise disposed of properly yet always nearby.

My first mobility session was spent in the classroom listening to instructions. My instructor was explaining how to use the cane, what the cane would and could do for the blind user, and how to use other senses to compensate for the loss of sight. There was the pattern to walk to, where to hold the cane, how to hold the cane, and what to expect to feel through the cane. There was getting used to holding the cane and feeling some new muscles strain and become accustomed to working differently. Ouch! And somewhere in the classroom process was a chapter or lecture on listening but I must have slept through it. This missing link would be discovered all too soon. The second mobility session found me standing in the hallway, cane at the ready, and lots of places to go see.

My instructor reviewed and quizzed me on cane techniques, asked if I had any questions, and insisted on a quick demonstration of my cane pattern and rhythm. Then he spun me around, pointed me down the hallway and said, "GO!" I took my first three steps and "Wham-O!" right into the wall! My instructor attempted not to laugh as he caught me and pulled me back into the middle of the hallway. Yeah, right! Back to the middle of the hallway, new grip, remember the pointers for cane techniques, spun me around to head down the middle of the hall, and three more steps. "Wham-O!" the other wall! My instructor ducked and laughed as I turned and swung my useless cane at him. He was fast. "Didn't you hear the wall?" he asked. Yeah, right! And suddenly the chapter on "listening" as it applies to cane techniques returned. Standing next to the wall I could hear it. At least I could sense it directly in front of me. Not only could I "hear" it but I could "feel" it, too. I tucked this away into memory for future reference. Back to the middle of the hall, quick pointers on cane techniques, spun me around to head down the hall, and away I went! I was extremely awkward and unsure, but I was mobile. I quickly found my own rhythm and off I went to discover the world behind my white cane.

As my cane techniques improved my territory expanded. There were several buildings connected by skyways. There were many new obstacles to encounter. The expanded process included different doorways, ramps, and strange stairwells. Soon after accomplishing the different buildings it was time to brave the city streets. It did not take long for me to experience crossing a busy intersection. This started out to be frightening. It was also entertaining for those watching. Still learning how to use my other senses to aid me in my mobility I forgot to listen to my environment and suddenly found myself in the middle of traffic. There was traffic in front of me, behind me, on my left side, and on my right side. Then I heard my instructor call from the curb "guess what happened?" The answer was too obvious. I had grown accustomed to making major mistakes in mobility (i.e., smacking the wall!) so I had become a quick thinker and reactor. I stuck my cane under my arm and started directing traffic. Soon I had traffic stopped enough in all four directions and I felt I could safely make one of the four corners. I resumed my working cane position and stepped forward across the street full of confidence. When I reached the curb I started to shake feeling the aftershock of my experience.

Once safe and sound back on the sidewalk it was time for another lesson on listening to what was happening around me. Someone once said "God watches over fools and children and God knows I'm a foolish child." Although it could have been disastrous in the middle of the intersection I somehow managed to dodge another bullet of fate. I was quickly learning how to use my other senses to assist my mobility.

As I got better with my cane techniques my humor began to take over. I started having fun with my mobility instructions by making little games out of each adventure. One of the fun games was a new form of "blind man's run." Another blind friend and I usually had mobility instructions at the same time. The objective of the game was to accomplish a predetermined course in the shortest amount of time. These courses might include different hallways, stairwells, and perhaps classrooms within the building on foul weather days, building and surrounding sidewalks in marginal weather days, and city sidewalks and bus-routes on sunny days. My favorite routes included a nearby university on sunny days. The instructor was always behind by a few paces watching, ready to assist if there appeared an impending disaster. It made learning a much-needed skill exciting and entertaining. The "blind man's run" part of the game was occasionally I would not pay attention and get lost. Then I would have to resolve my situation dependent upon my learned mobility skills.

One of the important rules of the game was I could not ask for assistance from a sighted person unless I was lost. If I determined I was lost I would tell the instructor following me. Now I could ask for directions from a sighted person if one could be found. Sometimes a sighted person was not to be found which made the game even more interesting for the mobility instructor, although nearby, would not offer assistance. I needed to learn how to solve my problems by myself since there would not always be an instructor close behind. However, a sub-paragraph to the rules and regulations for playing blind man's run included provisions if a sighted person offered to assist me in my mobility I could accept if I so desired. This became beneficial and provided me with several dates with some interesting women. This made my mobility instructors envious. I developed this "I am so lost!" expression, which increased the number of assists I got, both within the confines of the building as well as out on the sidewalks.

It made the game of mobility instruction much more interesting.

My favorite courses and mobility lessons took place through a nearby university. As springtime developed so did my opportunities of using my "I'm lost" expression. I got many offers for assistance and could choose whom I desired. One round in the game got interesting as I manage to slip away from my mobility instructor. The instructor had stopped momentarily to answer a question just as I approached a crowd of people. A lovely young woman in the crowd offered me assistance. I accepted. With a sighted guide we completed the predetermined course arriving at the destination much sooner than expected. When my instructor finally arrived my new friend and I had enjoyed a cup of coffee and had made plans for a date the coming weekend. My instructor decided I was proficient in my mobility skills. I had won the game of "blind man's run."

Getting use to my own mobility I started helping another friend not doing as well. He had been blind since birth and was not as familiar to the visual things of the world as myself. This issue proved to be a challenge to me as I began to understand how much of our society speaks in a visual oriented language which is not always accessible to people with visual impairments.

I began looking for different ways to communicate in a more visionless language, which helped me understand my own blindness. Mobility got better and more exciting.

One day my friend and I decided we needed some refreshments from a student gathering place a block from our classroom building. After quick planning and noticing we shared a couple of open periods near the end of the day, we decided to make a break for it. Once outside the building I discovered my partner had very little outdoor training and was feeling rather lost. When we got to the first street crossing he informed me he had not crossed a controlled intersection by himself. So I offered him my elbow as a sighted guide. Talk about the blind leading the blind. We made the crossing. I really did not think about all the complications that could have happened. I simply was faced with a situation which called for a response and I acted by helping my partner across the street. We crossed the street easily and headed up the block. The next situation we had to face was finding the door to the establishment to which we were going. Neither of us was sure which building it was but knew we were headed in the right direction. As luck would have it, two females heading for the same place approached us. They offered to assist us and together the four of us arrived at our destination. We treated them to refreshments and enjoyed fun conversations. An hour later our mobility instructors found us via a note we left scribbled on the message board and joined us. After short discussion we passed our lesson for the day.

The day came for my 'road-test." Passing this test would mean graduation from the mobility courses and a winning effort to the game of blind man's run. I accomplished my course in a record-breaking time. It included everything imaginable including cars parked across the sidewalk (parked there by the mobility instructors), city bus rides to prescribed stops, and travel in and out of buildings. I felt good about my accomplishment and offered to treat to refreshments at another local establishment which I had frequently walked to on my learning routes. For some it was a bit more difficult since it required crossing a river on an open grated metal bridge. This was always a difficult road-hazard for the open slots were prone to swallowing canes if one wasn't careful. But all of us made it and we had a good time. We laughed about our experiences, shared our stories, and then looked forward to moving on. For me it meant heading for seminary in a new community with new challenges and new courses.

I was almost done with my first semester in seminary when the big mobility disaster struck. I had been studying at a friend's apartment about a mile from my dorm. It was late and cold for a November night when I headed home. I enjoy walking and wanted the fresh air so I refused an offer for a ride. With cane firmly secure in my right hand and clipboard and tape-recorder under my left, I departed. I followed my normal route along a major street, finally crossing it at the stoplights. I turned and crossed with the second light and headed up a slight hill towards school. I used two intersecting freeways as audible landmarks to navigate by. However this night, because of the crispness of the cold November night and the lateness of the hour, the freeway sounds were different. I didn't make the proper adjustments. I walked along whistling and singing to myself. I made what I thought to be my last turn into the school property. When I felt I had walked the appropriate distance into the school driveway I began looking for my familiar curbs and landmarks signaling I was home. Suddenly I felt the familiar sound of a wall directly in front of me. Another step and I struck it with my cane. By the sound of my cane crashing into it I realized I was against a garage door. I figured I had gone past the front door to my dormitory and was down the driveway by the garage. I turned around, retraced my steps along what I assumed to be the campus driveway, and headed for my dorm. I could not hear my familiar audio landmark of the freeway but could hear a solid object to my left. I assumed this to be the dorm and after walking an appropriate distance turned and headed for the door. Wrong O! I found another garage door. What the hey? I now knew I was lost! I was not on the school property.

I returned to the paved street. I followed the curb until I found what appeared to be another driveway. I hesitated, listening to the traffic patterns from the freeway. They were definitely audible, but were they right? I felt confused. So I continued on. "Bam-O!" Another garage door! I was lost! Now what?

I went back to the street and started checking the curb with my cane. I discovered I had made a wrong turn and was on a dead-end street in the residential area near school. Now what do I do? I felt I could no longer trust my audible landmarks and decided to look for a front door. I started looking for a sidewalk knowing I would be waking some unsuspecting person late at night. I knew I was going to feel embarrassed but it was better than freezing outside in the cold November night. It was cold.

It seemed like I walked around the curb of the entire dead-end finding nothing. I thought perhaps I was back on the road leading out of the wrong suburb back towards the main street when I ran into another garage door. This time I found a sidewalk leading to a door. It was two o'clock in the morning! I knocked.

A dog started barking and soon I heard someone approach the door. I could sense the porch light went on. I stood there holding my blind identification card up. It was probably upside down. My own imagination pictured what the person inside the house must be seeing. A stranger; strange looking character standing on the front porch holding some card upside down, holding a tape-recorder, clipboard, cane, and wearing a large denim Stetson cowboy hat. "What a dumb time to be making a door-to-door survey!" I thought to myself as to what they might be thinking. Then I heard the dog go quiet, the porch light go off, and someone dialing a telephone. It didn't take me long to figure out they were probably calling the local police. I tipped my hat to the door to say "thanks," turned around, and headed back to the street. I was standing curbside when the police cruiser crested the slight hill and stopped in front of me. The two young officers got out quickly and then realized I was blind. They politely offered to take me home. I enjoyed climbing into the backseat of the warm police car. Moments later they escorted me into the dormitory and to my apartment. I offered them a cup of coffee for their assistance.

After the officers left I was not sure whether to laugh or cry. I remember feeling like a little child who has learned the process of potty training but forgets at the crucial moment and suffers a mess. I'm sure I turned several shades of red with embarrassment. But I did learn to listen better to my audible landmarks and not to assume everything is always the same.

We all have experiences to which we can turn around and laugh at ourselves. It is important to laugh at ourselves. It helps us remember we are human and prone to failures, disasters, and unique experiences. Being able to use my inner-self humor enables us to learn more quickly what we need to do to survive. Being able to laugh at our mistakes helps to make us more handi-capable. It equips the human psyche with the ability to learn from mistakes, risk trial and error, and become more capable of facing other adversities. I learned to laugh at my mistakes and by those experiences I am better prepared to move forward.

Laughter is contagious! When we can laugh at ourselves we can laugh with others. It makes life a lot more fun. It also helps us establish a good foundation for self-confidence. Self-confidence helps develop a solid faith upon which one can depend in a time of chaos. Self-confidence also makes one more handi-capable. When we acknowledge our limitations, disabilities, and handicaps and are able to adapt, work through, and look beyond, we are able to see the much larger picture of how our journeys influence others around us. As our self-confidence grows we are invited into new relationships. It is something we can share through our stories as witness through our faith.

"Those who hope in the Lord shall have their faith renewed;" (Isaiah 40:31)

We find more and more ways to grow in our relationship with the Holy Spirit as our faith develops. Our abilities to share our experiences enable others to grow in self-confidence. My experience of the "blind leading the blind" to a local tavern helped my partner to further his own mobility skills. My getting lost at seminary resulted in an invitation to dinner with the family I woke during the night. I believe for every event, regardless of good or bad, there is something to be gained, something learned. This is a big part of our hope in the Lord, that we will learn something of ourselves, of others, and of God's creation around us.

CHAPTER SIX:
GETTING NEW EYES!

"THE REAL VOYAGE OF DISCOVERY CONSISTS NOT IN SEEKING NEW LANDSCAPES BUT IN HAVING NEW EYES."

With my white-cane mobility skills increasing there still seemed to be something missing. I became more confident and comfortable with my mobility with each adventure out of the house. I could easily get to any of my familiar places without difficulty. I rapidly learned to trust the blending of a good memory of what things use to look like with a sixth sense of what I was aware of around me. I could "see" with my imagination the routes I was customarily taking. But there was still something missing. I continued to search for the missing link to fill the emptiness I was feeling.

There was quiet excitement and comfort when I discovered the missing piece. My mobility confidence was restricted to safe familiar routes. But there was much to experience beyond those routes. What and how would I do with my mobility when it came time to explore those new opportunities? What would happen when I would have to encounter different environments I have not seen? I was getting nervous about my mobility skills. I shared my concerns with my instructor. He suggested getting a dog.

Dog guides work for the blind. I was blind. Me using a dog guide? The thought had never occurred to me. Being a rookie in the darkened world of blindness, I had never given thought to using a dog guide. I remember thinking they were for rich famous people who could afford them. It wouldn't work.

I was given an assignment to explore some of the different training facilities. It became a mobility assignment instead of my daily walks around the school hallways. I conversed with several facilities throughout the United States. Each program had slight differences in their philosophies in training, the types of dogs they used, and their overall program for the individual. I took lots of notes and conversed with my mobility instructor. After I had gathered about as much information as I could I chose three programs to apply to. I requested application forms.

Applying to the training programs was fairly simple. Basic personal information, character references, and medical histories completed the forms and identified I was legally blind. I wrote a short narrative of what I thought a dog guide could do for me and how it would assist my mobility. Stamps all around and the applications were off in the mail. Within the month I received responses from all three programs. My applications were approved. I received more information about the programs, items I would need to bring with me and things each program offered. I chose Pilot Dogs, Inc. of Columbus, Ohio based on the opportunity I might receive a Doberman as a dog guide. The program sent me several options for starting dates. I was already into my first semester of seminary making Wintrim my first opportunity to train with a dog. My confirmation of starting dates arrived in the mail along with an airline ticket.

I have always been fascinated with airports. When I had sight I always enjoyed watching people. I always dreamed of being the one who got to take the trip on the big jets coming and going. I was excited when the day came for my trip. When I got to the airport and the call came to board I suddenly found myself very nervous. Faced with flying for the first time the excitement was quickly replaced with fear. My father kept reassuring me it was safe since he had flown several times. I felt like I was being dragged kicking and screaming to the entrance of the airplane. My limited education in physics struggled with the "lead balloon theory" that something as big as an airplane drops like a rock when it loses power. The second call to board was announced. Things suddenly changed for the better. As I checked my tickets at the counter I was greeted by a lovely, very attractive flight attendant who offered me her elbow and assistance to my seat. I accepted and moments later I was comfortably sitting, strapped to my seat, ready to fly, with her name and telephone number tucked into my pocket. Then I white-knuckled my grip of the arm rest for the short thirty-minute trip.

I arrived at the training facility just in time for supper. I barely had time to deposit my suitcase in my room, meet my roommate, and freshen myself before heading to the dining room. I was instructed to leave my white mobility cane packed in my suitcase, for it was no longer going to be used. I assumed we would be getting our dogs after dinner. The bell rang. No dogs. Use your imagination to picture what happened next. Six blind people accustomed to working with their white canes and now experiencing a strange environment where converging on the doorway into the dining room. Total chaos. People bumping into people. It would take us a couple of days to get used to walking through the hallways knowing others were there. We all found our way to the dining room and to our assigned places at the table.

One of my reasons for choosing Pilot Dogs was the concept of family living. The dining room had a long wooden table with straight-back wooden chairs. It reminded me much of my grandmother's kitchen table which could seat fourteen without being crowded. The room was comfortable and simple. After dinner we gathered in the "day room" to begin our formal training.

The day room was much like a living room with plenty of comfortable easychairs, an entertainment center, a piano, and an old style self-contained telephone booth. This telephone served two purposes: it was part of our training with the dogs and also my link back home. We started to get acquainted with each other realizing we would be living together for the next twenty-eight days. One big happy family. Our instructor started us in the process of learning what the dogs could do for us and what we would need to do for them. I got excited thinking we were getting our dogs. But it was late in the evening. Our instructor said goodnight and suggested we get plenty of rest. Still no dogs. I was disappointed as I retired to my room.

The next morning my roommate and I were rattled from our beds by a blaring local radio station. It was 6:30 a.m.! Breakfast was at seven. We were informed first runs with the dogs would always begin at 8:00 a.m. Table conversation continued about the dogs and how we would be working them as guides. After breakfast we gathered back in the day room. Again I was getting excited expecting to receive my dog any moment.

The first full day of training was spent in conversation learning about the dogs. Our trainer took each one of us for a walk through the neighborhood so he would get an idea of our individual walking habits. There was much more to learning about these dogs as guides than I ever expected. Yet, it was also exciting. In a unique way, each one of us was becoming a professional dog handler, as we would be high profiles in our respective communities. At the end of the first full day we were told the dogs would arrive the next morning. It was hard to sleep during the night.

We were all at breakfast early the next morning. By the time the bell rang we were all standing outside the dining room waiting. Excited? You bet! We quickly found our places at the table and waited for the good news. Then, the bombshell. A heavy snow was making travel difficult. The dogs would not arrive in the morning. We had a late morning discussion on giving our dogs a bath when they did arrive. Once the dogs were there they would be with us all the time. Lunch came and went with no word. I retired to my room for a short nap. It seemed only a few short minutes of sleep when I was awakened by a knock on the door. My trainer entered my room. I was mugged on my bed by a cold wet nose of a happy eighteen-month-old Doberman pup. Her name was Babe. She was ready to go. Training had begun. I was excited! My trainer gave me the end of her leash and left us to get acquainted.

She was a playful frisky pup and we romped on the floor and bed. Then it was time for her bath.

Somehow we both survived. During her stay in the large sink in the grooming room the water faucet got bumped pumping hot water into the bottom. Babe started to dance and then jumped to the floor escaping the painful ordeal. I got my bath attempting to return a resistant Doberman to the sink. We got the job done. Babe enjoyed getting dried. The more I wrapped her in towels and rubbed her dry the more she enjoyed it. This was a special time for our bonding.

The first walk was scheduled. Babe's training had produced a love for her harness. She quickly pushed her nose into the harness and wagged her tail joyfully as I buckled it firmly underneath her. After getting my coat on we headed outside to wait for our trainer. It was cold. It was January. Not cold enough to make it dangerous to work outside but cold enough to make it interesting. The trainer signaled we were ready and we headed out through the gate. Babe made the first corner and headed directly for another door back into the building. Babe did not want to work outside in the cold weather. The trainer corrected her and put us back on the sidewalk. At this point I was just along for the walk to get use to walking with a dog. The trainer and Babe would have all the discussions regarding our training. I was just there to listen and learn.

We started forward again and Babe saw another door back into the building. She headed directly for it. She did not want to work outside in this cold. The trainer corrected her again. A third attempt, another door, and the same results. This time the trainer scolded Babe in an appropriate manner. I quickly learned of the Doberman sneeze is a signal when they are miffed about something. I tucked this little piece of insight into the Doberman's way of thinking for future reference. Babe had a healthy independent way of thinking, much like my own. We would get along well together.

A fun little game developed during our training walks I like to call "bumper dogs." The dogs all knew each other for the same instructor had trained them. They seem to enjoy racing each other from curb to curb. It did not take long for those of us working with them to join in. As we stopped at a corner waiting for instructions, directions, or a green light we would all line up curbside. We needed to wait for the signal from the trainer to cross. There would be three or four teams waiting. When the signal came there was a rush to cross the street and head for the next corner one block away. The game had begun.

The objective was to be the first team to arrive at the next corner. Babe had a strategy for this game. She would hold back at the start allowing the other dogs to push and bump each other across the street, up the curb, and head down the block. As she followed the other teams across the street she would watch for her openings. Each one of us walked at a different pace and soon the teams would develop gaps between them. Babe would make her move. Babe and I were one of the faster teams in training. As she approached the curb across the street we quickly fell into our fast walking pace. We moved out, trailing the other teams. Gracefully Babe would weave her way through the other teams working to the front of the pack. Babe was the only Doberman and female in the class. I believe the other dogs wanted to chase her cute little tailless backside. As the other dogs would pick up their pace Babe would do likewise, staying well out in front. Another team might draw along side. Babe would effectively maneuver us into forcing the other team off the sidewalk and into the nearby snowbank. Thus the game, "Bumper Dogs." Babe and I suffered our own fair share of dead-ends in snowbanks and snowdrifts. When she lost the game she always gave her miffed snort letting me know she was not pleased. We worked hard together at learning how to be a team.

The training program for a first time dog user is twenty-eight days. On the twenty-fifth day we took our road test. The test was to follow a prescribed course which would encounter everything we had learned. We passed the test and prepared to head home. Our trainer escorted us back to the airport and sent us off. Arriving back home we entered a whole new world of mobility. Even though I knew the airport at home it was a different experience walking by myself through the concourse without the assistance of my cane or someone else. It was a tremendous sensation of freedom I had never before felt. The more we walked together the more comfortable we became with each other. Our relationship grew stronger. We learned how to trust each other in a unique way which helped us work better together. We learned each other's quirks and characteristics. Soon we could communicate to each other by feeling how we were working together. Many people were always amazed at how much she knew because they would not hear me give her the navigation commands we needed. When I felt tense Babe became more aware and sensitive to my needs for mobility. When I was comfortable she relaxed and even began prancing. Babe could show-off with the best of them. The stronger our relationship became the more independent we became and the greater appreciation developed for each other.

Babe and I were partners for over five years. Average working time for a dog guide is about ten years. In the summer of our fifth year she contracted an incurable liver disease. After three long weeks of highly specialized medical treatment and research through a nearby university's veterinary clinic and research facility Babe's life came to an end. It was a difficult decision for me to "put her down" but in the last hours I knew she was blind and having seizures. It was a difficult decision yet necessary since she was no longer able to work and we were unable to manage her increasing illness. Her body was donated to medical science to assist with further research to help other dogs. I was hurt and felt empty by her loss.

One week after Babe's ending we celebrated her work and ministry in a memorial service. Many people who knew Babe joined us for the service to ask God's blessing for her ministry. During the service one young girl who was very fond of Babe openly shared, "now Louie has someone to play with." Louie was her grandmother's dog who had died six months earlier. There would never be another Babe, she was my first. The next day I left for the training facility to get a new dog. A new dog would mean a new relationship and another new chapter in my life's journey. In stepped Lady Marge whom we called "Marge!"

Marge was an excellent worker. We learned quickly to work with each other and to trust. Trusting each other is so important. The dog guides are trained to work, which becomes the love of their life. Whenever I pick up the harness the dog guide is there, excited, and ready to go. The stronger our trust relationship becomes the better they want to work. Trust becomes the most important part of their livelihood. The more a person learns to trust their dog the better the dog performs. This has always been one of my greatest joys of working with my dogs.

Marge was an exceptional dog guide for the blind. She had become a unique story in her own way. Marge was rescued from a bad owner who abused both her and her daughter. She and her daughter were rescued by the local humane society and sent to a wonderful person who knows Dobermans, Ms. Joanna Walker. Ms. Walker has a program where she is able to de-program and retrain abused Dobermans with a lot of tender loving care. I had the pleasure of seeing her fine handiwork as I trained with Marge. Marge carried her own love for others and worked hard. Marge had a hidden secret which I was too late in understanding. Marge had the ability to escape when she wanted. There were several close calls which alerted me to be careful but I just wasn't seeing the whole picture. Then disaster struck.

On the evening of June 5, 1988, Marge hung herself in my van. She was attempting to escape by slipping her collar. It was a tragic night. When I found Marge it was too late. I felt this tremendous feeling of guilt overwhelming me.

Marge's tragic death happened eight years after my loss of sight. Yet, her tragic ending suddenly threw me into a new understanding of my blindness and the darkness which surrounded me. It took me nearly three days to finally venture out of my house alone, traveling again with my white cane. I quickly learned just how many obstacles there were in seven short blocks from my house to the busstop. I felt trapped and isolated. I remembered my first day of being blind and needing to make the difficult trip to the bathroom. All of those feelings of being unable to function were overwhelming.

My next Doberman dog guide was named Tildy. Like Babe and Marge, Tildy had this unique gift of enjoying people. Tildy had a disability. She was a Doberman. Many times I had to confront the stigma all Dobermans are attack dogs. So many people only choose to believe the bad about something. Tildy was a charmer and a lover. If I were to command her to attack she would sit down, pull out her pocket dictionary and look up the meaning of the word. She didn't know what the command meant and would not do anything to harm anyone. Most dogs which are trained to attack are often abused, mistrained, and improperly bred dogs. They are "junk" dogs. Dog guides for the blind are some of the most highly trained and specially trained dogs used in society. That is why they can go anyplace their master goes in public.

Tildy knew when others were watching her. She pranced gracefully with her head held high making sure those who were watching took notice. Tildy wanted to please. She worked hard and well for me. She also displayed a gentleness toward others which made her something special. In my ministry she was a unique gift. I enjoyed sharing her quiet personality by allowing her the freedom to use her gifts. We made a good team.

We both shared a motto: "If you're going to make a scene...why not be seen."

When I first lost my eyesight I felt trapped. In reflecting upon those experiences I realize the trapped feeling comes from within. If I want to be blind, then I am the one who makes me blind. If I fail to see the beauty of God's creation around me it is my own fault. Even though I cannot physically see, the trap lies within me. Despite the many obstacles which society places in front of me because of their failure or unwillingness to accept me for who I am with my gifts, handicaps, and disabilities I still have the ability to overcome the barriers in order to function the best I am able. This profound awareness of my abilities strengthens my character.

I make many appearances sharing my experiences and speaking about how the dog guides work for the blind. One of the most frequent questions asked is what I would do if I had to do it all over again. I believe these questions are directed at what kinds of things I would do differently to prepare myself for going blind. There really is not a good or right answer for these questions. I could have been better in managing my diabetes before the visual impairment set in. I might have seen an optometrist sooner. I should have stayed away from alcohol in college. All of these answers are "if" responses which is always hindsight. Hindsight is always twenty/twenty. Life just does not function with hindsight. I often times respond to these questions with "I'm still searching for the answer and I will let you know just as soon as I find out for myself."

I find a creative tension within myself between feeling confident about my skills as a visually impaired person and the feelings of being trapped or isolated. Many times these types of questions come from people who are worried about losing one of their senses. They are questioning themselves. I cannot answer their questions. What has worked for me might not work for someone else. We each handle adversity differently. There is uniqueness to my gift. I have adapted to my sightless environment and function quite well, thank you.

But do I function all that well? This is perhaps the better question to ask. In considering this I find myself looking at a creative tension between my self-confidence and my fears. My best example for explaining this tension can be seen in working with my dog guides. The dogs become human-like in their characteristics and personalities. I talk to them just as if they were human. They understand. They respond to many of the same influences which affect me. When I am comfortable with my situation the dogs are relaxed. When I am tense they are tense too, and alert to everything and anything happening around us. By learning what the dog guide is trying to communicate to me I am able to "see" with my mind's eye and imagine what is happening. My Dobermans have been very expressive in communicating with me.

I have had to learn how to use my memory capabilities better. I believe all of us have the capability for good memory; we just have to learn how to use it. In losing my sight I was forced into learning how to use my memory better. I had exceptionally good sight for twenty-two years of my life. Over the years as I became more aware of my gifts and talents I discovered I had near photographic memory. If I saw it once I could remember it. I learned to use my eyesight appropriately by being able to scan a large area and remember the details. This became very useful as a professional driver for I never got lost. I always knew where I was because I could remember the details of what I saw. If I went a particular route once I remembered that route from memory. I can still see in my memory many of these routes although perhaps some of the landmarks have changed in the past years. My parents always joked they would never be able to lose me for I could always remember where I was. They would often tease about leaving me someplace. Chances are I would return before them because I knew where I was. Most of the time you would find me navigating because I knew where I was, where we were suppose to be going, and I could visualize the route in my mind.

I learned how to use this gift in my educational process. I discovered with my near photographic memory I could visualize the concept on the pages of the textbook. If I read the chapter in the textbook I could recall the basic information from memory when taking a test. I use to spend hours copying my notes from class because the process committed the information to memory.

When I first went blind I felt lost. Slowly I began to discover I could depend upon my memory and my developing imagination to give me images of what I thought I should be seeing. Along with this discovery I also developed the ability for audio-graphic memory, memorizing different sounds associated with different things. This became especially helpful in remembering people's voices and associating them with names. Instead of seeing people in their physical appearance I see people by their voices. In developing the audio-graphic memory of associating sounds with different things my mobility increased. When I work with a white cane empty lots are notorious for swallowing a blind person. This happens because a blind person is listening to the buildings along the sidewalk. Suddenly the sound changes. If a blind person is not prepared to make the necessary adjustments the vacant lot swallows you and then you are lost. Corner gas stations are notorious for the same reasons. The blind person has to learn how to use their audio-graphic memory to be able to adjust for road hazards such as these.

Another example of the use between my memory and my imagination is looking at my Dobermans. I know what Dobermans look like from when I had sight. This is stored in my memory. I now experience my Dobermans through my sense of touch and by working with the dog every day. So it becomes very easy for me to see the dog in my mind. I have also learned to believe what my imagination is creating for me is reasonably accurate. This oft times confuses many people for it appears I really can see. I can be very descriptive and precise with what I think I see. Most time I am fairly accurate.

Another piece of my magical mystical dance in working so well through my blindness is I am an optimist and a dreamer. I look for the positive in myself and others. I make my dreams bigger than life so I am sure to push for them to become real. I am not happy sitting still. I am not a quitter. I always want to be doing something. I am an organizer and sometimes even an over-achiever. I sometimes fear if I let my mind become idle I will either fall asleep or be tempted by evil to do something I will regret later. A favorite banner which has become a good motto for me used to face us when it was our turn to do dishes for the family. The banner hung directly in front of the kitchen sink and since there was no window there you had to look at it. It read; "When a job has once begun, never leave it until it's done. Be the labor big or small, do it well or not at all." Keeping this motto in mind helps me to keep a positive outlook for moving forward and getting things done.

I hate leaving projects undone. When I get started with something I like to get it done, completely. Sometimes I get too involved and I forget to watch the time only to find out it is much later than I thought. This becomes hazardous to other responsibilities, which must be taken into consideration when getting involved in any project. I had one experience where I was working on the rigging of my boat. The project required I crawl into a narrow space in the bow. While I was working on changing some parts it got much later than I expected pushing me way past my lunchtime. Lunchtime is important to diabetics. I started to have an insulin reaction, my body needed food! But I was so close to finishing the project and if only I completed the task I would not have to crawl back into this tight narrow space. I went past my physical limitations and suddenly found myself helpless. I could not move. Fortunately my wife heard my panicked cries for help and brought me high sugar latent food. I had bad visions of someone having to cut into the bow to get me out. I learned the hard way about time consumption when getting involved in projects.

I do like getting projects done. I find when I assert myself my imagination and fingers help paint a picture in my mind which allows me to "see" what I am doing. This helps me to focus on the project and to accomplish said task. I prefer to do one project, do it well, complete it, and then move on to the next. I try not to get into more than three projects at one time. I don't like to over-extend myself.

One of my secrets to being successful is I am able to focus my attention and energies on what I am doing. When I am working with my dog guide she is my focus and project. I pay close attention to what she is communicating to me as she works. I feel as though I can "see" her doing her job. Consequently, when we are working together I believe I can see everything around us. Sometimes I think I can see us working together as though I were just another observer.

When I am sailing I become focused on what the boat is doing. As it responds to the wind, the sail, and the water I feel like I can "see" exactly what the boat is doing. This vivid and developing imagination helps me paint a picture of what I think I should be seeing. It has caused many a friend to doubt whether or not I really am blind. That is the joy of the magical mystical dance of getting new eyes.

An important lesson which I learned through my blindness was not to take anything for granted. I did not realize the potential of my near photographic memory until I was suffering the diabetic retinopathy. It was not until I needed to start developing my other senses that I found myself depending on them for crucial information. The same was found in relationships with others. Relationships cannot be taken for granted. Friends cannot be assumed. Each relationship, each friend needs the same focus and attention which enables me to "see." I must use the same creative tension to help me see the larger picture of my relationships just as if I were working on a project or a hobby. The magical mystical part of life's journey is learning to become aware of all the beauty which surrounds you before it is gone. This is the creative tension between my ability to function as a blind person and my fears. When I lost my sight I lost the ability to see everything around me. Now that I can "see" in a new way with new eyes I am more sensitive to my surroundings.

In learning to work with each dog I was constantly made aware of how sometimes I took them granted. Babe had a unique way of showing me she was upset by planting a "pyramid" next to the pedal-board of my Hammond organ. I loved to play the organ barefoot. If Babe felt she was being neglected she let me know by planting one of her famous landmines. Without fail I would step in it as I left the organ bench. Marge had a favorite tree across the street. If I were taking her for granted she would brush me against the tree. Depending on how severe or bad she felt would determine how hard I hit the tree. There were a few times when I had to stop to catch my breath! And Tildy was no different. If she felt neglected she would take her nose and throw my hands off the computer keyboard and onto her head. What a unique way of getting petted. The more neglected the more she would pester me until I would play with her.

It hurts when we discover when we have been taking something for granted. Whether it is one of our physical senses; sight, hearing, touch, taste, and/or smell, or if it is in the way we interact with our personal relationships, I believe it is never too late to change and make things right. Sometimes we have to learn how to forgive ourselves for our mistakes, other times we have to learn how to forgive others, and still other times we simply have to learn how to accept the adversities of life and go on.

I believe I am in a relationship with everything in my environment. I am in a relationship with everyone whom I meet. What I do influences and/or affects everything else. The beauty in the gift is I am able to "see" beyond myself and look at what is there, deep down inside.

As a visually impaired person the gift of the dog guides has been an "eye-opener" into my own faith. Isaiah 40:31 -- "but those who hope in the LORD will renew their strength. They will soar on wings like eagles; they will run and not grow weary, they will walk and not be faint." I needed to learn this myself; to trust I would have the strength to face whatever challenge lies ahead by trusting in God. The dogs helped me to trust in God by trusting in myself and others. I am only a small piece of a much larger whole. The harder I work on trusting all the pieces the better I am. I can find the strength to face whatever lies ahead because I know God is always with me. When I forget: Wham-O! It hurts! I then have to learn my lesson the hard way. I have gotten hurt when I have mistrusted or taken something for granted. This hurts much in the same way as walking blindly into a wall or telephone pole. My ability to function as a blind person and to function as well as I feel I do is I have learned to hope in the Lord. I trust the everlasting presence of the Holy Spirit in my life. I try not to take for granted the gifts I have.

CHAPTER SEVEN:
BEWARE THE
SEVENTH WAVE

The excitement of entering seminary masked the underlying fear of my new independence when I moved out of my parent's home and into my first apartment. There were many little details which needed to be worked out; little details such as filling insulin syringes, reading the mail, assistance with grocery shopping, and proofreaders to help with research papers.

It was up to me to find and develop the necessary support network to get these many tasks completed. The tasks which I needed assistance with required vision. My biggest challenge to adapting to my disability was discovering ways to function in a vision-oriented world.

I was looking forward to entering seminary. Deep inside my spirit was responding to the voice calling me to be a minister. Now, as a blind person, the voice was even stronger. I was discovering a new understanding and purpose for my ministry, to be a bridge-builder in helping others to see beyond without using their physical sight. I had many doubts about my capabilities of entering the unknown.

I spent two weeks prior to the start of the school year setting up my apartment. It gave me a good chance to explore the community around the seminary. I started meeting new friends as they moved into adjoining apartments in the seminary dorm. My network of support people developed. I had someone to fill my syringes, read my mail, help me get groceries, and assist me in the writing of my research papers. My fears and doubts lessened. I started getting comfortable and could feel my self-confidence growing stronger. Seminary started and I was on cloud nine.

At the end of the second week of classes my fears returned. There was an annual retreat after students had the opportunity to attend one session in each of their courses. I knew from others this was an exciting time in the life of the seminary. I was excited about attending and getting to know other classmates in a more personal and intimate way. I went with three close friends, two whom I had known before I lost my sight and the third whom I met moving into seminary. The three of them were very instrumental in my adjustments into the seminary community. The four of us became good friends, discovered we had some mutual friends outside the seminary community, and enjoyed being together. These three friends also displayed a unique and special gift of being exceptionally sensitive to my disability. We shared a gift in seeing the beauty of a person within rather than perhaps the mask we sometimes wear.

The retreat was excellent. The four of us traveled together to the rural camp where the seminary community spent twenty-four hours together learning to know each other better: students, faculty, and staff. Time was spent talking with each other, sharing personal stories and expressing dreams for the future. I was the first totally blind student to enter the seminary and people made a tremendous effort to making me part of the routine and process. I easily participated in volleyball games, square dancing, and sing-a-longs which frequently occurred during the retreat.

Adversity, disasters, and fears strike when we least expect them. My troubles started when word got out that an orchestra was being formed for the closing worship. I wanted to participate but there was no practical way for it to happen. Some things had been planned ahead and no one had a way of knowing my desire to participate. I did not feel good about pushing change just for me. I needed to understand there were going to be times when I simply would need to refrain from participating because of my disability and this was one of them. Nonetheless, it hurt! I felt myself sinking fast and fading away.

Music was an important part of my life. It had carried me well through the early stages of my blindness. When I felt depression moving in, felt bored, or scared, I would spend hours playing the piano, a new organ which had been given to me, or my guitar. I would move back and forth between composing originals to practicing old favorites. The more I played the more I learned to trust my hearing and discovering I could easily play by ear. Before I lost my sight I had always been dependent on reading music from the page.

Music was a gift, something I could share with others. Suddenly it felt like music was against me and I was backing away from the conflict. Once again I was feeling blind and very disabled. As my fears and doubts overwhelmed me and I started to bottom out I began considering the alternative of putting music out of my life. The very thought hurt!

I was making myself blind and handicapped. I was only looking in one direction; "I" wanted to participate. I was being selfish and filling myself with self-pity. I should have been attempting to find a new and creative way of participating but I just couldn't bring myself to do it. The pain was greater than the drive to deal with my handicap. Instead I was sliding deep into the grips of being disabled. I found myself held captive on a metal folding chair off to the side listening to the practicing orchestra. The tears were swelling from deep within and trickling down my face. I felt the heavy weight of the "depression monster" sitting on my lap. The old favorite hymns brought a heavier flow of tears and newer unfamiliar tunes pushed me farther away. At times I felt myself getting angry. Angry at everything I thought but really only angry at myself. The more I struggled for something to hold onto the more I felt I was fading away.

I was sinking fast when a gentle presence suddenly appeared. The burden of the depression monster disappeared replaced by a warm caring embrace and a sensitive gentle touch wiping away my tears. A comforting soothing whisper spoke. "You're much too much like a tidal wave. Be gentler. Don't crash into the shore but gently caress it." My tears stopped, replaced by my confused searching stare. I clung to the warm caring hug as my emotions said, "Please help me?" For an instance I left my fear and felt comforted by the presence of this newfound friend.

From the first moment I met Barb I began discovering God sends special gifts sometimes wrapped in small packages. Barb was shorter than I am yet had a heart bigger than the world. Barb had a beautiful gentle personality which was open, sensitive, and honest. She had a special genuine concern for others not always seen or readily displayed by many. Barb was able to communicate in both verbal and non-verbal ways many of the emotions which were present. Instead of feeling depressed I was feeling warm, friendly, and open. I found myself beginning to share secrets of my disability I am not sure I was even aware of myself. Her image of the tidal wave overpowering the gentle wave became a special part of my relationship with her as well as an important new understanding of me.

Barb was a beautiful person both spiritually and physically. As I learned how to function as a blind person depending upon my other senses for data not being received through my sight I continued to enjoy the development of my insight. Some call it a sixth sense. For me it provided two interesting practical functions: I always knew what time it was, give or take five minutes, and I would always seem to find good looking people by first seeing the beauty within. Barb was one of those beautiful people. Many of my male friends were always jealous because I always seemed to be found with the most attractive women. Some accused me of not really being blind, that I could see, because I was always finding the good-looking women. I found it to be a unique gift because my experiences with people, women or men were through their inner beauty and self-confidence. I could always tell a person who carried themselves well regardless of the difficulty of a situation one might face. Barb was one of those who had the inner beauty, the physical beauty, and the beauty of self-confidence. I like this in people because it is much the same way in which I tend to function.

So in a unique and special way Barb and I "clicked" the first time we met on the foldingchair on retreat.

When I first lost my sight I had this tendency to always be the center of attention. When I went to camp all the campers were captive audiences by first my mobility with the use of a white cane and later my dog guides. When I started seminary it was the fact I was going to be the first totally blind student to attempt the Masters program which would have many challenges and difficulties. I always seemed to step onto centerstage and into a single spotlight. My desire to continue forward with dreams, aspirations, and goals always seem to put me high on the crest of a large wave. My inward blindness was not allowing me the ability to see I was many times offending others. This was the tidal wave which Barb could see in me which was pushing me away from a lot of super neat people. The overwhelming emotions while on retreat suffering in front of the practicing orchestra were another one of the times when the tidal wave was building and getting ready to crash in upon an unsuspecting shore. Barb's presence on my lap and her ability to breakthrough my barriers de-powered the tidal wave. She could see the gentle person inside and could help me begin to see it myself.

I believe everyone needs a moment in a spotlight. It helps build self-confidence, an inner strength, and makes one feel good. I have had my moments in many different spotlights. All have been good and I do not regret being there. I usually find ways of sharing my spotlights with others. It is important for me to enable and empower others by sharing the center of attention. This helps both them and me. This was another piece of the larger picture which started happening when Barb sat on my lap and invited me to be gentler and less tidal wave in my approaches. I really enjoy much more the activity which takes place back stage, the planning, set designs, stage development, and preparing for the ultimate presentation. When the curtain raises I would much rather have someone else on stage with me watching from the wings or audience.

I am a take-charge sort of person. In realizing I was not comfortable being the center of attention I discovered I preferred working with others in making something happen. Many times I feel like people put me on a pedestal far away from the others. I much prefer to preach from the main floor or even while sitting in a pew rather than from a pulpit high, away, and set apart. I need to be in touch with those around me so we can work together. I really feel trapped when

I am set aside. Most times when I am set aside or put centerstage those watching really do not get to know me. They do not get the opportunity to see how I function, experience what I feel, or understand I am affected by the same things others are. Before I met Barb I was unfortunately caught on top of the tidal wave enjoying the attention. I was also pushing a lot of feelings; frustrations and angers out of my life. I had gotten used to the centerstage routine pushing and locking away the frustrations and fears of my disability. Barb's gifts of gentleness and sensitivity to me as a person helped me to start processing the feelings deep inside and sharing them with someone else. I was still afraid of my disability.

Barb and I went for a walk that afternoon, as I needed to get outside and away from the rehearsal. It was still painful not being able to participate but I was learning something about myself and my disability. The high levels of frustration and anger were slowly subsiding. We walked along many wooded paths and along the lake continuing to talk about the differences of being a tidal wave and a gentle wave. I could sense the gentle wave within her. I could feel the tidal wave in me. I started to share some of the struggles and fears I felt. She shared parts of her story. It felt good. I was experiencing the development of a close friend and important part of my support network.

Barb and I were best friends for the next four years. The academic challenges were tough yet our mutual support for each other was helpful. When I felt my world coming apart I knew I could find a sensitive listening ear with which I could share my inner secrets and fears. She was a warm beautiful sensitive person. When I felt afraid of myself I could always find a warm comforting hug in Barb. It was special. Her image of the tidal wave became a strong important image in my approaches with people in my ministry. Barb's friendship and support has helped me to cease the moment and enjoy the gifts the moment offers by being gentle. Barb taught me much of how to look within from outside myself to see how I was participating in the much larger picture. Later that first day when I met Barb I was able to participate in worship and celebration feeling the miracle of healing taking place within. I give thanks for friends like Barb.

I have developed Barb's image of the waves in several ways. First, there are the big powerful waves capable of moving large seemingly immovable objects. Second, there are people who are powerful like a tidal wave who push and move people out of their way in selfish determination to get done what they wish or desire and especially if it makes them look better than someone else. Third, there are quiet gentle waves which bring comfort, serenity, peace, and smooth sailing. These waves make us feel good. There are people who are gentle, quiet, peaceful, and full of serenity which enable, empower, and make others feel good. It is like these people I attempt to shape my ministry to others.

I love the many moods of the Great Lakes, especially Lakes Michigan and Superior. I have experienced the waves' threatening power as well as having seen them become calm, passive, and serene. I have shared experiences with others watching large powerful rollers crashing the winter beaches. I have sailed in some of the lakes' worse conditions. I have seen them show no mercy. I have also experienced moments of beauty, refrained, and placid, sharing peace and serenity to those who would dare to know their inner secrets.

A simple illustration and parallel of life is the image of a surfer and the relationship with the waves. A surfer is always looking for the "big" wave for the ultimate ride. There is a tremendous struggle between the surfer and the waves as the surfer paddles out past the point where the waves begin to crest. Next, the surfer regroups and recovers strength while watching and waiting for the one big right wave. The surfer may try several waves in hopes it is the big wave as it develops beneath the board. As the wave approaches, the surfer maneuvered himself to the point where he thinks the wave will begin to crest. If he is correct the wave will lift his surfboard and he will begin his ride. If the wave is right and he keeps his balance doing everything right, it is possible for him to return with the wave all the way to the beach. If something goes wrong such as losing his balance, the wave dies out beneath him, or an unknown disaster wipes him out, he either returns to the point from whence he began the ride or hopefully clings to his overturned board and return to shore for some other day of surfing. A surfer's ride might also be flashy and include "shooting the tube" or "hanging ten." These are the expert experienced surfers. A surfer is also able to cut the board back against the wave over the top of the crest thus ending the particular ride. Surfing is short lived and accomplished on waves of a larger scale. They only last but for a brief moment. Surfing cannot be done on a calm body of water. Floating lazily on an old innertube is more appropriate in calm seas.

I believe there is more to life's journey than always hoping to be the flashy surfboard rider. Some people go through the experience of struggling with life to get to a certain point where they think the action will begin. However, many times they get to the presumed point but do nothing more. Thus, nothing happens. They maybe content to simply wait, perhaps getting frustrated if nothing happens, perhaps content just to sit on their surfboard and do nothing. Some folks will take the opportunity of a ride on a big wave only to find themselves spilling in disaster because they were not prepared or the ride got too big. Some might try projects and activities far beyond their expertise only to lose the precious balance and wipe out in disappointment and frustration. Some will make the ride all the way back to the shore. Whatever the results may be, some will be content, some disappointed and frustrated, others will be flashy. But these moments are short lived, experiential, and not always conducive to riding the "right" wave through life's journey. Surfers need to be strong muscular experienced participants. The novice will know disaster before success.

There are times when I find myself on the cresting wave riding down its front. No matter how good the surging feeling might be, I can still see the pending end to the ride, the crashing surf before me. I know if I don't control myself I shall be slammed into the white foam of the pounding surf. I think too many times I have found myself trying to be the flashy expert surfer, riding high on the wave of being the center of attention, getting in way over my expectations and skills. Those times hurt. This is not me. Thus, entered Barb and her image of the gentle wave.

I have seen both Lake Michigan and Lake Superior become smooth like glass. I have experienced them in this way for days as well as just before and after tremendous storms. Just as I have seen the pounding waves alter and change shorelines I have walked those same shorelines of soft new sands and peaceful tranquility. I have discovered the aftermath of a raging storm. I have sailed the stilled waters with relaxing peaceful pleasures. I know and understand its inner beauty to be calm; I respect its ability to erupt in rage. I can work the waters of the Great Lakes, I can play upon them, and I can find rest. I also respect and know well enough how to survive so I will never try to out smart or beat it at what it knows best.

When I feel myself getting into situations, when I am a tidal wave and not a gentle caressing person, I think about Barb and our special friendship. When we first met I could not see the deep inner beauty which lives within each of us. Barb's gentle touch opened my eyes to a New World and helped me through some difficult times. The beginning experience and continued relationship was like the gentle caress of a slow small wave stroking the quiet shore. Her gentle touch was calming, soothing, relaxing. I could trust her. I could experience others in this more quiet way rather than being the one whose entrance was pounded by the crashing wave. Now, whenever I am in one of those places I see Barb in my own unique way; the gentle-stroking wave bringing peace and tranquility. I become comfortable with myself. Then I can see the outer beauty and the larger picture.

So I struggled with changing my perceived image as a tidal wave to being a gentle wave. I wanted to be a gentle wave, someone who empowered and enables others like Barb did for me. My experiences into seminary expanded and increased my personal search. Many struggles became celebrations as I learned about myself and others. The more I learned about myself the more I became the gentleperson capable of enabling others. The journey however was not free of setbacks, disasters, and roadblocks. I started to meet some other tidal waves, strong powerful people who used others for their own rewards. Some of these experiences were painful reminders of what I know I was once perceived as. Others made good references for stories like these.

There is one particular story and experience I share with you to illustrate my second point that some people want to be tidal waves.

My call into the ministry is different than any other. I believe everyone is called into some kind of ministry. Just being a friend to someone, being kind to a stray animal, and even knowing one is in a good relationship with the Holy Spirit is a type of ministry. The most important part of the larger picture of ministry is acceptance. Everyone needs to be accepting of others, despite differences, despite personality conflicts, despite differences of polity. To be a minister one has to be accepting.

Tidal waves are not accepting. People who choose to be tidal waves are not accepting. Usually by the time we realize we have encountered someone who is a tidal wave they are already past and we are left in the backwash attempting to figure out what hit us!

I had one particular experience which helped me become a strong self-confident gentleperson because I knew I did not or would never hope to be like this person. The unfortunate part of the story is I was swept away by the tidal wave and did not realize what had happened until it was too late. I needed to suffer through the pain in order to gain the positive experience.

I met a woman in the first couple of weeks of school in whom I became intrigued, fascinated by, and infatuated with. I eventually pressed the infatuation issue thinking this was someone I would like to spend a lot of close personal quality time with. We started serious dating. She had many personal stories and experiences she brought to seminary. These stories intrigued me. I enjoyed spending lots of time with her, feeling she was sensitive to my blindness and treated me like a real person, not some freak side show. We shared classes together, which lead us to study together. I was able to financially reimburse her for some of her reading of texts and materials needed for class. We became intimate with one another. But soon the relationship turned a different direction and we mutually agreed to part company. Ending a relationship is painful. Ending a relationship, when both still live, work, and play in the same community, is even harder and more painful. It felt like I was always walking on eggshells needing to be careful what I said or did in fear of meeting her when I least expected. In my pain I discovered gentleness through friends like Barb and found comfort in my support network. She chose to become a tidal wave and unleash her angry power at me. The tidal wave struck,

I was wiped out, and left overwhelmed thrashing in the churning aftermath of the crashing wave.

I accepted the ending of the relationship. Things were not going well and we mutually agreed to part. I experienced my pain quietly attempting to figure out what happened, what I might have done differently, and what I needed to learn from the relationship. She dealt with her pain in the opposite direction becoming very angry. She began venting her anger at me. First it was little personal attacks in class, in the seminary community, and among mutual friends. When these friends refused to get caught in-between a nasty lover's quarrel she pulled other little stunts just to irritate me. The most irritating was when she called my apartment every morning at four o'clock and hung up when I answered. She made the mistake of telling someone of her little trick, which got back to me. I faced the conflict, took the tidal wave straight on, and found myself thrashing once again in the after-wake. Then came the ultimate. She started a rumor amongst classmates accusing me of raping her. This was too much. My gentle patience left and my own anger exploded. When I received the telephone call from a good friend who had heard the rumor I was so mad I slammed my foot into the plastic garbage container in the kitchen of my apartment. The garbage can was setting next to a concrete block wall. I was wearing tennis shoes. The pain was horrible! I remember throwing the telephone receiver back onto the base and running outside. I needed to calm myself and get back in control of my feelings. What she had set out to accomplish was working. My foot began to swell.

A good friend and neighbor followed me outside having heard my explosion rumble through the apartment complex. Quickly other dorm residents learned of the rumor and following consequences and quickly rallied in my support. We attempted to peel my shoe off my throbbing foot. We packed it in ice. Hours later I was the proud owner of three broken toes. They cannot do much for broken toes and ever since then I have a constant reminder of my own tidal wave rage and anger. I had my very own "hammer" toe on my right foot. But it was a beautiful field goal kick of the garbage can. It must have gone theoretically fifty plus yards. My roommate and I discovered garbage in places throughout the apartment.

The next day I hobbled into the Dean of Student's office to face her once again. I politely sat quietly and listened to her tell a story of deceitful lies and rumors. When I was given the chance to tell my side of the story her anger erupted again and she quickly left. It was then I learned some people will choose to be tidal waves and to powerfully use people for their own gains. When she had discovered she could not control nor manipulate me in our relationship she turned against me. When I did not respond the way she wanted me to after our relationship had ended nor could get the desired effects she wanted she turned to deceit and lies to make herself look good. It only led to mistrust and deception by many others. Her forceful tidal wave approach towards people was painful and destructive. Some people simply choose to be tidal waves and others gentle caressing enablers.

The last two pieces of my illustration of being a gentle wave which offers peace, serenity, and tranquility and also the image of the wave who is an enabler can best be shared through two experiences I have had sailing Lake Superior. The first is a story of a sailing adventure shared by five adults in early June 1990. The second is an experience shared by four friends who crossed Lake Superior one night in the merciless pounding of unforgiving waves. I was the center of attention in both sailing adventures. But there was no spotlight for the gift was that I was the gentle wave which brought calmness in adversity, rest after struggle, and enabled others to go far beyond even their own wildest imaginations. I think I have finally reached the point of becoming the gentle wave I want to be. I was becoming the enabler like Barb had been for me.

It was shortly after eleven o'clock p.m. aboard the 28-foot sloop. The crew had all settled into their berths for some long awaited sleep. I was waiting for my own body heat to warm my sleepingbag and trying to find a comfortable position within the tight quarters. The temperature had begun to drop at sundown indicating a cold high-pressure front was approaching. It was not uncommon for drastic weather changes such as this for these parts of Lake Superior. The weather forecast for the next three days was not real good and we had anchored accordingly off the sand-spit on the southeast corner of Stockton Island, the largest of the Apostle Islands located off the shores of northern Wisconsin. The anchor had set well in heavy sand and I felt sure it would hold through the night. I had just closed my eyes when I heard the wind shift.

Having more than seventeen years of sailing experiences on the Great Lakes and two days into my fifth consecutive sail camp on Lake Superior I felt like I knew this massive body of water. It felt like a reunion of two close friends as I listened to the light waves slapping the motionless hull of the boat. I have always stressed to my crews you can play upon the waters, you can work the lake and survive, but you can never beat it. Besides my own experiences I have continued to study the sea and folklore of the Great Lakes learning from the experiences and mistakes of many who have gone before me. I am fascinated, intrigued, and curious about the Great Lakes especially Lake Superior. It is my escape from reality and the place where I go to get my spiritual batteries recharged. I felt confident and my crew sensed this making them comfortable sailing on Lake Superior with a blind skipper. I quietly spoke to the crew and said, "Here it comes." The other four crew members sat up in their berths listening to the dull and growing roar as the jetstream changed directions and came crashing down upon us from the northeast. At the same instance when they heard the wind I felt the boat pivot on its anchor rhode. I knew we were moving backwards and using the seventy some feet of anchor rhode left in the water and on deck. As the slack tightened and the anchor dug deep into the heavy sand bottom of the anchorage there was a sudden ending jerk on the boat sending all four crew members back into a lying position. From the sounds of a few hard knocks I could tell several heads hit nearby bulkheads.

"Ouch!" rang out through the cabin. The anchor held and the sloop tugged hard and the wind sang through the rigging the rest of the night.

By sunrise the temperature outside was near forty degrees. It was windy, rainy, and foggy. There would be no sailing today. The blanket of fog was thick and moving rapidly across the sand-spit. Off in the distance I could hear the pounding waves slamming hard against the opposite side of the island. Around the sloop the waters surged from the tremendous power being generated nearby but there were no waves. We were rather well protected. I slipped into my storm gear and made an early morning inspection of the deck. I rigged another anchor just in case we needed and returned to the cabin. The crew was starting to wake. I offered the opportunity for additional sacktime and four heads snuggled deep into their warm sleeping bags. Breakfast and lunch would happen much later than usual that day.

At noontime I made another inspection of the deck and anchor. There was no change in the weather unless perhaps it was a bit worse. The temperature had climbed to its high for the day, forty-one degrees. The wind pounded the island averaging better than 35 knots with gusts much higher. It was still foggy and raining so we stayed below in the warmth of our close quartered cabin. Because of the close quarters we as a crew learned how to communicate and share movement. Meals had become a group effort making them quick, efficient, and fun. Then we spent countless hours entertaining each other by reading Jonathan Livingston Seagull, singing countless verses of the theme to Gilligan's island, a half hour of train songs, and of course a verse or two of the Wreck of the Edmonds Fitzgerald. We laughed, cried, and enjoyed our being together safe from the rage of the elements outside.

Later in the evening the fog lifted for a time so we hoisted anchor and motored to the Park Service docks. It felt good to stretch our legs on solid ground. We decided to hike across the island to the point of the sand-spit opposite from where we had been anchored. At the end of our trail we could see the tremendous power of the raging lake as the waves crashed hard against the shore. The huge waves had some two hundred miles of open water behind them as they pounded the immovable object of the island. They had a lot of driving power behind them. As they crashed into the northeastern exposure of Stockton Island they sent a flurry of sand, water, and foam into the air. The wind gathered these small particles slamming them violently against the trees, rocks, and other shoreline objects. The exposed sides of the trees were smooth to the touch from the windy sandblasting of the storm. Driftwood was gathering high on the shorelines away from the natural waterlines. Only a very tight likens moss which could hold its grip to the sandstone rocks grew along this side of the island between the treeline and the shore. In all it's furry and rage the lake still had a certain beauty about it. We stayed for only a short time, as the force of the weather was chilling and damp driven through our protective stormgear. We retraced our trail across the island and returned to the boat to seek another anchorage for the night.

Early the next morning I took my normal deck-inspecting walk. The boat was tugging hard against the anchor rhode. The anchor was some seventy feet in front of the boat in ten feet of water still clinging tight to the sandy bottom. The temperature was a whopping thirty-nine degree. This would be the high for the day. The fog was heavier and the rain harder than the day before. We could not see the dock only a few hundred feet away. We trusted it was still there or perhaps at least we were still here. The anchor lines told me it was. The crew decided to remain warm and snug in their sleepingbags.

By early afternoon the wind started settling down and there were breaks in the fog. Occasionally we could see several islands to the south and west of our position. There was hope. We began studying the charts of the islands and soon discovered that approximately seven miles away was an island with a higher elevation. This meant more protection from the strong northeast winds. It would bring us much closer to our planned destination for the next day. But it would mean hoisting anchor and crossing some open water between islands. This would mean the powerful rolling waves from the northeast would be hitting us hard astern. We spent several hours discussing the many options, alternatives, and possibilities island hopping would and would not provide. It needed to be a unanimous decision to weigh anchor since it would involve all of us working together to make the seven mile trip. An hour later with excitement surging through our bodies we hoisted anchor all clad in our various colored stormgear and set course for Oak Island, the tallest in the group of islands.

The first leg of our journey was easy as we followed the shoreline of Stockton Island staying well within its protective cover from the wind and the waves. The second leg was the hardest. We set a course due west heading for Herman Island. I had two crewmembers in safety harnesses on the foredeck watching the island ahead. The other two-crew members were with me in the cockpit standing the helm and reading me vital information of compass, speed, and water depth. As we neared the midway point of the second leg where we were at the mercy of the huge waves crawling up our stern the fog set back in, covering both the island before and behind us. There was no turning back for it would mean an even harder trip against the huge waves. I was well aware there were a few stomachs among the crew which would not make it. A seasick crewmember is virtually useless. We forged on. Each wave seemed to grow as we pushed onward towards the mysterious point on the chart before us now covered in fog. The crew was watching through squinting strained eyes for any signs of the island ahead of us. We had to depend upon our charted course and instincts of direction to steer us steady towards our next point of course change. This charted point was crucial for it would guide us towards our next point, a bell buoy marking the tip of a shallow reef. To make life difficult and the journey more interesting each wave would gather the sloop from its starboard aft quarter, lift and push us forward through a surging surfing motion, and then deposit us behind only to be captured by the wave following. It was a rocky ride! Suddenly, through the howling wind and the questionable looks of a searching crew they all pointed in the same direction shouting, "There she blows!" They had either just seen Moby Dick or the island. Either was good enough for me and instructed the helm to the new course.

Approximately forty-five minutes later right on estimated time and charted course we passed the clanging bell buoy on our starboard side clearing the shallow reef. The fourth and final leg of the trip was calm and quiet as we approached the shoreline behind the protective high masses of Oak Island. We again anchored in a beautiful little cove with the anchor riding in heavy sand. After the deck was cleared and stowed for night we settled into the cabin for supper and reflection of our experienced journey. We lit a solitaire candle, shared some favorite Bible passages, and then our own thoughts and feelings of our trip. It was then I learned none of the crew had ever seen Herman island! They all figured it had to be there and we were close enough to turn. There was a moment's silence when I told them of how disastrous it could have been had we passed the bellbuoy to port. The charted water depths showed only three feet or less. We drew better than five with our keel. Survival time in the cold waters of Lake Superior would have been less than ten minutes. Then we laughed long and hard with a new understanding of community within our crew and how by working together we had made a safe passage. We shared in common prayers and private petitions before retiring for the night.

The next morning as we emerged from the cabin we could see the clear skies of a new day dawning. The weather front was rapidly moving away with the winds freshening from the southwest and warming. We decided to share breakfast underway and quickly set sail towards our next destination. By the time the sails were set and trimmed the sun broke away from behind the clouds bathing us in warmth and brilliant light. As we sailed forth we were calmly graced by the presence of a bald eagle which swept low to the water, snatched an unsuspecting fish feeding near the surface for its own meal and then with powerful yet graceful wings lifted skyward. It was an appropriate symbol of God's presence watching over our journey. "For those who hope in the Lord shall have their faith renewed, they shall rise as on the wings of eagles, they shall run and not grow weary, they shall walk and not faint."

The second journey began in the tiny lakeside harbor of Bayfield, Wisconsin, gateway into the Apostle Islands. A tiny sloop lie in wait tied to the public docks. The crew was uptown getting ready for their journey across the lake back to the homeport of Grand Marias, Minnesota. The hot summer afternoon was clear skies, slight southwest breezes, and a glass-smooth lake. We finally got everything together we needed, the extra gear removed from the boat which we would not need, and bid farewell to our friends. The ship's log entry noted sails were set outside of Bayfield harbor at 1615 hours; course heading northeast towards the channel up between Madeleine and Stockton Islands.

The next log entry was at 2115 hours noting the wind had died, sails were furled, and the sloop "Sitz En Laben" was now under auxiliary power. I noted in my captain's log the lake suddenly got very quiet. This made me nervous. The lake was giving me a sign which I have learned to trust and interpret. I noted the surrounding conditions in my log: clear skies in all directions, calm flat seas, and steady temperatures. I went below and listened to the weather forecast. Nothing of importance. Yet the signs were there. The lake was trying to tell me something, but what?

My eager young crew had learned quickly during the afternoon and evening how to handle the boat. In the near perfect condition I trusted them and felt secure to go below to get some sleep. I knew with an all night crossing on Lake Superior there would be much time later on I would need to be on deck. As sleep quickly overtook my tired body the last thoughts drifting through my mind were the definite signs the lake was communicating to me. The other three crewmembers were trusting souls. My firstmate Brian had made one previous crossing, the week before aboard the same boat. On that crossing we had absolutely no wind and spent twelve hours of motoring across hot glassy seas. The sun reflected heavily upon the smooth waters. The survival was not to get burned too badly and not to dehydrate. Now Brian was at the helm guiding the tiny ship into the darkening skies of night back across Lake Superior. The other two-crew members were on their first voyage: the first time on a sailboat, Lake Superior, and a difficult night crossing. There were feelings of doubt and excitement as the beautiful serene sunset was quickly replaced with darkness.

It was easier to see in the darkness by not using any more running lights than required leaving nothing visible except the white churning wake behind the boat.

The ship's log noted the "security" message broadcast for other lake vessels to be aware we were making the crossing. I felt assured the boat was in good hands and slept very soundly.

My first awareness something was wrong was a loud crack on deck. Instantly I was out of my sleepingbag and on deck. A somewhat confused crew, a dark threatening thunderstorm, heavy waves, and a cold, cold rain, greeted me. Not prepared for this I was wet in seconds. The loud crack of noise I heard had been the wind ripping the sailbag off the headsail, spilling its contents over the liferail. The sail began to unfurl causing the sloop to begin dragging sideways. I realized the greater danger was fouling the propeller with one of the trailing lines. Ryan and I climbed up onto the slippery foredeck and began hauling the wet saturated sail back on board. At one point the sail threatened to pull Ryan overboard with it but he quickly recovered. Being a high school wrestler he used his smaller body's leverage to help bring the sail back onto the foredeck. We cleared it from its riggings and passed it back to Mark and Brian. They shoved it into the aft hold and secured the hatch. Ryan and I finished securing the foredeck area and worked our way back into the cockpit. By now the thunderstorm was full-blown around us. Each flash of lightning lit the sky with a brilliant blinding light. Each clap of thunder rang deafening loud as there was nothing out there in the middle of the lake to rebound or sound off from. The waves had grown to better than seven feet crashing over the bow and washing back into the cockpit. We were all soaked despite our stormgear. Ryan and I went below into the main cabin to begin charting our course and our progress while Brian and Mark stayed topside working together to hold a steady course with a heavy helm. The ship's log indicated 2230 hours: Thunderstorm!

The storm was a battle! Brian and Mark had all they could do to brace themselves against the crashing waves over the bow and to hold the tiny ship straight and true. Meanwhile down below Ryan and I attempted to plot and chart our location for security reasons incase there was an emergency. Although I had changed my wet clothes I was still chilled to the bone. I would shiver the rest of the night until landfall. The next log entry indicated the storm seem to subside about 0130 hours. But the huge waves and cold chilling air was still there flushing down our throats and into our faces.

By 0200 hours I estimated we were running approximately one hour behind our estimated time of arrival. I broadcast another security message just to let others know we were okay. Then the seventh wave struck. One of the things I have learned about the Great Lakes is that approximately every seventh wave is going in a slightly different direction. This is usually a rebound wave or ground swell from the massive power being discharged by any storm. In this case with the wind and waves coming down on top of us the seventh wave came up from behind us. There was a definite different rocking to the boat. More serious, suddenly the auxiliary motor sputtered and died leaving us in total silence. Even I could sense the look of fear in young Mark's eyes and face. "Now what?" I reached across the cockpit to the control panel and flipped the switch. The engine sputtered a couple of times and kicked back into life. We all sighed with relief, attempted to clear our throats of last night's supper, and tried to return our focus to the task at hand.

An hour later the same thing happened. The boat rocked different from the seventh wave hitting us from behind. The engine sputtered. This time Brian quickly cut the throttle to idle and somehow managed to keep it running. Our hearts were beating rapidly high in our throats. We eased the throttle forward and the engine roared back to life and pushed us forward into the next wave. We all felt the same overwhelming sense of fear deep inside.

By 0400 hours Sitz En Laben's bow was pointing towards the entrance to Grand Marias harbor. The cold damp darkness of the lake was suddenly disappearing with the twinkling lights of the small city before us. Like some gigantic weight lifted, we knew we had made our destination. Twenty minutes later we were tied to a small dock and all systems turned off. We shed our stormgear for dry clothes and shoes, radioed our location and "all was clear." and walked into town for something to eat. At first our bodies reacted to solid ground with the sensation we were still bobbing up and down on the high seas. We conversed about our experiences and quietly realized we had all been praying to God for the strength to survive and the guidance to make it through the storm to our destination. Suddenly breakfast tasted so much more wonderful! We were thankful to be alive, to be stronger about ourselves, and comforted by the deepening friendships we shared among ourselves. There is a unique bonding which the four of us shared through this experience which has not nor will ever be duplicated again. It is a special feeling.

Whenever I think of these stories or share them with friends I always remember Barb and her images of the waves. Her peaceful and gentle touch reminds me of the mornings after the storms. Her beautiful presence as a friend in a time of my fear and need gives me a lot of strength to push forward regardless of the circumstances. I am reminded of how thankful I am for her support and support from others when the struggles have gotten hard. I remember from my experiences and struggles which Barb helped me to become an enabler, helping others to see a larger picture rather than just their own situation. The image of the eagle reminds me of the tension between the tidal wave and the gentleness God's grace seeks through me. The eagle, with its powerful wings capable of lifting a large fish from the watery depths yet to glide gracefully among the skies almost effortlessly brings both joy and comfort knowing I am not alone. When I feel myself getting too hard, too rough, too much like a tidal wave I step back and remember Barb's tender soft presence and images. I remember the doubting moments of the journey across open waters between islands. I remember the fear of simple survival upon the open waters of Lake Superior in one of its storms. I remember when there are moments of fear and being afraid my strength does not come from a mighty wave pounding the shore with destructive force but from a gentle trusting presence caressing my faith deep within.

Barb's images of the wave have become my images for a successful life. Whether I am struggling with myself, my handicaps and disabilities, or my failures and disappointments I have come to understand I must experience these struggles in order to feel the calming caressing presence of my faith. The experiences shared by those aboard the boats have made each of us a different, stronger person. Had we not experienced the profound depths of the situation we would not share in a new understanding of our trust and faith, both in ourselves and each other. In experiencing many people as many different types of waves I have found the same kind of strengthening of my faith and my person. I believe life's entire journey has a purpose, a purpose which we must discover, understand, and share with others. Like Barb, my purpose is to be an enabler. I think many times of her soft kind presence and what she did for me. I hope I am doing likewise for others.

CHAPTER EIGHT:
BROKEN TO
WHOLENESS

In my many years of diabetes, I have experienced several losses which have left me broken and seeking wholeness. As if my diabetes isn't enough of a disability, I have experienced loss of sight, an amputation of my right leg just below the knee, and have had five by-passes on my heart. I have also experienced the brokenness of a divorce, which has left me hurting and wanting to feel whole and good about myself. Each one of these experiences has taken me through the entire list of feelings from brokenness to wholeness and given me opportunity to learn something more about myself. The new understanding I have of myself and my limitations allows me to once again experience the feeling of soaring like an eagle above and beyond my disabilities.

I believe there are two kinds of brokenness and wholeness in a person. There is the physical brokenness which happens when a person suffers an injury or experiences a disability. This kind of brokenness can happen from some adverse accident of life, by not taking care of oneself, or the product of some strange and unexplainable act of nature. There is also brokenness which is emotional and can be just as devastating. Although not always self-induced and sometimes caused by the actions and reactions of some other person, this brokenness usually happens when we lose control of our feelings and/or our participation in a variety relationships. Whatever might be the case, physical or emotional brokenness, it is possible to gain wholeness through our pain. Spiritual wholeness is finding and understanding oneself through the pain, learning from it, and not letting the brokenness control who we are.

I believe everyone experiences brokenness in life. Some experience it more than others. Some find it painful and almost unbearable; others appear to handle it more calmly. Brokenness in relationships is always difficult. Brokenness in a relationship sometimes means certain uncalculated risks were taken and resulted in failure. Therefore, we may find ourselves alone and feeling isolated.

Through the process of losing my sight, I believe I experienced both physical and emotional brokenness. My greatest fear was being alone and lost in a world of darkness which was different from the world I knew with sight. I was afraid that because of my disability, people would not understand what I was experiencing. I felt isolated, having moved back home and away from my friends. My world was changing fast and closing in around me. It seemed like there was nothing I could do to stop or change its course. I feared being alone.

One of my first encounters of feeling blind happened during a simulation exercise while working with youth at a church camp. When the exercise was completed and the participants were removing their blindfolds, one remarked, "But Mark cannot remove his blindfold like the rest of us." I was amazed at the profound insight of this sensitive youth.   As time moved forward, I started to adapt to my disability. I began to appreciate others sensitivity of my disability. I was not nearly as broken as I originally thought. When I would take walks with sighted friends, our conversations opened a new world through their eyes and experiences. There was still a barrier which hurt because of my blindness. I was not what I wanted to be. The real pain came from within. I was experiencing both the physical and emotional brokenness of my disability. My fears of being isolated fostered my inability to face my reality, thus making me something which I was not.

In losing my sight, I often found myself alone with too much time to think. I discovered idle minds create idle thoughts and idle thoughts are open doors for depression. In the early stages of my blindness, I found myself struggling. The self-confidence was missing. The inner strength was not present. I doubted myself and my purpose.

I loss the fact I am a person who likes being with people. In my earlier experiences with people, I had developed a philosophy that, "If you're going to make a scene…why not be seen."   I was at my best when I was with others, whether it was going dancing with friends or quietly sitting on deck of a sailboat watching a beautiful, serene sunset. However, at this time, I was no longer making scenes.

Through my journal entries, I quickly discovered I was carrying unwanted baggage. No wonder my emotional arms were tired. This was not healthy. When I felt a new relationship starting, I was too quick to dump my emotional baggage on my new partner which scared them away. Reviewing my journal, I discovered numerous entries of emotions, mixed feelings in relationships, many of which were never shared. Many of the entries were letters never sent. Each entry contained another little piece of my own mystery which seemed to be driving me deeper into myself and farther away from others. I began to search for a common thread which might help me to understand all that was contained inside my baggage. In some ways, I discovered some common patterns of brokenness. There was a common thread through the process which started me towards wholeness.

An individual's life can be described as a tapestry which hangs upon the wall. From the front people see wholeness, beautiful scenery of experiences woven into many patterns which express the uniqueness of our individuality. Meanwhile, the backside has lots of brokenness, loose threads and knots which keep us held together. The image of the tapestry became important to me in understanding what others saw of me up front while in the background there were still many loose ends. There was still the fear of being lonely, isolated by my disability. Yet in finding the common thread which runs through my tapestry, I began to understand myself better and what I needed to change to make myself whole. It would take tracing through the many loose threads and knots on the backside to fully understand the display up front that others would see. So we must begin to search for that common thread through our tapestries of life and relationships that can and will lead to wholeness. That is where this story goes: brokenness to wholeness.

To begin understanding my brokenness and to get a hold on my common thread I returned to the prophecy of Isaiah 40:30..."Even youths grow tired and weary, and young men stumble and fall." This verse reminds me that too many times I have been impatient, wanting things to happen immediately, on my time schedule! Without doubt, every time I forced my impossible time schedule, the outcome has resulted in my stumbling and falling. Rushing into any experience and/or relationship only created a tremendous feeling of brokenness which left me feeling lonely and isolated. A better parallel example might be found when I am walking. If I am not careful in paying attention to what my other senses are telling me to compensate for my blindness, I usually discover many obstacles in the way. Wham-O! I stumble, fall, and fail. If I move carefully, I can walk as though I can see and miss many of the obstacles. Patience becomes a necessary and important ingredient to tracing the common thread through my tapestry. Through my many different life's experiences and relationships, I have learned the same thing. Each event and/or relationship must develop at its own pace, on God's time so to speak. Each experience becomes unique as it begins to share common threads between tapestries. When I start to run, I stumble; when I push too hard or fast, I fail. When I fail, I find brokenness. I seek wholeness. I must slow down.

Many of the entries in my journal are letters to friends never sent. In writing these letters to certain friends, I was able to share some of the inward and spiritual brokenness I was feeling. These feelings of brokenness were pain, fear, frustration, and loneliness. One of the common threads that I discovered running through my tapestry was a dark thread of rushing into relationships, stumbling, and eventually falling. The pain that accompanied the brokenness was tremendous. The journal entries were one way that I could share my pain without burdening others. Yet these friends, to whom the letters were written and to whom some were sent, were true friends who were sensitive to my pain, experienced my struggles, and helped me to understand myself better. They are people that I love very dearly and are very special to me. I owe them much.

I believe that through my written expressions of my broken experiences, I was able to find wholeness. It is my hope that by sharing the stories, connected to the dark thread that runs through my tapestry, you might find common points which may help you identify and understand your own journey from brokenness to wholeness.

Some of the first journal entries, after my total loss of sight, began to describe this dark thread running through my tapestry. I was in the fast lane driven by my fears of loneliness. I was overwhelmed by my fear of going blind. I started over-compensating for these fears by running away from my situation. I tried to hide within what I thought to be the perfect personal relationship. As my fears increased, I ran away faster becoming this huge tidal wave pushing everything and anything away! I became selfish and self-centered in my fears and pain. When reality set in, it hit hard, harder than any of the physical pain suffered through my loss of sight!

I kept returning to that verse in the 40th chapter of Isaiah's prophecy. Even though I was slowly learning from my mistakes in previous relationships, I was still in search of that perfect relationship that would erase and eliminate all my fears and brokenness.

When I started dealing with the more serious problems with my vision and realizing the severity of my situation, I started to cling to what I felt was the only female/male relationship I had. With the fear of going blind fueling my drive to be a whole person, I was running away from my reality and piling much of my unwanted baggage onto the relationship. I am sure it was a heavy load! My own emotional arms were tired and so I could imagine what she was feeling. Up front I was attempting to be strong and appear independent. Behind the scene I was hurting and afraid. She began understanding the unraveling of the knots and loose threads behind the tapestry. She was able to keep a safe distance most of the time but when we got together I pushed to make more happen than was humanly possible. Fortunately for me, she was a spiritually strong person and in her own unique way she helped me to begin understanding what was happening. I was desperately clinging to more in the relationship than was really present. I was smothering her.

One of the things I discovered in my brokenness was that fear was often times more emotional pain than physical pain itself. When I discovered this clue, through the threads running in and out of my tapestry, I was able to start grasping my own wholeness as a person. As I discovered more and more of my wholeness as an individual without sight, I was also able to explore and examine closer my brokenness in relationships. This became very helpful in giving me patience with others, which was a badly needed virtue on my part.

One of the issues that I have discovered in defining brokenness is that when we suffer a physical brokenness it is often something that is not within our control. Losing my sight, although my own fault for not caring for my diabetes properly can be part of the blame, there is still the reality that many diabetics suffer some form of eye disease simply because they are diabetic. It was the same with my heart by-pass surgery and leg amputation. I was playing by the rules, yet losing because I was a diabetic. Physical brokenness can happen when we break a limb from a nasty fall, suffer from any one of the many different diseases, and the list goes on and on. The only way to heal is to be patient and let God's healing take place. This healing and wholeness comes with a responsibility that we must participate and learn to do what is necessary to increase the healing process. The difference between feeling physical brokenness and emotional brokenness is that the physical aspect can be more readily defined and addressed. Whereas in emotional brokenness, we feel more loss of control because we do not always fully understand what we are feeling and how to deal with those feelings. For some of us, loss of control can be a tremendous, sometimes overwhelming experience.

As I continued to learn from past mistakes and move forward on my journey from brokenness to wholeness, I discovered another unique and special person walking along with me. Her laugh is what first caught my attention. On the way home from camp, we stopped and shared an ice cream cone. We found that we had much in common, enjoyed each other's company, and felt a unique connection that was unexplainable. School separated us, yet the relationship grew through many countless hours of taped letters. I started writing letters to her in my journal when pressures in seminary began to overwhelm me. A new twist to my old pattern of writing now happened where I would actually send her my thoughts and feelings expressed on the page. She was supportive in many ways, including praying for me. This took me to a new level of understanding myself and helped the relationship grow. Yet this time I held back because I did not want to stumble and fall.

Time passed and our friendship grew. We continued taping letters, sometimes getting into lengthy multiple tape discussions. The subject of these lengthy discussions was our personal faith stories. We shared many common beliefs, yet came from different approaches. I always found her letters to be most helpful in keeping my focus on my vision for ordained ministry. She possessed a unique and special way of helping me see and understand the perspectives of faith from the pew side of the story rather than always from the theologian and/or scholar part of me struggling through seminary. She was extremely helpful through her faith stories and experiences. When vacations, long weekends, or necessary escape breaks were taken, we would get together. I soon found that my dark thread through my tapestry was not so dark anymore. I was not rushing, was not trying to make something out of nothing, and not just living the relationship internally. We were communicating, sharing, exploring, and enjoying each other. This new found level and understanding of wholeness felt good!

My seminary career continued and one of my second year projects was a term-long paper known as "Constructive Theology." This project and paper was an expression of our personal faith story presented both orally and written. The paper was an expression of self, my understandings of my personal life and faith journey, and how I interpreted God working in and through me. It was not an easy paper. The unique part of the process is that it helped me along my journey of understanding my brokenness and moving towards the wholeness I sought. Part of the process was to periodically share our papers or sections of our papers with fellow classmates in a small group setting. I chose a particular discipline of liberation theology and landed in a small group with one other male and six females. It became a unique challenge for my male classmate and I to express, sometimes defend ourselves, through the disciplines of liberation theology with six women holding us accountable and responsible for our feelings. Rising to the new challenges along with the support of my close personal friend, helped me grow and I felt that I stepped to another new level of wholeness within my life. It made me stronger. It helped me face some of my internal conflicts so that I became my own best friend.

As my new relationship with myself grew, my relationships with others got better. When my faith was challenged, my interpretations questioned, or issue taken with a particular way in which I presented myself, the volley of other's comments, their interpretations and questions helped me look at things more objectively, more openly, and more carefully. A new experience began to develop. I felt myself starting to turn that important corner of understanding my brokenness and moving towards wholeness. Instead of retreating to lick my wounds from disappointing failed relationships and running from self, I was able to see the larger picture of how relationships need to be nurtured, cultivated and treated with special care.

There are lots of loose threads and knots tangled across the backside of my tapestry. Without these experiences woven into the fabric of my tapestry, I would have not learned how to deal with my fears, frustrations, and doubts. All pieces are necessary for me to understand myself and become a better person. Beginning to understand my wholeness helped me turn the corner so that when I feel myself running away I have the strength to turn and face my conflict. My past relationships both broken and continuing remain important pieces, threads woven into my tapestry of my journey from brokenness to wholeness.

I believe that each one of us has a unique way of healing that makes us whole. There is a process that we go through learning about ourselves that moves from the brokenness to wholeness. The tapestry that we display to others is the ongoing product of our trials and errors. Sometimes the loose threads and knots begin to unravel. We become afraid that we will not appear to be as good as we would like others to believe. These are the times we begin to run from ourselves, seeking a place to hide and lick our wounds. Being able to understand our process of moving from brokenness to wholeness gives us strength, the strength that is necessary "to run and not stumble, to walk and not faint".

Being a whole person involves a tremendous amount of risk. There is always another experience, another encounter, and another relationship on our journey. There is always the potential to stumble and perhaps fall. If we come from too many experiences of brokenness, we are less likely to take the risk and put forth the effort necessary to make a relationship work. It takes much energy to take that risk to be involved in a good relationship. When I entered relationships rebounding from the brokenness of the one before, the new relationship stood in harms path, in jeopardy of being pushed away by the tidal wave of my fears. Then I started to discover the wholeness within me, started to relax, stopped running, faced my fears and internal issues, and saw the tidal wave disappear.

When we discover the process that works for us to move from brokenness to wholeness, we begin to understand the much larger picture of how we participate in life. We are always participating. We are called as spiritual beings to participate with ourselves, with our Creator, and with others. This is one of the unique pieces that make us so wonderfully human. There is still the process of trial and error, celebration and disappointment. As we understand the tapestry of our lives and how they are woven together, we discover the ability to move from our brokenness to wholeness.

In looking at the many knots and loose ends of threads on the backside of my tapestry, I discovered that one of my problems that led to brokenness was being selfish and self-centered in a relationship. I was taking my philosophy of "If you're going to be seen...why not make a scene" way too seriously and consequently pushing others out of the way. In selfishness, I wanted all of the attention. Being self-centered, I did not know how to give to a relationship appropriately but sure knew how to take. It took a long time before I began to grapple with my brokenness and this flaw in my tapestry. The first part was the most difficult, admitting that I had made myself my own victim by being selfish. Most brokenness in our lives is the direct result of our own selfishness. Experiencing three broken engagements and a divorce was my prime example. I was pushy and selfish. When I started to ride the crests of new job opportunities and special accomplishments, I forgot many of those that were important to me. I expected too much and assumed wrongly. I was my own worse enemy, in that I wanted to stand out in the crowd and all too quickly forgot that I had not gotten to that achievement by myself but with the help of others, many who were and are very important to me. The pain of brokenness caused the common thread connecting my sorted relationships to darken. This thread through my tapestry was weak. It also became an important thread through my tapestry that constantly reminded me of my mistakes.

This common thread that runs through my tapestry is that brokenness can become wholeness. I am just as much a part of each mistake and disaster, just as I am part of my celebrations and successes. I must learn from the experiences in order to enjoy the accomplishments. My searching through prayer and reflection helped me discover how important the people, with whom I have had a relationship, have helped me understand who I am. I discovered that I could not deny my brokenness if I was to experience wholeness. Moving from brokenness to wholeness gives me strength, gives me hope, and gives me the ability to dream. Discovering wholeness gives me the courage to "run and not stumble, to walk and not faint."

It has been painful struggling with my identity of who I am and what I bring to a relationship. One of my downfalls has always been that I had a difficult time accepting gifts, compliments, and activities done for me. Too many times my pride got in the way. I wanted to be independent and lost the vision of sharing interdependence with people I loved. I could easily give but discovered that I gave too much in wrong ways, which always became smothering. Smothering in a love relationship does not work for it stifles the other person. I stand guilty as charged. The guilt became my brokenness. I then began to discover that my healing process towards wholeness happens when I acknowledge and witness to my brokenness. I must experience the profound depths of my own brokenness before I can look forward with new understanding and insight of what I can offer.

There are still moments in my experience of wholeness when I feel broken. Sometimes I feel afraid of my disability. There are times when my blindness makes me feel trapped and isolated. Experiencing heart surgery has left me much more aware of how I need to take care of myself. My leg amputation leaves me wondering what is going to happen next. Knowing that I am no longer independent helps me rely on the schedules of others. When fears of isolation start to overwhelm me, I see that dark thread surfacing in my tapestry, sending red flags in many directions. Yet God's grace prevails, patience enables, and I continue to learn by my mistakes.

As I started to understand my own sense of wholeness and could vision myself beyond the limitations of my disabilities, I began to soar like an eagle. I was able to achieve a new sense of independence based on inter-dependencies with others. Relationships became important gifts of sharing, mostly giving, and finding that what I was receiving was significant for my wholeness. Out of this identity of wholeness, I realized that in my relationships with others I must treat the other person as a unique gift, sent by God, the likeness of which will never again be seen on the face of this earth. In realizing this thread through my tapestry, it made me feel whole, feel loveable, and feel significant. It made me a compassionate person, sensitive to the needs of others, while still remembering my limitations. I could offer myself to any relationship whole and complete because I knew that I had put the pieces of my brokenness back together with a new image of self to present. People can now see the tapestry up front for what it is while I know what lies behind in all of the knots and loose ends.

The important piece of the larger picture is that I need to be sensitive to my broken past and continue to learn from my mistakes. This is what wholeness is about. My wholeness is found in being my own best friend. I have learned not to go looking for a perfect relationship but to be open to making a good relationship work. I understand wholeness by being sensitive to my experiences, by offering all that I am, and by receiving graciously that which my partner has to offer. I am experiencing the joy of marriage and continue to grow spiritually. The dark thread connecting my past relationships with the present is getting lighter and blending back into the patterns of my tapestry. I feel good about myself and can feel my wings spreading and lifting me in a soaring way. Dreams are things to share. Struggles are pillars of mutual support strengthening and encouraging each other to move forward. In wholeness, my relationships inspire many good things to happen. From the profound depths of my brokenness, I learned to experience and enjoy wholeness. As I move on, I leave you with these words from a poem and song of which I am the author.

"Falling in love's not easy when you're miles away from the one you love. Dreaming a dream is not easy if you dream that dream alone. But falling in love was easy when you came along. Dreaming a dream got easy cause you dreamed along. So let's get together and spend some time.

Yesterday, today was tomorrow, and I was here standing all alone. Then you came along, and look how far we've gone, so let's get together and spend some time.

In the wind I hear your voice calling. In the sunshine I see your sweet smile. In the coolness of the rain I can feel your warm touch, so let's get together and spend some time."

CHAPTER NINE:
TOO MANY
QUESTIONS, NOT
ENOUGH ANSWERS

Isaiah 40:29, "God increases the might of the poor and gives strength to the weary."

Being a child of God makes me a person of faith who believes that for all things there is a reason and purpose. As I move forward through my life sharing and displaying my tapestry to others, I am always learning to look at the larger picture. I believe that as a child of God I am in constant relationship with myself, others, and the Holy Spirit. There is a reason why things happen. Whether it is a normal routine of "for every action there is an opposite and equal reaction" or the adverse and tragic accidents of life, there is always an answer. Sometimes I do not understand the answer at first, for it is complicated. Other times, it takes learning and time before I can see the real purpose. And then again, there are times I do not ask or am afraid to ask the right questions. I might be afraid of the answer. Or, I sometimes have a hard time accepting the answer. Whatever the case, I do believe that the larger picture holds a reason and purpose for the events that happen to me.

There are still times when the load of my disability seems more than I can carry. I get frustrated when projects and activities take longer because the process is altered by my disability. I find myself constantly needing to compensate and adapt. When I forget, I stumble because suddenly the task becomes a burden. I get scared when I feel trapped because of my blindness. I become angry when I experience injustice through my disability and feel that I am helpless to do anything about that injustice. Sometimes there are just too many questions to ask and not enough answers to satisfy.

Being a child of God helps me understand that all things are possible in God. Still, sometimes, I find that it is difficult to sit back and let something happen that is beyond my control. I am a person who responds, who fixes, and makes things happen. I am always looking for something I can do to help. Yet when I am at my weakest point, those times when I feel helpless, I find myself relying on the strength of my faith. I find that God continues to work through me and still has much to reveal. My helplessness is only a sign that reminds me to continue trusting in what God has yet to do through me.

When my faith has been tested by life's unfair events, I have discovered that I am only as strong as when I am at my weakest. When I feel dysfunctional, unable to operate, I must remember that God increases the might of the poor and gives strength to the weary. Even in moments when I cannot do a single thing, I can still trust in God's presence, and my patience will help me through. So when my path becomes darkened with fear, danger, and the threat of the unknown, there is still the ability to wait in the Lord.

All of us experience losses in our lives. Sometimes it is easy to understand old age, terminal diseases, and even tragic accidents. Other times we do not understand. Losses in life are part of the magical, mystical dance. If we do not understand our loss, fail to accept our loss, or find that we are unable to ask the right questions to help us understand, we become angry, dysfunctional, and complacent.

Too many times I have seen dysfunctional people turn their pain and confusion inward, where it becomes anger and depression. Suddenly they become so withdrawn, they are almost impossible to reach. Because I believe that all things are possible through God, it is important to continue to reach out and help. When I first started having problems with my vision, I continued to think and believe that I was invincible and that I would overcome my problem. I would learn differently.

The first moment I began to realize that I was not stronger than when I am at my weakest point was shortly after the first of five major surgeries on my eyes. A week before surgery, I began suffering the tremendous pain of what was eventually diagnosed as vascular glaucoma. The pain was very intense and focused just behind my left eye. It felt like someone had pierced my eye with a large stick! I was taking some powerful painkillers and yet somehow managed to participate as the best man in the wedding ceremony of two close friends. Two days after the wedding, I underwent surgery.

The morning following surgery, when the doctor removed the bandage, his suspicion proved true. During surgery, I had suffered a major hemorrhage inside my left eye. This is a known high risk for diabetic retinopathy patients. There were slim hopes that the eye would be able to recover from the hemorrhage. I was quickly discovering what it meant to be totally blind in one eye. My depth perception was the first to go. I needed to compensate for this loss as I was constantly knocking over glasses of water, bumping things onto the floor, and clipping corners too sharp. A week later the glaucoma returned and another surgery was attempted. This surgery was successful for the glaucoma. However, it became evident that the eye was not going to recover totally. I was down to one not so great, but functional eye.

As I grappled with the pain of losing sight in my left eye, I also began realizing just how much I was missing in other arenas of my life. One of those arenas was realizing that my engagement to be married was over. My fiancée and I had put plans on hold as my vision problem developed. Things were happening so quickly that we both felt we needed to give ourselves time to sort through and understand what the future would hold. When I lost vision in my left eye, my pain turned inward and I closed my fiancée out. I realized too late that I had hurt her; she had every reason to slam the door on me. I was doubly devastated. Not only was I losing my sight but also my girl. I became angry and depressed and started to withdraw. I did not understand. I did not know the right questions to ask. I was becoming dysfunctional.

By the time I was faced with losing the rest of my vision, I was beginning to understand. I knew all the medical terminology involved. I even began to see and understand the reasons and purposes that caused my situation. I was willing to accept responsibility. When total blindness occurred, I was ready to step forward on my new journey, for I firmly believed that in God all things are possible. I also understood that as a child of God, God would increase the might of the poor and give strength to the weary. This faith helped me understand the loss of my fiancée. I started to look forward once again.

Life moved forward moderately well with just the normal trial and error experiences of attempting to understand myself as a blind person. I also went through several relationships that felt important to me, yet I mishandled them and consequently lost. Even though most of these relationships redefined themselves to being good friends, there was still the pain of their loss. I continued to work on trusting my faith and believing that all things are possible in God.

My next stumbling block arrived when my Grandfather Schowalter died. I knew all the reasons. I did not understand the feelings. I remember sitting on a kitchen floor at a friend's house when I received the news that he had passed away. I expected it, since he had been placed in the hospital just a few days earlier. After I hung up the telephone, I cried. Something felt like it had cut cleanly through the tapestry of my life. I was not sure I could mend the pieces together.

At the wake and funeral, I was scared. I was afraid to go near the casket that held my grandfather. Yet strangely enough, I also felt attracted to it. The magical mystical dance of my life was confusing. I remember feeling this tremendous amount of pressure deep inside as I greeted and visited with more relatives than I knew I had. The pain increased. I looked for answers, reasons, and the purpose of why I felt this way. I remember the fearful feeling of responsibility which now rested upon me to carry on the family name, as I was the oldest grandson. At the end of the evening, I went forward to say my last good-bye. I was suddenly compelled to hold my grandfather's hand. I found myself praying for his journey. Big tears streamed from my sightless eyes, yet I felt as if I could see everything.

As I prayed for his safe passage and new journey into the promise of eternal life, I felt my father's hand resting over mine. In that moment, it all became clear. I now understood how grandfather had taught me to live in relationship with the earth through the many years of farming together. I now understood why his purpose on earth had been fulfilled and he was moving on. I understood what was and was not expected of me. The pressure and pain deep inside left and I felt my faith rejoicing in celebration for Grandfather's life. The reasons and purposes were all there.

The next moment of confusion in understanding the purpose of life came five years after I had started working with my dog guide Babe. Babe was a special dog. She was my first guide and taught me what a guide for the blind can do. She faithfully sat through countless hours of seminary classes, mumbled her own words of prayer during worship services, and always had a warm and friendly greeting for whomever we met.

Shortly before I graduated from seminary, I taught her to shake paw. Some classmates made her a stole in the seminary colors, which she wore with great dignity for the procession and graduation ceremonies. When I received my Master Degree, Babe received a degree for "Helping Master Through." Amidst the standing ovation that both of us received, Babe stopped and lifted her paw to shake hands with the seminary President. It was a special moment for both of us and my family. She was a precious friend.

Babe was a hard worker. She knew her job and loved to do it. She also loved to play. When given the opportunity, she would stretch her muscles by running as hard and fast as she could. Many times friends would describe her beauty and grace to me while she ran. In my mind's eye, I could see exactly what they described. Babe adopted every friend as a member of her family. I know she never forgot a face. If she met someone once, she always remembered them.

Upon returning home from a summer vacation in Maine, New York and Pennsylvania, I discovered that Babe was losing her appetite. A full physical examination by her doctor indicated all the symptoms of hepatitis. Babe spent five days in the animal clinic receiving treatment. Babe's veterinarian was exceptional and further blood tests revealed that her illness was more serious. He recommended taking her to the University Animal Clinic in Madison, Wisconsin. After exploratory surgery and more tests, we discovered that Babe suffered from a disease called "Wilson's Disease", a terminal liver condition. Experimental treatments were all that could be prescribed. We needed to take one day at a time.

When Babe came home from the hospital, I was at camp. Someone brought Babe to camp because she enjoyed the people. All the campers, over the years, had become her "kids" and she was excited when they greeted her in the parking lot late that evening. The entire camp understood the importance and seriousness of her disease. Babe did not care about her situation but greeted every camper. There were many special things we needed to do to care for her. Upon reflecting through my confusion, I knew that she was concerned about me. Dogs are tremendous barometers of human emotions. Babe knew I was scared. I could sense that Babe was happy to be at my side. This is where she knew she belonged.

Our last two days together went painfully fast. During her last few hours, Babe lost her own sight and started having seizures. This was hard on me. When the seizures would start, she would bury her head into my stomach and attempt to curl up on my lap. All I could do was hold her and comfort her through her pain. This was difficult for me. Babe had been my eyes for five plus very good years. It was hard for me to see her suffering. Yet in her own pain, she knew me. She constantly wanted to be by me. Late that last night, we rushed her back to the University Clinic, about a two hour drive away. It was the longest two hours I ever spent in my van.

On Monday, June 23, 1986 at 1:20 a.m., while comforting her in my arms, Babe went to sleep for the final time. After we arrived at the clinic, her doctor discovered there really was nothing he or anyone could do for her to sustain any quality of life. The only thing he could suggest was experimental treatments that would be costly and yet provide no real future. The doctor could see the special relationship that Babe and I shared and he was afraid to suggest that I put her down. In my heart, I had already made my decision. I understood the outcome. Babe and I had celebrated together and we shared our pain. I invited the doctor to put her down. There was not a dry eye in the room. My parents, a brother and his girlfriend, and a close friend were all present at the clinic that night. Together we prayed for Babe's safe passage to her promise of eternal life and gave thanks for the ministry she had provided. Her final moments were spent pressing her weakened head into my stomach, knowing that I was there to hold her. At last, her body went limp and she was gone. I slipped her collar from her neck. I said my last good-byes and then quietly left her. Suddenly, I was overwhelmed by my own loss and felt myself slipping back into being totally blind all over again. I wept for a very long time.

Once again in my blindness, the fear of the unknown darkness surrounded me. I was scared! There were so many questions to ask, yet fear pushed answers away. The harder I tried to find reasons, the more I felt lost. My struggles in searching were hard. Even though, a week after Babe's death, I was back in training with a new dog guide, I was still suffering with pain and confusion.

We celebrated a memorial service for Babe's life and ministry a week after her death. Friends came from many places to participate. I know some thought it was not appropriate to hold a memorial service for a dog in the sanctuary, but it was important to me. Babe had served her entire career as a dog guide in the Church. The Church and its many friends were her life. For those who gathered, it was important. There were stories shared, poems read, and prayers offered. We celebrated Babe's ministry, not only to me, but to everyone that knew her.

Part of my healing process happened during the worship service. An answer appeared in the voice of a little girl who was a member of the church. She loved Babe. There was silence throughout the sanctuary as she spoke. God often times speaks to us in mysterious ways when we least expect it. This was one of those precious moments. Her message was simple and complete, "Now Louie has someone to play with." Louie was her grandmother's dog who had died about seven months earlier. Although I was filled with many questions, here was an answer that I could understand and hang onto: "God increases the might of the poor and gives strength to the weary."

The day after Babe's memorial service, I began training with my next dog guide, Lady Marge. We called her Marge for short. A new chapter and adventure in life was beginning. Marge was lovable and was quickly filling the void left by Babe. However, I soon found myself trying to work with Marge with expectations of how Babe worked. I was not working. I found myself tripping, stumbling, and falling because I was not paying attention to Marge. I began to realize I was not asking the proper questions to find the answers to my grief of losing Babe. Marge was a different dog with a unique personality. Marge was not Babe. I had to let go of Babe. The answer was rather simple, especially after Marge got my attention by walking me into the same telephone pole for the third time. I realized I needed to move on.

Marge was a terrific dog guide. She had her own set of unique characteristics. From the moment I realized she was not Babe, and she had her own way of communicating, she gave me everything she had to offer. She even seemed to understand when, by accident, I would call her Babe. We spent two weeks training and passed with flying colors. The flight home was not her cup of tea and she spent most of the ninety-minute trip on my lap.

As Marge and I grew closer as a team, I learned about her horrible background as an abused dog. After she was rescued by a local humane society, she was sent to a wonderful woman known internationally for her work with Dobermans. Ms. Joanna Walker was able to deprogram Marge, and Marge's daughter Duchess, and then retrain both as dog guides for the blind.

When Marge and Duchess were ready, they went to be trained at Pilot Dogs, Inc. of Columbus, Ohio, where we started as a team. Upon returning home, I soon realized that one of her skills was being an escape artist. Because of her previous abuse, she hated being left someplace without me. There were several occasions when, for her own safety, she was left in the van while I tended to business. Three different times Marge made her escape. The first time she pushed herself through a small vent window and followed me into a wedding reception. Her second attempt was not quite as successful as she tried to push herself through a window that had been left open to provide ventilation. The window was only open perhaps five inches and she managed to get all but her right hindquarter out. This left her hanging upside down on the outside of the van. She was quite sore and stiff the next couple of days.

There are questions in our lives that we never find answers too. At least not the answers we want to hear. I learned this painful lesson in Marge's third attempt. It was a warm summer's evening. I was visiting friends at their rural home for a summer barbecue. When the time came to go inside for dinner, I left Marge in the van with all the windows open so that she would have enough air. There were cats present on the farm.

Marge hated cats. This was another unfortunate piece of her past. Knowing that she was an escape artist, I had a special tie-down cable attached to the back seat of my van. This allowed for Marge to stand up, turn around, and reposition herself back on the floor between the seats. It was getting dark and the evening was getting comfortably cool so I left her alone for a couple of hours.

It was dark and quiet as I prepared to leave. My driver went to take some things to the van and to let Marge out for a last run before returning home. The passenger side of the van was opposite from the front door. As my driver turned the corner of the van, she screamed! I almost jumped out of my shoes! I ran to the van only to discover Marge hanging out of the open front window. I'm really not sure what happened next. I remember telling myself to breathe. It felt like my heart was beating inside my head and my stomach was caught in my throat. My first instinct was to release her collar. Her limp lifeless body fell to the ground. The sudden release of tension allowed the air trapped in her lungs to escape, creating an eerie groaning sound. Thinking and hoping that Marge was still alive, in my panic, I started mouth to nose resuscitation. As the chill of fear and disappearing hope left me, we all began to realize that Marge was gone.

For days I blamed myself for her tragic painful ending. I kept returning to the van trying to figure out what happened, how it happened, and perhaps why. I blamed myself for leaving her in the van and for not checking on her more often. I never even heard her cry for help. My own pain and my returning blindness overwhelmed me. The pain was empty and bottomless. I could not think clearly. I was lost and angry at myself for this tragic accident. Marge was such a good dog, which made it even harder to deal with. I was filled with questions but found no answers.

I often remember Marge in her final resting place. The night of the accident we buried her body near the cemetery of many of my ancestors. My friends and I held hands and prayed for her safe passage to the world beyond, that which we knew. The more I thought about the tragic accident, the harder I cried. I searched long and hard, but found no comfort.

Finally, I had to get myself out of the house for my own sanity. I got my old trusty, rusty white cane out of the closet and headed out the door. I had never used my cane in the community where I was currently living. It was a tremendously anxious filled moment. I walked the seven blocks to the bus stop. I was headed for my office. I was awed by the discovery of telephone poles, parking meters, and other obstacles along the way. For the previous two years, Marge had navigated me through the maze. I quickly learned how much of her work I had taken for granted. She was a real gem.

When I would suffer through some painful mobility mistakes, the anger about the accident would flood through me. Even though, in my head, I knew it was an accident, my heart found it difficult to forgive and forget. The painful memories of the accident bothered me for many weeks. Even knowing that Marge was an escape artist, and perhaps it was her own fault, brought no comfort.

Losing my sight, and then Babe and Marge, taught me a painful lesson in life. Sometimes there are tragic accidents that cannot be explained. There is no fault, no blame, and no reason. They simply happen as a part of the magical mystical dance we call life. Each time we experience a tremendous loss in our life we are thrown back into the depths of our spiritual wells and we must begin again. The path back is difficult. There are always more questions than answers. That is part of the search, part of our journey.

When I lost my sight, I had plenty of questions and very few answers. I kept asking myself the question, "what did I do to cause my blindness?" When I realized the answer, it was painful. The answer was mismanagement of my diabetes and abuse of alcoholic beverages. The hardest piece to accept was giving up driving. I was a professional chauffeur. My eyesight was my ticket and resource to assist my financial obligations. Driving was something I enjoyed. It was relaxing for me. Losing my sight required surrendering my driver's license and giving up an independence that meant much to me. I now had more questions and still not enough answers.

When I lost both Babe and Marge, I again lost my independence. I was filled with self-pity. I had the same feeling when I lost my sight. I searched for answers that I wanted to hear with questions that had no meaning. I would learn this time and time again, as I experienced different losses in my life. When I have lost special people, special relationships, and unique experiences, it has always meant that a part of me died. It has always reminded me to return to the foundations of my faith. God increases the might of the poor and gives strength to the weary.

The magical mystical dance we call life, is sometimes filled with tragic adverse events that we have no control over. I believe that we must turn to God for the strength and guidance to help us understand. I do believe that there is a reason and purpose for every event. If nothing else, every unanswered question eventually gets asked in the proper way and we do understand. Understanding expands our horizons, makes us a better person, and strengthens our weariness. Sometimes the question to the unanswered event is simply trusting in God for that strength to make it through. This also increases the might of the poor in spirit and gives strength.

My experiences of loss have always been the most painful when I ignored the signals along the way. Sometimes, my own independence became an unhealthy co-dependency on my fears and doubts. The harder I tried to be strong, the weaker I found myself becoming. When I reflected through my journals, I found that another common thread through my tapestry was an attempt to be strong, to be the fixer, to be the one always trying to help. I found patterns of being able to give but not able to receive. This became another part of the magical mystical dance of my life. I had the answers but did not know the questions.

It took me a long time to learn that independence is not healthy, nor is dependency. I began to realize that the happy medium was inter-dependency. I have much to offer. I also have needs. My understanding of grief and loss is learning that inter-dependency is necessary to be able to understand the reasons and purposes. Now, when I experience the pain of loss, I know that I will grieve, that I will feel bad, and then I will begin to understand. If I am to blame for my mistakes or bad decisions, I accept the responsibility. If the pain is caused by a tragic and adverse accident, I remind myself through prayer that God watches over children and fools. God knows that I am a foolish child. God will increase the might of my spiritual weakness and give me strength. The deeper the pain the more I have learned to trust in the faith that has been given to me.

CHAPTER TEN:
MARK, MUSIC, AND MINISTRY

There are many lines, paragraphs, and songs written about dreams. Some of my favorites that come quickly to mind are "To dream, the impossible dream," and "I like dreaming, because dreaming can make you mine," and "Don't fall in love with a dreamer".

Each thought expresses a slightly different feeling of the author and many times becomes a borrowed expression of our own feelings. I am a dreamer. I know this because I have the tendency to look forward, to vision a much larger picture of myself, and to work towards the reality that always seems to be one day, one step in front of me. I believe in dreams. Dreams are important to our emotional health for it gives us the motivation and determination to push for something that we really want. As soon as I began to understand who I was and accepted the reality that I am a dreamer, I began to discover that "Mark, Music, and Ministry" were very much part of my dream and part of my reality. They began to work in concert with each other. They began to tie things together that helped me function as a person. "Mark, Music, and Ministry" helped me to find the necessary ingredients I needed to survive and be successful.

I have three mottoes that help me focus towards finding and keeping a proper balance in my life. These mottoes are little helpful reminders that I am not perfect, that I am constantly involved in some sort of relationship, and that my journey is always going to have some form of tension within, just to keep it earnest. The first of these mottoes is ""If you're going to make a scene…why not be seen!" The second is "I seek to serve," and the third is "God doesn't make junk:

just look at a giraffe, platypus, and me!" I admit that they may seem strange to you but after we visit for a bit about what these sayings mean to me and how they help, I think you will understand. I also think you will probably know a few yourselves, that help you.

Your journey will never be the same as mine. You will encounter different experiences, go different places, meet different people, do different things, and see things differently than I do. That is the unique piece of the puzzle to the magical mystical dance we call life. We may share similar paths for a brief period of time, we may even encounter the same experience, but I guarantee that you will see life in a slightly different way than anyone else. That is what makes the dance so much fun. All of the different experiences that we encounter are important and become blended into the mixture of who we are. These experiences are woven into the fabric of our tapestries. We can perhaps pick and choose those experiences we wish to share with others, which we put out front on display. However, all of our experiences, good and bad, are woven into the fabric and become part of us. We then must discover the balance in our life by studying our experiences, relationships, successes, and failures as we see them. As we learn about ourselves and when we are ready, we can shake out the wrinkles and once again display our tapestry to the world, boldly proclaiming; "This is who I am! Look out world, here I come!"

Each one of us develops and grows in different places at different times. For me, High School and those dreaded "teen" years seemed like the worse. One thing I remember was feeling that I didn't belong. I wasn't a socialite, a super jock, or a gear- head. Dating was occasional at best, most of the time, just for the big events such as Homecoming and Valentine's Day. I enjoyed participating in group activities like intramural sports, pep band, and music performances. I was never the most popular guy or a person who stood out in the crowd; I was just an everyday person, always around and maintained the status quo. I spent much of my free time working part-time jobs and learning to sail.

One of those impressionable memories from my high school career was learning to dance in gym class. Every Friday of the second and third semesters was spent learning ballroom dances because the weather did not permit us to go outside. Everyone had a favorite partner, who we would attempt to dance with during the hour. We also had those partners with whom we dreaded dancing. If you missed your desired partner, and held back in hopes of not getting picked, you could end up dancing with one of the female teachers. I was never sure which was worse, dancing with an undesirable partner or with a teacher. If you were unlucky and ended up with a teacher, you also knew that you were going to be the "display and example" for the day. Now truth being told, there were a couple of female teachers who were not bad. There were some to be approached cautiously. So if and when fate struck, and I had to partner with a teacher, I tried to make the best of the situation. It was at this time that I began to develop my motto, ""If you're going to make a scene…why not be seen!" Needless to say, I'm a fantastic swing and ballroom dancer of the fox trot, cha-cha, jitterbug, two-step, polka, and schottische, just to name a few. Once a month, we were lined up on opposite sides of the gym for the "grand march." This meant fate, happenstance, luck, or misfortune would pair us as we marched to the beat of the music. As we marched to the music, we would end up in squares of four couples for a day of square dancing. Sometimes you got lucky and sometimes personalities clashed! Consequently, I also loved square dancing. Now when I go to a dance, be it a wedding reception, nightclub, or chaperoning teen dance, I have a blast showing off. ""If you're going to make a scene…why not be seen!"

I have also discovered that there is a new definition for "closed ballroom position." I like it!

High School was an eternity! I was a late bloomer, more shy than assertive, content to stay with the status quo rather than to make waves or cut my own trails. That was too bad for me. I look back now and wish I were then what I have become now. It would have been much more fun. But then again, that is not me. There was a purpose for things happening to me the way they did. I was in training, a student of life, watching, testing, taking notes, and waiting for the right moment when I would get my chance. I can reflect and find many good things about high school that I missed. I enjoyed concert band, marching and pep bands, radio broadcasting, and marriage/family relation's courses.

In the early 1980's, I started listening to a Saturday morning television program called "Saved by the Bell." Although many times I wished I were like the characters of Zachary Morris or A.C. Slator, I found myself relating more with the character of Screech. I could relate to many similar experiences and shared a common thread with the character portrayed. I did well academically and seemed not to do as well socially. I always had a crush on the prettiest, best looking girls, who would have preferred that I disappear. I guess, all in all, it was not as bad as I thought. I survived. I continued developing my character through my motto of "If you're going to make a scene...why not be seen!"

I worked a variety of part-time jobs. I started by cutting lawns around the neighborhood, then moved into food services as a bus boy and dishwasher, started building some muscles in a warehouse job, delivered flowers, and eventually worked in an industrial fabric shop. All of these jobs provided me with a variety of different skills that would eventually become very helpful. When I went to college, many things started to happen and happen fast. My first day on campus, I was offered a job as chauffeur for the college. My previous experience, as a flower delivery person, made me well acquainted with the community. I was perfect for the job of chauffeur. I loved driving! It took me only four days to study the manual and take the written and road tests for my license. Six days after being offered the job, I was officially a chauffeur for the college. I became very popular through my chauffeur skills; polite, responsible, and reliable. As I got better at my job, I became more popular, which made me work even harder. I got most of the unusual calls; odd hours and unique trips which allowed me to meet many interesting people. The promising career utilizing my driving skills helped me find a balance somewhere between studying, work, and the ever-popular college party.

In high school, music was always a hobby for me. It was fun and I enjoyed performing. I hated practicing. In college, I began to discover a new balance in what I was becoming. The motto "If you're going to make a scene...why not be seen" became a fun and motivating force. I found myself majoring in music with an emphasis in performance. I started a Dixieland type band that became popular. I loved being out in front, leading the group and getting audiences to participate with us. When I first went to college, I left my trumpet home hoping to shelve that part of my life, and then suddenly found myself a leader of the band. "If you're going to make a scene...why not be seen." My music expanded to musicals and then theater. Soon I found myself a student of the theatrical arts and rehearsing for my first lead in the spring musical. I was devastated when the doctors told me I had to quit dancing, due to a stress fracture in my right leg, and I never had the chance to learn tap dance. I did end up in the pit orchestra as lead trumpet. I enjoyed myself and my popularity increased. I was learning how to make things balance in my life; studies, work, play, and relationships. College was becoming more fun with exciting new friends.

College became a great testing ground for my newly found talents, skills, and gifts. The love for the stage, the ability to perform and make people laugh, and having fun making a scene and being seen, I now began to realize that there was this tiny little voice speaking to me. It was calling me to do something, yet I was not clear in my understanding. That would develop later. After college and having lost my sight, I felt I was no longer making scenes. After I struggled through the depression and knew what my purpose was in life, I was back on stage. Once a performer has the smell of grease paint, can hear the roar of the applause, and sense the excitement of centerstage, the actor always returns. I could find ways of using my disability to make a scene. Not a bad scene, not a scene that put others down and says, "Look at me! I've got an ego a mile wide and a chip on my shoulder to boot." Rather, I found ways to use my disabilities to effectively make a scene that could help others understand disabilities and handicaps more clearly. My blindness helped others to see. My insight helped others understand themselves. Thus, "If you're going to make a scene…why not be seen."

When a person such as me travels with a dog guide, you always stick out in the crowd. Make that dog guide a Doberman and you get twice the visibility. I am constantly being stopped and asked questions about my blindness, about the dog, and "Hey mister, is that really a Doberman?" I love spending time helping others realize that blindness is survivable. I enjoy helping people understand that not all Dobermans are trained to attack, shred, and ask questions later. In fact, most are surprised when they learn that there are more documents of Dobermans rescuing people than hurting them. Vicious Dobermans are products of ignorant people who are insecure. The mass media makes money on stories of bad news and a bad situation festers into mass hysteria, and the poor helpless Doberman gets blamed. So with my dog guide faithfully and loyally doing her work, we follow the motto, "If you're going to make a scene...why not be seen."

My first semester at college started to open my eyes to the needs of others. I developed many new friends who had as varied a background as there are stars in the sky. I became involved with one group of guys known as the Zeta Chi Fraternity. Some will say that I was destined to be a Zeta, since my father was an active member when he attended college. He still has his fraternity paddle, with all the names of his fraternity brothers inscribed into the polished wood. I knew the educational principles of the paddle through my youth, having well deserved the engraved fraternity emblem on my butt. My learning process through the paddle had taught me the five virtues of my fraternal order: spirituality, scholarship, service, strength, and mercy. Although I was to be considered a legacy of the fraternity, it was the motto of this brotherhood, "I seek to serve" that captured my attention.

When I joined the fraternity, many of the active members were involved in the leadership of the campus. Presidents, Vice-Presidents, and other leadership positions were all active fraternity brothers throughout most of the other organizations on campus. I was impressed! I also believed in what they stood for as an organization, a fraternity of loyal brothers. I wanted to serve others. In my driving, I was doing that. I pledged the fraternity and was accepted. The desire to "seek to serve" grew within.

Another seed that had been planted the summer before I started college started to grow. It was the seed of ministry. As my college career developed, the seed sprouted, the voice got louder, and I had to start paying attention. Many friends who know me will tell you that I admired my father as a minister from as far back as age three. Since my ordination, I have recovered a letter about when I attend my first church meeting when I was five days old. How was I to know that I was going to be a minister? Although there have been many detours along this journey, the roots of the seed have been lying in wait for the right moment. With my college career developing and the influence of supportive friends in the fraternity, the magical mystical dance was awakening. I began to focus my studies towards being a minister, something that many of us in the fraternity felt called to do.

Growing up as a "P.K.", preacher's kid, I spent much time around the Church. The church was a special place for me. I experienced the Church as a place where I was always accepted. It was a place filled with wonderful stories about extraordinary people. It was an unbelievable warehouse of human resources. As a child, I saw it as a big adventure. As I grew older, it became a friend, a place of challenge, and a place of quiet comfort. I always admired my father as friend, preacher, teacher, and Pastor. It was a unique relationship. Through him, I was learning, watching, and testing my own skills. I was learning how I could seek to serve.

In my family's experiences in the Church, there was always the element of fellowship. We were constantly doing things together. Whether it was work or play, there was always fellowship. It made the work easier, more exciting, and less of a task. It made play a special reward for just being together and accepting one another for who we are, not what others think we should be. The feeling of "I seek to serve" became an accepted part of life, something that I always felt I needed to do. For example, when an elderly woman needed help with her storm windows and screens, I was happy to assist and would not accept payment. Snow shoveling in winter was another incentive to help others, especially those who could not handle the job themselves. It was easy to find many places to do something for someone else and not expect payment in return. The more service performed, the better I felt about myself.

The summer after my senior year in high school found me attending a "Leadership Skills Camp." The camp was a familiar place to me. It was a part of the Church that I had frequented many times. I enjoyed spending time there with friends. I had been attending camps for many years, finding and enjoying the different weeks, facing challenges and new growth with my peers in the Church. Whereas in the public arena of my high school I felt left out, at Church camp I was accepted. I could simply be myself. It was here at this particular camp that I believe the seed was planted, that would eventually lead me towards becoming an ordained minister. I was beginning to understand the meaning of "I seek to serve."

The voice spoke loudest to me on the last night of camp. It was an emotional night for many of us as it was the last night that we could be campers. The next time any of us would return to this campsite we would be staff, counselors, and/or directors. I was sitting outside the chapel at camp with a close friend. Emotions were running high and wild through the seventy plus campers there. We were sitting on Vesper Point sharing some tears, fond memories, and expectations of what lay ahead. There was a storm approaching from across the lake, which kept most of the group close to the chapel. As we sat in the darkness watching the storm approach and talking quietly, I started to see a vision on the lake. The rain was moving across the water toward us. I could see the rain line approaching and moving on shore where we sat. As the rain began to touch us with its quiet, gentle presence, I believe that I saw an image of Jesus reaching out and asking me to follow. Before I ever understood the fraternity's motto "I Seek to Serve", I believe I was being called to serve by Jesus Christ. Although the rain was cool, I felt a surge of warmth go through my body. Suddenly, everything was in balance within me and I felt better about myself. For a few short moments while sitting in the rain, I felt I stepped back and could see the much larger picture of my life, my relationships, and my purpose. Something inside was set in motion. I shared my experience with my friend. She embraced me with a warm hug. The affirmation helped me understand and hear the voice, within me, calling.

Moving on from that night at camp into my college career, I began to see things differently. Instead of focusing on myself, I was beginning to see a wider picture, including others around me. The journey was not always focused on attending seminary and becoming ordained. I had many avenues to explore where I could seek to serve others. Through my college education, I was changing my tapestry. I was redesigning myself so that others would see the person I was becoming. I was changing my tapestry so that people would see three important pieces; Mark, music, and ministry. New energy was developed, new skills and talents tested, new opportunities explored.

Many of my fraternity brothers and I were considered "pre-seminary" students. We were considering some form of ministry as a chosen career. Our fraternal motto of "I seek to serve" always reminded us of our focus as we offered service projects to the campus. Many of us were involved in the leadership positions of the campus, carrying on the traditions of those who had gone before.

The seed that had been planted much earlier was growing rapidly. The still voice inside of me was speaking louder than ever and I was responding. It was exciting. It was also a struggle. I was not totally sure of what lay ahead. I felt confident about what I was doing and that gave me strength. The more I discovered the talents and skills in myself, my music, and my ministry, the greater sense of balance I felt. These days in my college career were important days of developing the foundations from which I would be able to struggle through the trials that were yet to come.

After I struggled through the pain and depression of losing my sight, it was once again time to work with my three mottoes. By the time I was totally blind, I was ready to start serving others. One of the ways I could serve was to be an example as a blind person. So my motto of ""If you're going to make a scene…why not be seen" grew stronger. I began using experiences as examples to help others discover and understand their own disabilities and handicaps. From the depths of my own pain and depression, I was able to develop a sense of patience and humor that became my medium of communication. Moments of chaos and misunderstandings became moments of teaching and learning for both student and teacher. My skills as a minister strengthened, my music became important, and my own self-confidence increased.

The third motto began to develop; "God does not make junk; just look at giraffes, platypuses, and me." Giraffes and platypuses are unique creatures of God. Although they appear to be oddly designed, they have been created with a purpose and ability to adapt to their environment. A giraffe has such a long neck that it can eat the necessary leaves and foliage, required in its diet. I also wonder whether or not a giraffe is the first one to know that it is starting to rain. Plus, think of the observation capabilities of being up so high. It has been designed by God to adapt to its environment so it can survive. It is the same with the platypus. A platypus is unique in that it is the only mammal capable of laying eggs. It has a duck-like bill so that it can eat the necessary plankton and other water insects required for its diet. It has webbed feet for swimming, a beaver-like tail for its warning communications system and for packing mud in necessary places, and four strong legs capable of cruising over land at an adequate pace. How unique to be one of a kind, capable of adapting to its environment for survival. Which brings me to me?

I am a unique individual, the likes of which have never been seen before nor will ever be seen again. I guess that puts me into the same category of strangeness, weirdness, and uniqueness as the giraffe and platypus. Yet I am confident to proclaim, that," because giraffes, platypuses, and I are able to adapt to our environment in order to survive, God does not make junk." Rather, God has made something so special, given it life, and given it a purpose for existence. The secret to the larger picture is discovering what the skills, talents, and gifts are that help us adapt.

My life has not always been easy. Nor has it been hard. I have had many successes as well as many failures. Sometimes, the best way that I have learned something about myself, has been through trial and error, taking the risk to attempt a task, and learning from my mistakes. I am not a complainer because I am fully aware that many have it much more difficult. Yet I also want to be sensitive to others by realizing that life is not always a picnic, a barrel of laughs, or a humorous story. Sometimes, there are successes that need to be shared and celebrated. Other times, there are adversities, difficulties, and frustrations that must also be shared and experienced. These are the times when I depend upon my little mottoes to help me survive.

I would have to be the first one to admit that there have been many times when I was scared and ready to quit. I have known many times when the pain, both physical and emotional, has felt like it was too much to bare, too much to handle, and that I would not survive. Survival is the name of the game. I believe that we all wish to survive. I believe that all of God's creation wishes to survive. What makes us humans different than any other creature is that we seek a balance in our life, a balance that enables us to enjoy life. I believe that beyond our own survival is the balance that helps us to experience pleasure, whatever that pleasure might be for each individual. My balance provides pleasure for me. It gives me enjoyment, strength, and courage. My balance comes when I am able to blend music and ministry with myself and offer it to others.

The key to my survival has been finding the balance of things that work for me. Logic has taught me that I can no longer be a chauffeur because I cannot see.

Blindness has also ruled out airline pilot, railroad engineer, and cruise ship captain. I would have a difficult time taking the medical board exams to be a brain surgeon. There are simply some things that I cannot be. However, it does not mean that I cannot dream about being something. Finding what works for oneself requires that we become dreamers, visionaries, and people who look ahead. For me, it meant mixing the music and ministry with my skills and talents, making me the best I could be. It was taking the "If you're going to make a scene...why not be seen," "I seek to serve," and "God doesn't make junk..." blending them into me, Mark, in order to make things happen. I had a dream, a vision, something to work towards.

It is important to dream. Dreams help us to form visions of ourselves for tomorrow, which gives us the necessary goals, desires, and determination today. Dreaming is becoming a "visionary." Visionaries are those who are able to blend their talents, skills, and gifts into a dream that encourages the balance of who and what we want to become. Being a visionary, gives us the freedom to take our past experiences and test the waters, so to speak, of what we might like to do in the future. Although we exist in the present, working, playing, sometimes struggling, sometimes celebrating, we have the capability of seeing both forward and backwards to gain a perspective of the much larger picture. Visionaries are able to test theories, practice role models, and presume certain characters to see whether or not it fits right. Sometimes, we discover what is right and other times we know it is not yet quite right. It can happen on the first try or it might take some time, some different attempts, and sometimes even beginning the whole process over again. Becoming a visionary enables us to use and increase our God-given gifts, talents, and skills to help ourselves.

I am a dreamer, a visionary who looks forward more than anything else. It makes me an optimist. It gives me a positive attitude. It gives me the ability to look at the better side of things, rather than getting bogged down by the bad. I do not think I get lost in my dreams or lose touch with reality; I am able to keep my head above water when things get rough and keep moving forward.

An important part of dreaming is that one finds the right dream of whom and what they want to be, and they make that dream bigger than life. This will give the dreamer the energy and determination to push hard towards becoming that identity. When I was developing my goals of what I might be while in college, the blending of my music, theater, and desire to serve others, I began to dream about becoming a minister. I made the dream larger than life. The more I dreamed about the ministry, what I could offer, what talents I had, and the skills I would need to acquire, the louder the voice inside of me spoke and empowered my drive and determination to be a minister. Sometimes, I thought about other possibilities of what I might be. However, because the dream was larger than life, I always returned to ministry. Other times, there were barriers in my way. For example, when I was in the depth of my depression while losing my sight, I thought that ministry was out of the question. But the Holy Spirit spoke loud and clear to me through my larger than life dream and the determination and drive was still there. I had to continue pushing forward, working, sometimes struggling, sometimes wrestling with my own sense of worth, yet always trying to be the best minister I could be.

Much of the time I spend with youth and younger adults I find a lost sense of dreamers, people who are not visionaries. Economic difficulties, overcrowded employment markets, and unreal expectations for salaries seem to deteriorate the necessary drive for imaginative dreaming. I can remember being in that same place when I was losing my sight. Following the lost of vision in my left eye, I took a job as a Youth Coordinator with a local Church. I was excited to get the job. But on the day I was to start working with the youth of the Church, I found myself in the hospital undergoing surgery. Losing the sight in my left eye, I found myself feeling I was in a tailspin I was not going to survive. My ability to dream, to be a visionary about my life, was failing.

It was not that I did not dream. I had plenty of dreams. I had dreams about things that I had once wanted to become. I was having trouble looking forward with a positive attitude. For example, I had dreams of what it was suppose to be like getting married after college graduation, going to work to support my wife while she finished her college education, and then following my own dreams of seminary and becoming an ordained minister. Those dreams fell apart as my vision continued to get worse instead of better. I had dreams of becoming a professional driver, driving the big over-the-road semi-tractors and trailers, driving the large charter coach buses, etc. With my own sight failing, driving was becoming restrictive and would soon not be possible. My dreams became dreams about the past and never about the future. I was no longer able to be a visionary.

The contemporary songwriter and performer Billy Joel, has written a song titled "Everybody Has a Dream." Although this is an older song, it still carries an important message today. I, likewise, believe that everybody has a dream. Everybody has something that is the ultimate goal in their life. Everybody has an idea about what they would like to do in their life. I am no exception. I still have dreams of things I might accomplish, places I might go, and people I might meet. I believe that this is one of the special things about being a visionary. Being a visionary and having dreams about tomorrow is not limited to the young but transcends all ages.

History is full of visionaries and dreamers. Jesus spoke of a New World possible in God's promise. Jesus' vision was of a world where truth and justice would prevail, where evil would have no place. Many of us still dream and strive hard to achieve that world. More importantly, the Apostle Paul followed in Jesus' footsteps by writing, "there are many kinds of spiritual gifts, but the same Spirit gives them; and there are many ways to serve God, but the same God is served; and there are many different abilities to serve, yet it is the one and same Lord that gives the ability for service... we are all members of the body of Christ, is not one more important than the other, for all parts of the body are needed for the body to function." (1 Corinthians 12) Like Jesus, Paul had a vision about tomorrow that would unify the body of Christ, the Church, by bringing all Christians together as sisters and brothers.

Presidents of our great country all had visions, dreams of a better tomorrow. Many of the great leaders, of our time and before, had visions about how things would change and life would be so much better. I marvel at the reality that I am able to write and edit this book's manuscript on a talking computer, of which the likes were not around just thirty short years ago. Someone had a dream, a vision, and a glimpse of the future, made that dream bigger than life, and then pursued it as far as possible. We can transplant the human heart, put a human being on the moon, and send pictures, letters, and other data around the world in a blink of an eye, just because someone had a dream. Dreams are important.

One of the great leaders of my youth and still of this day was Martin Luther King, Jr. In his famous speech during the racial riots of the 1960's, King spoke of having a dream. It was his dream that someday all men would live in harmony, that some day there would be no segregation between peoples of different race, tongue, or creed. King had a dream where some day "righteousness would flow like a mighty river and justice would roll down upon us like water." (Amos 5) And at the very prime of his dream, when equality was becoming reality, King's life was extinguished by gunfire as he was assassinated at his hotel. Just like Jesus Christ and the Apostle Paul, they were all visionaries with a dream about tomorrow. Someone was scared of their tomorrow and took it upon themselves to eliminate these great leaders. There were also others: Abraham Lincoln, John F. Kennedy, and his brother, Robert Kennedy. They all had dreams and were willing to risk everything, including sacrificing their own lives to see their dreams for a better tomorrow become reality.

I share these examples not to scare you or to be morbid, rather to let you know that dreaming is risky. Sometimes we do get involved in pursuing a dream and the cost gets exorbitant. Part of being a visionary is to realize that sometimes the dream, the expectation, is too costly and we must alter our ultimate goal, if we are to achieve the desired success. We must also be practical in our expectations of ourselves in order to pursue our dreams. Someday there may come a time when we will be required to lay our life on the line and sacrifice everything to stand for a value or an issue that, in our dream, we know is right. These are what the above named leaders were willing to do. I believe we have all benefited by their sacrifices. However, my caution is more of keeping in perspective the talents, gifts, and skills each of us have as individuals, and blending them into our dreams so our visions can be obtained.

One of my biggest fears about dreaming is that my dream gets out of perspective and cannot be obtained. For example, ever since I started sailing I have dreamt about sailing around the world. A movie titled "Dove" was popular when I was in high school. I saw it at least six times. The story was based upon a book written by Robin Christopher Graham about his journey of single-handedly sailing his sloop "Dove" around the world. I started to apply my own principles of making that dream larger than life, but had not yet realized that it is also important to keep all things in perspective. I began to understand my dream, of solo sailing around the world, was not practical. I have better things to do with my money. Being diabetic added other complications. I had no desire to be a blind sailor, to solo around the world, just for the sake of being a blind sailor, to solo around the world. I no longer had the drive or motivation to follow that "bigger than life" dream.

Now the dream re-formed. I began visualizing ways my dream might become a reality. I found myself dreaming of sailing the Great Lakes. This was more feasible, practical, and within reach. Sailing the Great Lakes became the bigger than life dream, and I began to find the determination and motivation to follow this dream.

With the modifications in place, I have spent at least one week per summer sailing the Great Lakes. I have no desire to sail solo around the Great Lakes, for my greater pleasure is sharing the experiences with others that desire the same. My dream becomes a group effort, which pulls people together into a new and different relationship from which we all gain. The opportunities for success have been far greater, the rewards many, and my dream continues to live. I am able to blend my talents, gifts, and skills into a common purpose of pursuing my dream and continuing to make that dream bigger than life. The determination and motivation are stronger than ever. Being a visionary is to be keenly aware of our capabilities and use them to our advantage.

All of us are dreamers in our own little ways. Whether or not we dream about who will ask us to the next high school prom or of becoming President of the United States someday, we all have dreams. Dreams are important, for they give us future hopes on which to focus. Dreams help to guide us down the paths we believe we must take; dreams also light those paths while we are on the journey. Dreaming enables us to become visionaries, seeing what we will someday become, by helping us to blend our talents, gifts, and skills into one functioning product, called "us." We are the best we can be when we vision ourselves in our tomorrows and work on it today, with keen memory of where we have come from yesterday. Keep on dreaming!

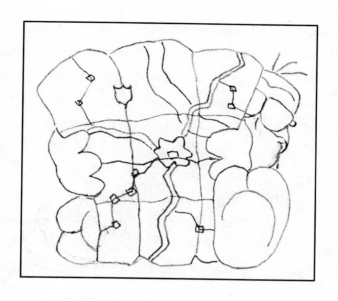

CHAPTER ELEVEN:
GETTING THERE IS HALF THE FUN!

An important understanding of successful living is working through the task, towards its completion. I believe the fullness of the accomplishment is only satisfied by the effort placed into the means of reaching the end result. For example, happiness is luck, happenstance that occurs by a stroke of positive fate, while joy is experienced through consistent work of positive energy. "What does he mean?" you are asking yourself. The premise for this chapter is to share stories that point in the direction of the emotions and satisfaction that takes place in working hard at accomplishing tasks, almost to the point where the work at doing the task is more rewarding than the result. Getting there is half the fun.

I have three ongoing projects in my house I use for pass-time activities. They are hobbies and much more. One of these projects is writing books, journal entries, and letters to friends. The second project is related to music, composing, arranging, and performing. The third project is a hobby train layout. All three are sometimes very frustrating, but mostly very rewarding. I can spend hours working on them, sometimes even forgetting to go to bed or to eat. The important connecting thread between the three is working through the process towards the results, which is more rewarding, than the actual end. And if I had a garage, I would have a fourth, boat-building.

Writing is a piece of practical therapy for me. I find interesting ways to express myself, hidden feelings, and unrecognized emotions. In writing this book, I have discovered new things about myself. Sometimes, I had to stop writing to cry for awhile feeling pain from things of which I was previously unaware. Other times, I have burst into laughter, because of experiences relived and/or remembered. Working through each chapter, writing and editing, has been helpful for me to understand myself. The process has been rewarding and important.

Letter writing is a lost art. With modern day conveniences, such as cell phones and computers, letter writing is no longer as frequent. Yet, I find writing letters to friends one of my most rewarding experiences. Sometimes, through a letter, I might get very romantic and express my feelings of love for another in words otherwise unspoken. Other times, I get creative and imaginative and short stories fill page upon page. When a close friend of mine was attending seminary in the east, I would write fictional stories for him, to help break the tension and pressure from his required reading. Today, if anyone would have discovered these stories, one of us would have gotten locked away. Still, at other times, letter writing helps disclose plenty of information that would otherwise take lengthy telephone conversations that are not always practical. So part of my love and desire to write letters is of a practical matter under the authority that "necessity is the mother of invention."

That is to say that lack of time results in less telephone usage and more time writing.

Songwriting is more of a part-time hobby. Occasionally a verse, poem, or experience will start formulating itself into a song. For me, the process is generally simultaneous in that the words and music will happen, different themes and motifs will bounce around in my head, and then all of a sudden take shape on the page. Many times this happens while I am out walking with my dog guide. Since she is doing all the guiding, I have a tendency to allow my mind to think about other things and work through situations in my head. I like music, especially singing, so I do spend much of my walking time singing, whistling, and/or working out new songs and arrangements as I go. The fun is getting there, working through the process, getting to the end results.

My model train room is much the same. I also call this my prayer room. When I feel that I need some quiet time alone to talk with God, I like to go into the train room, close the door, and for the next few hours spend some quality quiet time conversing. While I am talking with God, I work on the train layout. The process of establishing a particular layout, putting the tiny pieces together into a single working unit, and then eventually getting the train to run the circuit, is a great satisfaction. Once the layout is complete, it is time to disassemble, alter, or add to the layout. It is the process of taking many little pieces and making them a whole that is rewarding. Again, I can spend hours at a time working in the quiet of the train room, simply enjoying the work of using my hands to be creative.

In the many years that I have been blind, my main purpose has been to adapt to a sighted world. If one pays attention to our language patterns, it is easy to see how much we depend upon our vision. Our entire vocabulary is based upon our ability to see. Common everyday phrases such as 'see you later,' 'did you see that,' 'well, you see it is like this', are phrases we use almost without thinking about them. I do the same, use the same phrases sighted people use. People have become accustomed to speaking with the presumption that the other person listening can either see what they are talking about or have at least seen it previously. It is a visual world in which we exist. The challenge for me becomes adapting to the visual world in order to function as a blind person. The reward comes when I am able to share with someone the process of what I do to adapt from a blind world, so that they might understand a little more clearly what it is like to be without sight.

It is the process of getting from the dark world of being non-functional, because of my disability, to being capable of working with other resources available to me. If and when we work together in this process, we both feel the satisfaction and fulfillment of accomplishment.

Outside observers experiencing me for the first time often think that I am not blind because I respond, react, and interact just like a sighted person. There have been times when I have left people spellbound and wondering about my blindness, even after a week-long experience together. And there are some that will even go so far as to accuse me of faking my blindness. Believe me; no one would be able to pull that sort of nasty trick for these many years. I am totally blind. My inter-dependent functioning has been a learned skill in adapting to my environment and my disability. Part of that learned skill is identifying and witnessing the parameters within which I must function. It is within these limitations and challenges I have found the most reward. Sometimes, I step outside of the parameters just to make things interesting. For example, because of my blindness one would assume it is safe to say that I do not drive my vehicle. Guess again! Every summer that my vehicle makes the trip to camp in northern Wisconsin, we have a ceremonial drive into the parking lot. Whoever is driving when we enter the campground, via the upper parking lot, we stop and switch places. Then, I proceed to drive the remaining distance down the hill, around a slow bending curve, and into the lower parking lot, bringing the vehicle to a successful stop within its required parking space. As I enter the lower parking lot, I generally drive the vehicle in a large arching circle encompassing the full diameter of the parking lot. This is accompanied while I am blowing the horn, waving at the people, blowing the horn, waving at the people, etc. As I stated earlier, "If you're going to make a scene...why not be seen." And, so I do!

There are many stories when I have left people baffled as to whether or not I am blind. One particular instance was at a Senior High camp. While I was taking my shower in the bathhouse, the campers swiped my white walking cane. I discovered the cane missing when it came time to walk back to my cabin. Realizing that I was the subject of a playful prank, I headed out the door empty-handed. I needed to work my way through several parked cars, across the parking lot, and down a narrow path to my cabin. With my head held high, as to not allow the pranksters any form of satisfaction, I walked straight ahead listening carefully. Along with my other sense of touch, I could hear and feel where the cars were parked before colliding with them. In the open area of the parking lot, I could sense nothing near and moved rather quickly, imagining what I might or should be seeing. When I entered the narrowed path, I could again sense the surroundings both by hearing and touch. Finally, when I reached the steps into my cabin, I turned around, removed my traditional Director's Hat, and graciously bowed to the pranksters watching from the balcony above. They were baffled! Stunned! And disappointed! They had at least wanted to see me smack the side of a car, get lost in the middle of the parking lot and do circles for a while, or at least stumble off the pathway to my cabin. Sorry, no show today! I made it safely and quickly, as though I could see every step I made. They really were not sure I was blind.

Later that same week of camp, I caught two campers out after curfew. Breaking curfew is something most every camper attempts. At my camps, they get caught. That's why I'm the Director. At night, darkness is to my advantage. Here's my secret: I have been attending this particular camp for over a quarter of a century. I know just about every inch of that camp. I know where all the good and favorite hiding places are and even a few that have yet to be disclosed. I'll keep them that way, too. But I know the campground. By removing the collar and leash on my dog guide, I move with little or no sound. This makes me very dangerous in the dark shadows along the wooded paths.

I had heard the couple planning their late night adventure during supper. At curfew time, I was already out along the trail hiding in the shadows. One of my counselors came along to experience the hunt and capture of the game. Soon the couple walked directly in front of me, close enough that I could have reached out and touched them. They had no idea I was there. I then followed them to their favorite spot and observed them, for ten minutes or so, involved in a long liplock. I was almost afraid that I would have to supply mouth-to-mouth resuscitation, if they didn't surface for air soon. I sat on the other end of the platform quietly listening. Then, I started tossing acorns, sticks, and small pieces of bark at them. Several times, they stopped kissing and looked around trying to figure out what was happening. They kept shining their flashlight up into the trees above, but never to the side. Finally, I could not take the humor any longer and cleared my throat to say, "It's past curfew!" He ran straight off the embankment and into the lake, while she scrambled up the hill with the flashlight. My dog guide and I went to the water's edge and offered him assistance. We caught up with her shortly thereafter along the trail back to camp. Until I let them know, they had no idea of my presence. I also threatened to tell all, if they did not offer an apology to the rest of the camp community at breakfast the next morning. My Co-Counselor laughed for a good, long time and there were no further curfew violators that week.

My adapting to a visual world is universal. From domestics within my home to camping in the outdoors, from traveling independently across the country to sailing, I must find the way to adapt to my environment rather than expecting others will adapt to mine. It is an unfair assumption, for any person with a disability, to expect someone else to assume their position. It is simply not practical. It is unique and special when someone shows empathy for my disability and makes earnest attempts to be sensitive in their understanding. But, it is unrealistic for me to expect that they are the one who must change, rather than me. I have met many differently-abled people who expect others to change, and quite frankly, they offend me. They give differently-abled folks a bad name. It does make the challenge more difficult sometimes. But the harder the challenge, the greater the reward, when the adaptation is successful.

I had an encounter, while sailing one summer with a group of teenagers. They were eager to learn how to sail the tall rigs of the Great Lakes and I was happy to teach them. This particular sailing excursion would take us around Isle Royale, located in the northern waters of Lake Superior. Isle Royale is known for its beauty and splendor in large glacier-formed rock formations and luscious thick forest to water's edge. It also has a long history of claiming vessels and lives, when Lake Superior gets rough. It can be a sailor's paradise or a sailor's demise. For us, it was paradise.

During the week, we had joined a couple of other sailboats from different places, making the same trip. One of our skippers was well-versed in the island's history, so evenings were filled with stories of sealore and tales of the high seas adventures.

The other visiting boats had their suspicions that I was blind, but they were never sure. I generally never used my cane on shore, instead using the elbows of my crew for sighted guides. It simply looked like we were friends. On the water, they would see me at the helm controlling the boat, barking commands, and plotting courses. Again, they had their suspicions and started keeping a close eye, hoping to catch me off guard. I became aware of their observations and played along. Finally, one day, our boat had left the pack for a longer sail out into open waters to refill some freshwater tanks. This gave the other boats considerable advantage time to enter the narrow passage into a hidden bay where we had planned to spend the night's anchorage. With our task of filling the tanks completed, it was my turn at the helm and port-bound we sailed. We had a beautiful, favorable, trailing wind. I got excited and quickly commanded the crew to hoist as much sail as we had available and could carry. The boat lunged forward with increased speed. The other boats, already tucked away behind the large rock cliffs, watched in amazement as we approached flying wing'n'wing, a unique and skillful set of several sails. This is not recommended for the average or novice sailor, for a sudden wind shift or course change could spell disaster with a capital "D!" Having the necessary experiences and required skills to maneuver the sloop, we came screeching past the entrance of the narrow harbor taking down all of the sail and starting the auxiliary engine in preparation to slowly work our way through the narrows and shallows of Chippewa Bay. With sails stored and vessel under control by power, we began our approach. I stationed different crewmembers around the deck of the boat with each giving me visual information and data as we slowed and skillfully navigated our way up into the tight bay. I knew that once we cleared the large rock shallows and narrow entrance between the high bank cliffs, the bay would open wider with deep quiet waters. As we rounded the last channel marker, my crewmate on the instruments called out the "all clear" and that depths were again increasing. We could now see the other boats already dockside with folks gathering to where we would dock for the night. The folks who had their suspicions about me were feeling let down and began believing that I really wasn't blind. With my crew verbalizing necessary data, I eased the thirty-five foot sloop gently into its dockside berth, allowing the point deckhand to easily step ashore. The other crews applauded.

After the boat was secured for the night and all things stowed properly, the crew disembarked. I finally came ashore to meet with the other adults and sailing crews, popping my flexible cane into its rigid working position, and tapped my way along the dock. I found the other boat, upon which everyone had gathered, and requested permission to board. Again, they were surprisingly confused and I playfully left them wondering "is he, or is he not blind?" It had become a playful game of teasing wonder among the visiting boats that knew me not. My crew was sworn to secrecy. We spent many hours discussing experiences of disabilities. Some of the stories were fun, exciting, successful, and positive. Others were bitter, angry, defensive, and painfully negative. All were important, and by sharing, became experiences from which all of us could relate, understand, and ponder. Later that evening, after supper, I used my cane and returned to my boat.

The next morning we were getting ready to leave. Unfortunately, the tidal changes had caused our boat to run aground, backing away from the dock. We found the necessary clearance by getting the crew off the boat and walking it backward along the pier. Then my slip happened and everyone officially knew that I was blind. I was working the boat from the bowsprit, making sure we would clear the pier and swing properly towards the open channel. The rest of the crew was quickly climbing on board, as the water depths increased. They forgot to tell me how close I was to the end of the pier. I thought I had at least one, if not more, steps to go but "kursplash!" I took ye ole spill in der brink! I ran out of pier, I wasn't hanging onto the boat, and then I was wet. A roar of applause and cheers rang out from the crowd as I surfaced and waved to the crowd that I was "A-O.K!" The boat inched forward and I climbed aboard and we moved out into the channel. I went below and changed. For the rest of the week, my humor was well shared by many, as they now knew I was blind. It also made them more impressed that I was able to adapt through my disability and still accomplish something I enjoyed doing. Getting to that point of respect, as a qualified sailor, was the best experience I could share with the new sailors I was training.

My work ethic has become my faith ethic upon which the strength and foundations of my abilities to cope began. When I was a youngster, there was a small banner that hung over the kitchen sink. It read, "When a job has once begun, never leave it until it's done; be the laborer big or small, do it well or not at all." In my family, washing the dishes came as frequent as every fifth evening meal and more often on weekends. My brothers and sisters invented every excuse to attempt avoidance of this dreaded activity; from planned incoming telephone calls, to life or death exams and homework to be accomplished, to overly extended stays in the bathroom. Now, as I reflect back, I don't think it was so much washing the dishes, but more having to face that banner. It started to grow on me. The more dishes I washed, the more that banner became engraved on my brain. Soon I found myself saying the phrase to myself, while doing other homebound chores. Then it got worse; I started thinking and saying it during other projects. I remember saying it one time, while attempting to accomplish the rope climb in gym class. I only got three feet off the floor, failed the test, but remembered every word of that banner.

When I left home, I thought I left the banner hanging on the wall over the kitchen sink. One day, I found myself getting bored in class and soon the phrase developed in mastered script on one of the pages of my notebooks. Then it grew onto a poster made from a picture, made from a slide I had taken. The phrase now became a constant reminder, facing me every day on my dorm room closet. Then I discovered that, when my tasks in college got difficult, I would remember the short and sweet saying, and it would help me focus on my task. It became a helpful tool.

When I started to regain my determination, after losing my sight, the phrase returned. This time, upon its return, it began to blend both my work ethic with my faith, giving me a new inner strength to press on.

Although the task was not yet clear, it was evident that this little phrase was here to stay. It would always be with me. So, as I grew in my courage to face the unknown of adapting my darkened, sightless, world, to the visual world around me, I always remembered to never give up. If I started a project, it became the most important thing in my mind to finish. If the task got difficult, it was important not to abandon the job, nor give in, by using the excuse that I couldn't do it. If I started it, I completed it. Not completing the task meant the challenge of adapting to a new way. This simple little teaching phrase, found by my mother, became my work ethic.

In processing many of the different experiences I encountered in losing my sight, I found an interesting blend of my work ethic with my faith ethic. Both are very similar and, when woven together, are very important. The ability to start, work through, and complete a project, is necessary for us to build a good sense of self-worth, self-confidence, and self-esteem. Faith in ourselves is necessary for us to be able to work. Working at our faith is necessary to insure it will always be there. Soon, I found many parts in the previous phrase were inter-changeable. For example; "when our faith has once begun, never leave it until it's done; be the faithful big or small, work at it faithfully or not at all." That was something to think about and held truth within.

Our faith never leaves us; we abandon our faith. Our work never goes away; we walk away from our work. Our self-worth is always there, sometimes slightly tarnished, a little dented, or perhaps a bit obscure. Yet, be it work, faith, or ourselves, if we are willing to work at it, it grows, increases, expands, and accomplishes itself as success. That is how I became handi-capable in adapting my sightless world to a world full of visual things.

In my learning process of how to adapt to a world that was different than mine, I was the one who was changing. I had a guiding guru, a friend who was both a confidante and an inspiration. When I felt down in the dumps, frustrated by failure, or just in a bad place and in need of someone, my guru could make me laugh, remind me that the fruits of success are the direct results of our hard labor, and by talking out difficulties with others, would help me find the solution from within. He provided many a time of help, was always available, and most importantly, a good friend. His name is Peter.

Peter and I first met my junior year in college. He was transferring into school and became a resident in the same dorm, in which I lived. My first encounter with Peter was through an informal introduction by the Campus Minister, who was a close confidante, friend, counselor, and religious professor. Peter was entering the same "pre-seminary" program, in which I was participating. But, the introduction was not being made as a fellow classmate of the religion department. Our meeting was more in the form of a request for emergency assistance, if in the event Peter needed help. One of these crucial avenues was that four of my fraternity brothers from the Zeta Chi became responsible for seeing that Peter got outside in the event of an emergency building evacuation, such as a fire. Peter is a paraplegic. He is quite mobile, both in his wheelchair and with the use of special braces and crutches. I immediately admired and respected this new-found friend for, despite his disability, he elected to reside on the second floor of a building most definitely not made accessible for the handicap. There were no ramps, no elevators, narrow doorways, etc. There were other options on campus, which would have given him more accessibility, yet he elected to join our merry group of fellows living in one of the oldest dorms on campus. From the first day of our meeting in his room on the second floor, it became a daily routine to stop and say "hi" on my way up or down from my room on the third floor.

Peter was outgoing and special. Born with an open spinal column, he had very little use of his legs. I remember listening to him share part of his story with some friends. When he was born, the doctors told his family that his chances of making it past age fifteen or so were very slim. How painful, I thought to myself. But, Peter would quickly change direction and crack a fast joke, catch you off guard, and talk about his different experiences of adapting from his disabled point of view. At the time, I was an outside observer not realizing that someday I would become a student, looking for guidance and assistance in my own adaptive process. Peter had plenty of stories of adapting to the environment around him.

The first thing I learned, about Peter and from Peter, was that even though there was the pain and frustration of being different because of his disability, he blamed no one. He had made the spiritual decision from within that he would make the most out of his life, view life as a precious gift, and look for ways to use his disability to his advantage to help others. Sooner than any of us would expect, he would be teaching me.

There were many ways in which Peter had to adapt to our campus environment. The campus was not equipped for a wheelchair. There were only two elevators on campus, one in the science building and the other a freight elevator used mostly by the kitchen staff in the student center. An old plastic-covered desk chair on wheels was placed in the shower for personal hygiene, as there were no bathtubs in our dorm. Occasionally, he would have his parent's car on campus and I remember marveling, probably in an embarrassing way, how he could drive with the adaptive hand controls attached to the brakes and accelerator. His wheelchair appeared to be nothing special. Although, to see Peter in it, you could almost swear the darn thing was capable of flying. I remember always looking at it with a curiosity, as to where he hid the caterpillar tracks that allowed him to climb the many stairs around campus, and there were plenty of stairs to climb.

Peter's spirit and jovial presence always commanded favorable respect and attention. He was a good actor and soon became active in the theater department on campus. I'll always remember his starring role as the main character in the campus production of "Whose

Life Is It Anyway?" At college dances, it was not uncommon to see Peter in the middle of the dance floor, swinging with the beat, on the two large rear wheels of his wheelchair. I swear the darn thing could fly. And, when Peter went home for the weekend, the place was always empty; something special was missing.

We got the chance to prove our worthiness of responsibility, as one night the fire alarms sounded. It sent the residents of the dorm scrambling for clothes and heading out as smoke was filling the hallways. I remember Peter waiting at his dorm room door, in his wheelchair, as the four of us arrived on our way down and out. Each of us grabbed a firm hold on his chair, and down the stairs we went. Once outside and clear of the building, we got a chance to catch our breath, and watch in hopeful expectation that our belongings weren't about to disappear in flames. I remember laughing hysterically, as Peter went from person to person, thanking them for helping him out, and wondering what his mother was going to say because he greeted the firemen in dirty underwear. Fortunately, we never had to meet the firemen, as dorm mates were able to extinguish the blaze allegedly set in a garbage can by some prankster. A short time later, the four of us picked up Peter's wheelchair and carried him back up to his room. He was much relieved that he did not have to be seen by the local fire department in his dirty shorts, which would please his mother greatly.

The first time I met his parents, I began to understand more of his spirit and faith, and his ability to adapt to the environment. They were good people, who made you feel warm and welcome. Many of us knew, when we were passing through Milwaukee, we were always welcome in their home. They were kind, patient people with hearts of gold. They were supportive and went out of their way to help others. It all culminated within Peter, who took it serious. Peter was the same. He always had time for others. His difficulties never appeared worse than a friend's problem and he was ready and willing to listen. There was something special about him that words could do no justice; it was a presence, a spiritual happening everyone experienced when meeting Peter.

I continued to watch and grow with Peter, as he showed me how to adapt. Although I still did not know I was in training, I did realize the secret to his success at adapting was his humor. He had a tremendous sense of humor. He could laugh at himself, despite himself. After I lost my sight, I discovered the power of humor. His jokes were never offensive and, if the joke needed a subject upon which to focus, it was Peter himself.

I remember one evening, when there were some new perspective students on campus exploring the possibility of attending school. A fraternity brother and I were busily frying bratwurst behind the campus center, below a fairly large incline to the cafeteria doors. This was the closest thing we had to a ramp on campus and its purpose was simply of aesthetic value. The perspective students were gathered on the yard below the hill, near where we were working. Out of the corner of my eye, I saw Peter in his wheelchair, heading for supper up the incline, towards the doors of the cafeteria. The unsuspecting perspective students were totally unaware of what they were about to encounter. Suddenly, Peter veered sharply off the paved walk and started to roll down the steep embankment toward the now panic-stricken crowd. As they watched in horror, the front wheels of Peter's wheelchair dug into the soft ground, spilling him head over heels out of the chair and down the hill. I have to admit watching this sent a shiver of fear through my body. My fraternity brother and I dropped our cooking utensils and ran to his assistance. Peter, tumbling down the hill with his wheelchair close behind, paralyzed the observant crowd. Before my friend and I could reach the point of his tumbling fall, Peter landed, bounced up on one knee, imitating the late Al Jolson singing "Mammy!" with his arms spread. He got what he deserved, a round of applause, although the wheelchair did need some minor repairs and a slight touch of the welding torch. His ability to please a crowd was amazing. I was always amazed how I never saw him as being disabled, just different.

Another situation availed itself to our need to adapt to the environment in which we existed. It was during finals week of our first semester, about a week or so before Christmas break. We decided at two o'clock in the morning to relocate from campus to a nearby all-night restaurant. We needed food and beverage, to continue cramming for exams. I went out and started my car, warming and defrosting the windows, while Peter got ready. I brought the car around close to the door to meet Peter. He was on his crutches and I assisted him from the dorm to the car and across some thin and slippery ice. Once behind the wheel, I discovered we were stuck, caught on a slight incline that was covered with ice and we could not get enough traction to move forward. Placing the car in reverse, I was able to back down the incline. Unfortunately, it was on a driveway that had no exit; it led to the college president's garage. I got some distance from the point of trouble, put the car back into forward, and gunned the engine. We shot forward, but still could not quite make the last little ridge to freedom. We tried several times, but with no success. There was no one else around the darkened campus. What to do next? It was Peter's idea that, if he got behind the wheel of the car, he would have enough control to steer and accelerate the car, while I pushed. Sounded like an idea to me. I got out and he slid in behind the wheel. I did not have the adaptive hand equipment necessary to give Peter full control of the car, so we propped his foot on the accelerator. Then, as he applied pressure, I ran behind and started pushing. The car reached the incline and began to slip on the ice. I applied my shoulder to the rear end of the car, gave it all I had, and the car crawled out of the driveway and headed down the road towards the backside of campus. I was left behind, in a heap on the ice. It suddenly occurred to me that Peter had no way of stopping my car! In an instant, I was up and running after my car, which seemed to be accelerating away from me in fast idle. I managed to catch up with the rolling car and work the driver's door open, as Peter continued steering while moving from the driver's seat across to the passenger's seat. I firmly grabbed the door frame and climbed inside. Having regained control of the car, we turned around and headed into town. To this day, we laugh about our experience of getting stuck on the ice in the college president's driveway.

When the process of losing my sight became most serious, it was Peter who first showed his loyalty to my situation. Our friendship grew and strengthened, as we now shared a new commonality; we both had a disability. When I went through the first of several surgeries in which I lost the sight in my left eye, it was Peter who was there to lift my spirits, tell me jokes, and help begin my conditioning for what lay ahead. When I would return to campus during the many different procedures I was experiencing with the medical community, it was to Peter's room I went for my comfort and spiritual strengthening. I still admired his command of his disability and his ability to adapt to almost any situation. When I went through my last sight-losing surgery, it was Peter and three other fraternity brothers that spent the day with my family supporting, encouraging, and praying for my welfare.

In the spring following my onset of blindness, Peter and I took a long, late-night walk around campus. The memories of what I would have been seeing were fresh in my mind, although the vision was now gone. In the cool spring night air, I pushed Peter in his wheelchair and he steered. He told me different things he saw and I shared my fears and anxieties of what lay ahead. We talked much that night of the similarities we now shared. I thanked him for all he had been teaching me over the past two years, although I had not realized it at the time. When my blindness became my reality, it suddenly all made sense. Through the power of my own humor, and faith in myself in relationship with the one above, I would be able to adapt and move forward if I kept a positive attitude. In the dark, wee hours of that special morning, I heard the words of my mother's banner loud and clear; "when a job has once begun, never leave it till it's done; be the laborer big or small, do it well or not at all."

The following morning, I had an interview with an official from the seminary of my choice. It also became my approval for acceptance as a candidate for their Master of Divinity program. The task was now set before me. It would be a difficult journey with many frustrations, stumbling blocks, and barriers. The adventure would require an almost constant process of adapting, as I would be the first totally blind student to attend United Theological Seminary of the Twin Cities in Minnesota.   When the task seemed to large or heavy, the frustrations and disappointments too great, and failure seemed more the routine than success, I would remember the silly little banner that hung over Mother's kitchen sink and the inspiration Peter taught me, and move forward!

CHAPTER TWELVE:
PUT ONE FOOT
IN FRONT OF THE
OTHER

I do not remember taking my first small steps as a little child many years ago, but after watching my parents and family working with my eleven nephews and nieces, I can probably imagine what it was like. As each of these youngsters has developed, one at a time into my family, they have received much assistance from parents, grandparents, uncles, and aunts. To watch each youngster holding tightly to gentle helping hands and awkwardly taking those first steps, always with a big smile of success, is quite the wonderful sensation. I imagine I was the same when it was my turn to learn. Eventually, the time comes to walk "solo" and although shaky at first, it requires the important process of "putting one step in front of the other." Failure to do this results in a disastrous fall in which we say thank you for bulky diapers, providing padded crashes, and those helping hands which were always ever so close. Soon enough attempts are made, the process secure, confidence installed, and we make that crucial first step. Success! Our balance improves, our confidence strengthens, and soon those helping hands are hurrying in front of us to move everything out of reach. Before we can walk, we learn to sit, crawl, and pull ourselves to a standing position to strengthen developing legs. When we go for our first steps, we know by experience that it takes putting one foot in front of the other. Our success and safety comes in the form of our family supporting us in our endeavors.

I have been blessed with the most wonderful family. From the moment I began taking my first steps through the present, they have always been supportive, helping me to learn the process of putting one foot in front of the other. They are understanding, forgiving, and fun to be with. They are a special group of people. They are a gift, a free gift, no strings attached. They are precious to me. I enjoy crying, laughing, celebrating, and working with them. I enjoy sharing them with others. They are my best friends and I am glad they keep me around.

I am a big fan of our NASA program of space exploration. When the space shuttle is in the news, I am glued to my radio and television gleaning as much information as possible about its voyage. In 1969, the excitement was the voyage of the Apollo moon mission. I can remember being focused on my television, watching and listening to the reports as the "Eagle" landed on the surface of the moon. Shortly thereafter, the world watched as Neil Armstrong stepped from the lunar module onto the dusty moon surface proclaiming "one small step for man, one giant leap for mankind." At first, I only saw the spectacular glory of being the pilot of a lunar module and someday landing my own spacecraft on the surface of the moon. Then, I realized the tremendous support network of people who made Neil Armstrong's walk on the moon possible. To this day, I still dream of piloting the space shuttle around the world, just to do something different. In a way, NASA is a large family with each person carrying their own special responsibility to make each mission happen. They are smaller parts of a much larger whole. So it is my family; a whole unit consisting of many parts interdependent on each other to making life work!

My successes and failures would have never happened, nor had any purpose, if it were not for my family. They have always been there when I needed someone. When I needed help, they were there. When I needed encouragement, they were there. When I needed comfort, correction, or someone to celebrate with, they were there. When I needed help putting one foot in front of the other, they were there. I owe them much. Sometimes, I wonder what the bill would be, if a pricetag for their services could be attached. Then again, I do not wish to know, for it takes away precisely what makes the family unit so special, its genuine ability for that free gift of love given with no strings attached.

Many times, I learn about people and families who have put a pricetag on their love. The pricetag becomes more than they can ever afford and guilt, pride, ego, and selfish greed tear the family unit apart. My biggest fear in life is the loss of family love and the destruction of the family unit. I believe that the greatest sin is to separate ourselves from the love of God and the most common place this separation is seen is in the family unit. There is salvation for this sin of separation, which is family love, a free love, given as a gift with no strings attached. And so I write to share with you my family.

There are so many things that are given within a family unit that often are taken for granted, never fully appreciated, and seldom the words of thanks expressed. I know that I am guilty of not saying thank you enough. A family such as mine that is founded in the true and sincere sense of the word "love," is a gift. When someone begins to take them for granted, feelings are hurt, separation happens, and something crucial and important to the fulfillment and satisfaction in life is missed.

My participation within my family's structure was not always good. In fact, at many times, they would have had every reason to kick me out and leave me behind. When I think back to some of the things I did in my earlier years, I am surprised they still call me son, brother, and friend. It is painful for me to reflect and write about some of these experiences, but it is also important.

I believe it becomes important to be able to identify mistakes and wrong decisions, failures and disappointments, in order to learn from the path less traveled and realize what can be done to change. Change is an important part of our love for life, the magical mystical dance and celebration, for it is the way we interact with each other in relationship. Relationships are the chords that bind our families together; they are the necessary glue. Welcome to my family, the greatest people I know.

When I was in junior high and high school, I was rebellious and impossible. I was a diabetic, which made me different. I hated being different. Many times, my rebellion took the shape of anger striking out at people I cared about. My family took most of the hits! When I look back now and realize just how much the anger controlled my life and how it exploded unexpectedly, I can see why my brothers became more athletic than myself. They were constantly finding themselves the target of my exploding anger and running from me in hot pursuit! These many explosions were times when I was looking for someone or something to blame for my diabetes.

I believe there was a cause and effect relationship in my anger that often held me hostage. Many times, anger kept me at odds with my parents, brothers, and sisters. It seems like it was almost a constant struggle. I remembered when my family moved across state to a new community, a much larger community than where we had previously lived. It was not a move I wanted to make. In the new community I suddenly realized that, as a diabetic, I was much different than many others. Sometimes the differences were very oppressive, not allowing me to participate in fair and equal ways. Then again, who said life was suppose to be fair, right?

I fear much of my anger grew the more I felt oppressed and threatened by this larger community. I fought back. I struggled, wanting to return to the smaller community, but that was not going to be possible. The fight turned inward, which became uncontrollable anger. Uncontrolled, it could and would explode towards the people I cared for the most, my family. Any and all of them were targets. When my anger exploded, it was harsh, fierce, and destructive. How they managed to withstand the furry of my explosions is almost incomprehensible. But then again, it is also witness to the strength and sincerity of my family's love, which makes them so special. It is precisely this strength, this faith, and this ability to ride out the storm that makes us unique. We have our problems and misunderstandings, but we also know how to forgive. When we learned how to forgive (no actually it was when I learned how to forgive) my family became my best friends!

In the next paragraphs and pages, I want to try and capture a little piece of my family to share with you. I am somewhat reserved about how to share them, since it is through *my* experience from which I write. Yet they are so good to me I just have to share them with you.

The special bond that holds my family together begins in our favorite home, the Church. My father is a minister. That makes us "P.K.'s" (preacher's kids). As a minister's family, there were many times when, at least my siblings and I, felt we were on a pedestal. There were times when we all felt closely watched and scrutinized. Yet my parents had a unique way of helping us understand how we could help others. The best way was to bring them home with us; anybody. I really think, perhaps at times, we abused that offer for there are many stories of Mom's house being full of unexpected overnight guests. But somehow there was always a place at the table and a place for them to lay their head. It is a way my family shows its love.

Mom and Dad are special. They have always been there through thick and thin, always offering their expert advice, opinions, and thoughts. They are always available to help pick up the pieces when disaster strikes. I realize, in this day and age, my parents are a rarity, an experience many do not have. This saddens me, for the gift and ability of love they share is so profound, so awesome, words cannot explain! You simply have to experience them! Mom and Dad are my friends, role models, guidance counselors, sounding boards, and challengers. They have suffered through the worse with me as well as danced in celebration of the best. I wouldn't have it any other way. This may sound almost unbelievable and unreal. Yet giving credit where credit is due, Mom and Dad have the best marriage and relationship I have ever experienced. Their relationship is so good they had the courage to have four more children after having a character like me. Now that's amazing!

Wanting to be protective of the privacy and uniqueness of my relationship with my family, I will attempt to weave into my tapestry our interconnectedness. I start with my mother, Joyce, who has been the silent worker behind the scenes. Mom is special, since she is the one who brought me into this world. Stories revealed in collections of scrapbooks and conversations with relatives, document I was not an easy baby. I was the firstborn. Mom, Dad, and I lived far away from the Grandma's and Grandpa's. We lived in the eastern region of South Dakota. I arrived in the month of December. I understand there was an excessive amount of snow when I decided to make my grand entrance. The hospital was thirty minutes away. Yet Mom, being the strong, farm-raised gal that she is, made it through and thought I was pretty special. A letter, supposedly written by me at that time, describes how my Aunt Gloria, dad's sister, came to help after Mom and I came home from the hospital.

Mom and I didn't always see eye-to-eye. I was stubborn. There were plenty of times when my idea of what direction I wanted to go, was in direct conflict with what she thought. Yet she always hung in there, never giving up on me. There was always a welcoming smile when I returned home and walked through the door. She made our house a wonderful home. Even after I left home to attend college and would call announcing my return for Sunday supper, there was always room for two or three additional guests around the table.

Mom has many special gifts and talents. From my observations, she is the model homemaker capable of great meals, mending clothes, planting and cultivating a plentiful garden with Dad, and a tremendous hostess.

She could organize and orchestrate the moving of our tribe of seven, not an easy task. I once observed her prepare countless numbers of canned preserves, bake four or five dozen cookies, wash several loads of laundry, and prepare and serve a meal for a house full of guests in the same day. In between it all, I noticed she took a few moments for herself and played a game of solitaire with the deck of cards she kept on the dryer.

Church was Mom's home away from home. Although she did not attend seminary, like Dad and myself, her theology was just as deep and wide formed from her practical experiences in her faith. She was the silent partner to Dad's ministry and I believe much of his success. Sometimes, she wasn't silent. On Sundays, you could always hear her beautiful voice leading the hymn, stronger on the hymns that weren't as well known. She sang in the choir and enjoyed the music of Christmas the most. When she sang one of my favorite songs at my ordination, we promised not to look at each other. We both knew we would cry because of the magical, mystical dance and celebration. To this day whenever she sings the hymn "How Great Thou Art," I am reduced to tears of joy, realizing the wonderful love she has always given me. There were many times when she answered the phone for Dad, took his messages, kept supper warm because he was late, and helped us kids understand why perhaps a family trip suddenly got canceled because of a Church emergency.

Her firm foundation of faith really shined when my father needed critical open-heart surgery. As a family, we were all scared in the last moments together before the operation. It was hard to find the words to express the fears. Tears flowed freely. It was Mom who grabbed our hands in a family circle of love and began to pray. Mom is great. There are few like her.

Mom and I had some rough times, especially during my high school years. When I reflect on those years, I find it was my own struggle with diabetes that caused me to take out my anger on my family. This hurt Mom. We had some severe arguments. I didn't realize how much I hurt Mom or how special she really is, until I went off to college. When she wasn't there every morning when I got up, when she wasn't there making sure that I went to Church on Sunday, and when she wasn't there when I returned from class, I missed her. Then, I hurt. I began to understand the significance of our relationship and I changed. We became friends again. I could talk with her about anything and that was important to me. We eventually got to a healthier place in our relationship and she accepted my invitation to become a staff member at a summer church camp I was leading. This added to the depth of our relationship. Once again, I saw her never-ending love reach out to those around her. I have a super, special Mom. Thanks Mom!

My Dad, George, is pretty cool. I remember as a youngster admiring my father in his life as a minister. I think I have a good role model to follow. There are some folks who have known my family, who tagged me to be a minister from my early days. The letter I supposedly wrote when I was five days old, told Grandpa and Grandma I wanted to be a minister after attending my first Church meeting. Although the Church was Dad's career and life, his family always came first. I can remember many hot summer evenings when, suddenly, the announcement was made we were going swimming. Soon we would find ourselves playing in the backwaters of the Mississippi River at a local state park. Other times, the announcement was made to attend a professional baseball game and, if you didn't move quickly, you might miss the ride to the ball park. Dad loves his family and he loves to play. He is awesome on the volleyball court; in the water he scares the fish. I always admired his patience to take at least five kids and sometimes a few neighbors fishing. He managed to keep all the hooks baited at the same time. Dad also loved camping. Every summer he and Mom planned another new and exciting trip. Camping was always an adventure that created many fond memories.

Not many sons get to enjoy the unique relationship that I share with my Dad. He's my Dad, pastor, friend, role model, guidance counselor, colleague, and one of my regular Staff members at summer camp. In every facet of our many roles, we always share a common thread of faith that bonds us together. I know from experience, I can always turn to Dad for friendly advice, logical and rational discussions, and challenges that would make me stronger in my understanding of self, the Holy Spirit, and others around me. When I celebrated my ordination, the most precious moment was when we shared a hug of love and kinship following the laying on of hands. It was in that moment I felt the true presence of God's Spirit.

Dad and I have had our differences. There were times when I felt I hated him for what he said, what he did, or what he wouldn't let me do. Now that I am older and have a greater understanding of life, I love him dearly for his decisions and anger were always right, always appropriate, and always tools for teaching me to be better. I only hope that the fire of his fatherly spirit has tempered me into the strong steel of a dependable, responsible, loving, caring, teaching, guiding, and challenging father, friend, and minister like him. Dad is great. Thanks Dad!

My first sibling was my sister, Lou Ann. We were two years apart. In the early years she was a good friend, buddy, and playmate. When my next sister arrived, I felt threatened and out-numbered. I started to act accordingly. But then again, they were girls and I was starting to reach that age where girls were... well, you know girls. Being two years apart, Lou Ann and I generally had the same teachers through elementary school; that meant there was no avoiding being seen together. By high school, we shared some common friends and even had some classes, such as concert band, together. Now, being seen together was no big deal. We had our differences and at times I think my angry outbursts went far beyond normal brother/sister rivalry. Although I feel that my anger was directed at her intentionally, she was an innocent bystander and easy target to my own fight with my internal differences. When the arguments got more intense, it simply meant she was fighting back. She had the ability to fight back, which I respect. Sometimes I would get confused in the heat of the battle, having been out-maneuvered and wondering if I was supposed to be on the offense or defense. Now with my guard down, she would score her victory by clobbering me good! I had to watch myself.

We shared some common time at college, which strengthened our relationship. We became closer by sharing some friends, traveling back and forth to school on weekends and holidays, and sharing a car on campus. When she changed institutions, I felt empty; something was missing. When she left college, she stayed connected through a mutual friend and fraternity brother, Dan.

When Lou Ann and Dan announced their impending marriage, I was angry. I was supposed to have been married earlier that summer, but my engagement fell apart. Now she was getting what I had so desperately wanted and I was jealous. She showed me what brothers and sisters are all about. She helped me understand how God's grace is always with us. She asked me to read scripture for her wedding service, knowing that I could possibly suffer a hemorrhage in my eye at any time, due to my diabetes, and not be able to read. I think she knew that I could do it, regardless of the situation. She was right. My worst nightmare started when I left my seat during the wedding ceremony to read my part. A major hemorrhage occurred rendering me incapable of reading. God's presence enabled me to adapt and recite my Bible passage from memory. I realized her confidence in me soon after and celebrated a new loving relationship as brother and sister.

More recently, I have admired and enjoyed the way my sister has become just like Mom. Lou Ann has the patience of a saint, the energy of a nuclear power plant, and the wisdom of the ages. I have seen her prepare my nephews Matthew and Joshua for school, care for my nieces Sarah and Victoria, help manage the family's construction business with her husband Dan, do laundry, prepare dinner, and still have time to give me a ride to run an errand. I wonder if she ever has time to play a game of solitaire with a deck of cards kept on her dryer. She amazes me and I admire her with tremendous respect. Thanks Sis!

And that leads us to my sister, Karen. When my family left a small farm community in western Wisconsin, Karen silently allowed her spirit to stay. She was quiet, athletic, and the best worker of us all. She never complained and always accomplished her tasks with time left over to help someone else. She had a playful spirit and knew when it was an appropriate time to tease with a squirt bottle fight or practical joke. As we all grew older, I soon realized I was outnumbered, and picking on either sister simply meant I dealt with both.

One of the things I admire most about Karen is that she says what she thinks and means it. Not that she was looking for a fight or a healthy argument, she simply stated what she felt and believed, and that was that. She was also the best listener. I admire her for that. She was excellent in conversation, avoided the pitfalls of gossip, and challenged when challenge was needed. When her self-worth was tested, she knew she could rely on the strength of her faith to sustain her. When she graduated from college, she went back to the small farmland community in Western Wisconsin, where her heart had always remained. There she established her home and family. I have always been envious she was able to return to that place, a piece of the past we all shared. Sometimes my other siblings and I wish we could move back to that place, but know that we cannot.

Karen met and married Gabriel (Gabe) and they made their homestead in the rolling hills of the Mississippi Valley in Wisconsin. Gabe was an instant winner in the family as he enjoyed volleyball and could hold his own against the family team. Soon a new arrival showed us a different, seldom realized, side of life. My niece, Joy Marie, arrived a little too early but came in screaming. It brought our family close together and again showed us how life can be precious and fragile. Karen took it all in stride, just like she would, and only like she could. Her strength and presence has been a model and support, upon which I have drawn many times. I know it is never said enough times or as often as it should be, but thanks Sis!

My brother, John, and I share an interesting common thread. We were both born on the same date, only six years apart. I use to consider John a birthday present although, at the time, I was hoping for a bicycle not a baby brother. Over the years, I have enjoyed our growing relationship. The bicycle would have been outgrown rather quickly.

John became all the things I wanted to become; good looking, athletic, strong, and funny. Whenever entertainment was needed, John's innocence provided many hours of laughs. However, in the early years, our age difference made a natural barrier that did not allow us to be playmates.

When we moved to a larger community and I entered high school, I had the privilege to coach John's junior league football and basketball teams through the local

YMCA. This started to make some new connections that brought us closer together. We had a respectable team in both sports and won many games. As John grew bigger and stronger, he started to catch up to me and we began playing together more as brothers. There were many times when he was yet another target of my explosive anger. Often, I could be seen chasing him. I don't ever remember catching him, making me believe that is the reason he was more athletic than I.

After high school, John worked at several jobs before entering college. He attended the same school as my parents, my oldest sister, and me. He joined the same fraternity, making another brotherly connection, and our friendship grew.

Tina came into John's life after college. She is a talented artist in ceramics. She enjoys working in her home studio where she keeps a close eye on her two boys. Tina and I enjoy lengthy discussions and debates on many topics. She has brought a joy to John's life that is appreciated by the whole family.

John has a unique way of making me stop and look at the major screw-ups in my life. Shortly after my second marriage engagement dissolved, we had an interesting discussion and argument of how my haphazard decisions and hasty retreats were hurting many people.

He enabled me to see my mistake more clearly, which helped me to temper my maturity and look much more carefully before making a major decision. Likewise, he has asked my advice in similar situations. I am sure glad that he is my brother and in my corner. It means much to me to say "thanks bro!"

When I needed to return to my parent's home in the midst of the battle with my loss of vision, my brothers and I got closer together. They became my main providers for transportation away from home. We started doing more of the fun things that brothers often times enjoy including water skiing, sailing, working on cars, and chasing around just for fun. The pain of the past was replaced with a brotherhood and relationship where all of us knew we could depend upon one another in a time of need.

Last, but not least, is the youngest of my siblings, my brother, Joel. Joel is the tallest of the gang and definitely not the one to face opposite the volleyball net. Out of all my siblings, Joel and I are the ones who look the most similar although I think he is the better looking between the two of us. He is often times seen and observed as the quiet one. I know differently. Joel has a special gift of being able to see the humor in anything and being able to crack a friendly joke that binds our family closer together. Sitting next to him during a family dinner includes a constant running commentary in response to every other conversation happening around the table. Although perhaps spoken tongue-in-cheek, he slips his entertaining and delightful humor into the conversation, keeping us all laughing.

He decided after high school that college was not the path for him at that time but perhaps later. He became employed and continues to works faithfully at doing his best. When I was preparing for one of my surgeries, scheduled to retain my sight, it was Joel who assisted me in physical conditioning. We would jog around the local park, as he served as my sighted guide. He was also one of my main drivers for roadtrips when I would provide pulpit supply during summer vacations. In fact on one particular trip, he commented that he could give the sermon as he had already heard the same sermon three previous weeks in a row. It was this kind of encouragement that turned me to preaching from the prescribed lectionary text and changing my message from Sunday to Sunday, regardless of the congregation.

Joel and I shared an interesting week of sailing on Lake Superior. We started out by flying north across the lake in forty-five minutes and then spent the next twelve hours making the return trip by sailboat, which began a week of sail camp. The rest of the time was spent in hot summer weather, helping to teach fifteen teenagers how to handle the tall rigs of the Great Lakes, even though our boat was only twenty-five feet long. By the end of the trip, shaggy from avoiding any razors for a week and desperately needing an hour long shower, we returned to port feeling much closer in relationship with each other. Events during the sail camp caused us to work as partners dealing with our crew of teenagers. We were able to understand each other's thoughts, as we responded to the campers' silly and inquisitive minds.

Joel had recently married Jill. Jill has become an important part of our family. Jill and I have shared some common life experiences, which helped me understand myself better and brought us closer. There are stories shared by the three of us that have drawn us together. Joel's and my relationship has allowed us the freedom to enable each other. Thanks bro!

As I alluded to earlier, I couldn't wait to move out of the house and go to college. It was another time in my life when I needed to put one foot in front of the other and begin a new step. When I got to college, I missed my family's daily routines and activities. Suddenly, it was all so different, awkward. I especially missed the family evening meals. I was not aware of how precious those times were to me. To fill the emptiness inside me, I started bringing friends home on Sunday evenings for Mom's good cooking. College was just a few miles away and did not provide Sunday evening meals. I was also employed by the college to pick up returning students at the local bus depot, which was on the way. So, just about every Sunday for the first two years, I would bring at least two other friends along for an early supper with my family. On the return trip, I would stop at the bus station for passengers and arrive back at campus with plenty of time for activities and study. My extended family grew.

In early March of my freshmen year, a tremendous ice storm swept the college campus, causing much damage. The school decided to close for student safety and sent people packing for home. Some could not make it to their homes, as the roads were bad or the distances too far. Guess where they ended up...Mom and Dad's house. The irony of the situation is that ultimately my roommate and I were stranded on campus and unable to return to town. I had made three previous trips to the bus station and a few other local stops to deliver students. Upon returning after my third run, it became my last. The storm was getting worse and, as I turned off the main road onto the campus driveway, to my horror I watched as the weight of the ice snapped all of the telephone/electric poles along the road, effectively trapping those of us remaining. A few feet farther down the driveway, in front of the bus I was driving, was a more critical emergency as four students were trapped in their car with a sparking, high voltage wire lying across the hood. With help from proper authorities, the wire was removed and the students spent the night with the rest of us, trapped.

It got cold that night. I remember feeling jealous of my friends who were warm and comfortable in front of the fireplace at my parent's house, while my roommate and I struggled to stay warm. We finally went to bed with as many clothes on as we could find, covered ourselves with all the blankets and sleeping bags we could get our hands on, and dreaded the thought of maybe having to leave the shelter of our cozy, little room. As we use to say; "dem the breaks!" After the ordeal was over and my roommate and I had spent a good portion of our time working to reopen the campus, I realized that the process was another important piece of learning how to put one foot in front of the other. There were many of us that worked together as a unit in order to make it work. Each one of us was just as important as the other, as we lent our skills and talents to clearing the campus so that students could return.

After my second year of college, my parents received the call to move again and Mom and Dad started packing. This time I would not move with them, as I was putting one foot in front of the other and beginning to establish my own roots. My self-confidence was getting stronger and my dependency upon my parents and family were changing. I would stay in that community as I had two years of college to go and was now feeling much more comfortable about my identity as a diabetic, a maturing adult, and a responsible person. I realized it was not going to be the same, not having Mom and Dad just a local phone call away, but the challenge was necessary for me to stand by myself. It was time for me to let go of those wonderful, helping, safe and secure hands, and step off by myself. To celebrate, all of my friends, all of whom had shared a Sunday supper, and many that had spent a night, threw a big party. The picnic table seemed to stretch the entire width of the backyard. Dad was in his glory at the controls of the barbecue and the mouth-watering aroma and blue haze of bratwurst smoke hung heavy. I think Mom and Dad enjoyed all of their extended family "kids." In fact, I know so. When my brother graduated from the same college, an even bigger party was to be had.

A special time for my family was vacations. Many times, we spent two weeks on the road seeing the sights. Some of my earliest memories are of camping along the shores of Lake Superior, which is one of the reasons I enjoy returning there now and sailing the crystal clear waters. Other times, at least two weeks were spent on the family homestead farm. It was Dad's place of origin however Mom's parents lived only two miles away. As kids, we found farming exciting for about two days. Then we needed a break and went to town to be with the other grandparents. Fond memories are kept of all of my cousins, uncles, and aunts being "down on the farm" during the summer. We baled hay, pulled weeds in the dreaded potato patch (which is why I probably like potatoes so much), and played in the creek.

I remember one muddy March when I was into model rocketry and all of the cousins were present for the big launch. Lift-off was perfect! The brightly colored slim-line rocket scorched high into the air. When the parachute deployed, so did the wind. The rocket started to drift far out of the drop zone and the chase was on. About a mile later, I recovered the rocket in a muddy cornfield having run the distance to keep it in sight. After recovering the rocket, I turned around and saw just about every cousin either stuck in the mud fighting to get their boots free from the strong suction or having abandoned their boots and returning to the road in stocking or bare feet. Somehow I knew I was going to get blamed for this mess. I did. But it also made for some good times and fond memories, special memories of how special my family has always been.

Another favorite place for my family to play was at summer Church Family Camp. For many years, Dad and Mom were the directors of the camp for the week. This was always an exciting time of swimming, hiking, canoeing, and playing volleyball, which was a biggy for my gang. The week spent worshipping and playing together with other families, saw the extended family grow. There are some folks that we met through family camp, with whom we still stay in touch. As we kids grew older, summer jobs became necessary and soon we were no longer going to family camp as the family unit we once were. It was sad when we stopped going for a few years. Eventually, we returned to family camp for a weeklong reunion at that same location. This time it was exciting and even more special, as new spouses and the next generation joined us. We went swimming, hiking, canoeing, and played lots of volleyball. It was just like old times yet it was also new times! It was the best of times!

My journey continued as I put one foot in front of the other, moving forward in my goals and dreams. When the day arrived to graduate from seminary, the first church pew behind the graduates, was filled to the brim with guess who…my family. There was not a dry eye in the row, as my dog guide Babe and I crossed the stage to the roar of applause and a standing ovation. I had made it! It was all because of their love, their support, and their ability to forgive and forget. I still marvel at why I should be so deserving of their gifts, free gifts, given with no strings attached.

Several weeks later, we celebrated in the service of ordination. When it came to the most important point in the worship service, the laying on of hands, it was my family that made the inner circle of people. It was important to me to have them there, my parents and siblings, to be the first ones to lay their hands on me for the blessing of the Holy Spirit. Mom had sung a solo, it was Dad's church, my friend and an uncle read scriptures, and our extended family danced in celebration. It was the best magical mystical dance of life that one could ever experience.

There is now one in my life who shares the center of existence along with God. She is my wife Sue. She is the one I wish to grow old with because she assures me there is always something better yet to come. Sue is my friend, my confidant, my partner, my driver, my sounding-board, my leaning-post, and inspiration. She brings me joy and laughter when I am down, she cries with me when I am hurt, and she dances with me when the music of our souls sings the loudest.

I like to tell the story of how Sue and I met. I was seeking employment in the wider church. Sue was the Co-Chair for a search committee of a congregation seeking a Pastor. While I was reading and studying information about her church, she and her Co-Chair were reading and studying information about me. After several telephone interviews and an on-site visit, the new congregation called me to be their pastor. My teasing bit is that I claimed that while one Co-Chair was looking for a Pastor... the other was looking for a husband. I made them both happy.

Actually, at the time of our meeting we had no idea, nor intentions, about the other. Both of us were working through relationships that had failed. We became good friends, sharing many different activities with other friends. After a period of time, we started to discover a special mutual feeling for each other. As time moved forward, we found ourselves spending more and more time together, and feeling empty when apart. We got engaged and married, one of the best day of our lives!

Sue is my pillar of strength to lean upon when the chicken part of my life is prevalent. She is my soaring partner when the eagle is dominant. When we are apart, I am not complete, there is something missing, I feel empty. When we are together, we compliment each other, we are a whole unit, and we join in that magical mystical dance called life. With Sue, God blesses our marriage, grants us satisfaction and fulfillment each and every day, and establishes our home in peace!

I believe all of life has a cause and effect relationship. We can only experience the heights of our successes and celebrations by knowing the depths of our pain, sorrow, and sufferings. My family has seen and experienced much, been through much, and continues to look forward with hope. When needed, we are there for each other. In times of pain we cry on each other's shoulders. In celebration we dance to our hearts content. We play, work, share in prayer and eat together, sing, worship, and most importantly, love each other, for who we have become. We are there, just as we have always been, to assist with helping hands as we each put one foot in front of the other, so that we might move forward and grow. I am constantly reminded of a favorite Bible passage I believe best explains the love of my family. It is found in Romans 5:3-4..."Let us also rejoice in our sufferings, because we know that suffering produces perseverance; perseverance produces character; and character produces hope." Thanks for the love of God that is given; given as a gift, a free gift, with no strings attached, from the members of my family!

REVELATION:
FROM CHICKEN TO EAGLE

"I do not trouble that infinity is greater than my power to comprehend or that but vaguely I discern the end toward which we journey through eternity.

Should I expect that God whom I adore limit himself to my intelligence? Or feel too humble since he GAVE me more capacity with each experience?

As on stern brazen portals, old and dull huge sculptured figures like dark shadows cross until a ray of sunlight shinning full to pristine radiance may one shade emboss, giving the dimness one bright memory?

So I caught flashes of God's brilliancy."

-- Annabel Gray

Chickens are afraid of their own shadows! Chickens scare easily! Chickens are so ugly, that they are cute enough only for the frying pan. Chickens are weird. Chickens do not trust themselves, and therefore have some major emotional problems. And why do I know this you are now asking yourself...because I am a chicken! I am as much a chicken as I am an eagle. I have discovered, through many of life's events, in order for me to be an eagle I have to remember I am also a chicken!

Life gives us mountaintops and valleys! Mountaintop experiences are where we are comfortable with ourselves, confident in who we are, strong in our personalities. Mountaintops are where we soar like the eagle and feel closest to our Creator God. Valleys are where we are afraid of ourselves, lacking inner self-confidence, fearful of what lies ahead. Valleys are filled with clouds of doubt, shadows of darkness, disappointments, and frustrations. Valleys are where chickens gather to hide from the eagle that soars overhead.

I believe everyone is part chicken. Each one of us has within us a part that is insecure, lacking in confidence, full of doubts and fears, and afraid of what lies ahead. Even trying to deny we don't have a chicken hiding someplace within still makes us a chicken, because we are trying to hide something or from something that scares us. Chickens do not like eagles. Eagles like chickens especially when they are hungry. Chickens are afraid of their own shadows because shadows make them vulnerable to the unknown, the uncertainty, the mystery of change which they cannot control. We have something we are afraid of, something that makes us vulnerable, something we wish to hide. Being a chicken makes us uncomfortable and when we are uncomfortable we begin to lack our inner confidence. So instead of soaring like an eagle, we run like a chicken.

In our roles as chickens, we hide things. Hiding things is a character defense to protect ourselves from being vulnerable. Some people think being vulnerable is a weakness, however it generally means we are afraid of some unknown and don't want anyone to know what it is; most of the time, we are not sure of what it is ourselves. This simply complicates our chicken status and pushes us farther into the darkness of being afraid. These fears, we attempt to keep hidden, are what make us chickens and haunt and scare us!

I like to consider myself an eagle, capable of soaring beyond the confines of any limitations, free to accomplish whatever it is I set out to do. However, I can only be an eagle by admitting part of me is a chicken. The height of my soaring can only be accomplished by identifying and understanding my limitations and boundaries, which shape and define my fears. In fact, my experiences with life have taught me that when I think I am mostly the eagle, I am really more of the chicken. Yet, when I am able to admit to myself that I am the chicken, afraid of what has been held back, I sprout new wings and soar like an eagle.

I am constantly changing between an eagle and a chicken; constantly going from mountaintop to valley. Through my experiences of losing my sight and learning how to live with diabetes, I am learning I am constantly bouncing between the mountaintop experiences of success and the valleys of failures and depression. When I find the balance between the eagle and the chicken, the mountaintop and the valley, I am most confident about myself. If I attempt to push myself beyond the mountaintop and fly a little higher than where eagles dare, I find myself crashing and burning and being more of a chicken. The quest of my journey is to find middle ground between chicken and eagle where my inner confidence resides, so I can be comfortable in trusting myself. This inner confidence is a marvelous tool that can do many wonderful things. It can cause us to soar high like an eagle with great inner personal achievements. It can also cause us to sometimes risk more than we have to offer, leaving us vulnerable. Then we crash and burn, we get hurt, and our inner confidence begins to dwindle, pushing us back toward being the chicken.

I have discovered my ministry exists somewhere between chicken and eagle; sharing with others my stories of being an eagle and a chicken; celebrating my accomplishments despite my failures; being strong because I can be vulnerable. My strongest moment is when I am most vulnerable to failure. Failure is success if something is learned. I believe my successful ability to adapt to the different adversities I encounter, which makes me an eagle, is because I am willing to be a chicken, vulnerable to the pain risk involves.

I have no special secret, no magical potion, or mystical way of surviving through life. I only have bumps, bruises, pains, and scars from adapting to the adverse and diverse experiences of my accomplishments and failures. It is these experiences that allow me to take yet another step forward in life, always seeking middle ground between chicken and eagle. There is always motion within, always something yet to accomplish, something yet to discover, something I am still seeking that brings me to middle ground. I feel I can never quit searching for this middle space. I do not quit; there are still too many mountaintops and valleys to experience.

Within me, and surrounding me, where both the eagle and chicken dwell, exists my faith in the mighty One, God, my Lord. This faith enables me to realize the chicken and experience the eagle. It is this faith that allows me to believe in my past experiences so I can adapt to the adversities I yet must face. It is this faith that allows me to risk what I am for what I will be moving forward in my journey.

Sometimes, in our experiences, we use the opportunity of chicken to gain attention for ourselves. Like the little child who throws a temper tantrum at the most opportune time and in the most inopportune place, we can use our feelings of fear as an attention getting scheme. This can be very effective in gaining attention, as it creates a false identity of who we are. In most cases, playing chicken for attention-getting purposes can also hurt us. Playing chicken as an attention-getting device means we are lacking in our own confidence, trying to create some sort of false confidence around us for others to see. Ultimately, we have to admit the whole scheme was just an act and confess to ourselves this is not who we really are. Playing chicken often happens when we are afraid; we try to surround ourselves in self-pity, hoping someone will rescue us from our crisis. We can create anything within our minds, that which we want to believe, that which we fear, that which is both real and unreal. Sometimes we create the fears, which are unreal simply to make ourselves the center of attention. Playing the chicken, rather than simply realizing sometimes we are chicken, ends up hurting ourselves because we are not being truthful. If we use something for inappropriate behavior, we get hurt because it is not real. This is when I believe people cannot find success in their failures because they fail to learn from the experience of which they are afraid.

Instead of using the role of chicken as an attention getting device, I like to believe I can use my realization of being a chicken to learn more about myself. My tool for discovering more about myself is writing, keeping a diary of experiences, a road map of where I have been in my life. This road map allows me the opportunity to reflect, remember, and respond to both the moments of chicken and eagle. I try to keep these three images in mind when I write; reflect, remember, and respond. It is a simple way of reflecting upon the experiences by remembering the important pieces and responding accordingly as I move forward. Writing helps me to identify some, if not most, of the markers along the way of who I am, why I am, and what I am. Sometimes things seem to happen so fast, I am left dazed and confused, overwhelmed with too many things to do, and not enough time to do them. Writing helps me settle down and regain control of myself, so I can continue forward and rediscover that sense of accomplishment that, for me, accompanies my journey forward. When I find myself struggling through experiences, of which I am unsure, I feel as though I am clinging in fear to the side of a mountain. I fear I will fall. Writing in my journal, with the images of "reflect, remember, and respond", helps me regain control. Now I can either let go because the bottom was only a step away from where I was clinging, or I find the necessary strength to keep holding on until such time I can continue to climb upward.

I believe our learning process of who we are is the task of collecting memories through events and understanding how those experiences fit together within ourselves. Each moment, each and every moment we encounter whether sleeping or awake, is part of us and part of the picture we paint for others to see. The journey then becomes the process of putting these events together and understanding what we are from within, so we can tell our stories. The eagle will see things the chicken never experiences. The chicken experiences things the eagle never sees. But somewhere in that space, the place between chicken and eagle is where we exist. It is how we work and play, learn and fail, love and suffer, that we define ourselves. Making discoveries through reflecting, remembering, and responding to my collection of stories helps me to grow and move on.

My life has been an ongoing process of learning, adapting, and expanding my boundaries. Living, with several disabilities, has been challenging, frustrating, and disappointing. These same experiences have also been rewarding, significant, and inspiring. My balance in life comes when the eagle and chicken are able to share equal space within and I am able to identify and admit to both. This is my inner place where I am at peace with myself and the world around me. This peace becomes involved not with the passing of time, but with the use of time, making the most out of the moments that I have been given. This inner peace makes me relaxed, allows me to enjoy what I am doing, and helps me find tremendous satisfaction and fulfillment.

Using the images of reflecting, remembering, and responding, helps me find my inner peace. By writing my experiences as part of the reflecting process, remembering the important pieces of those experiences, and looking for the appropriate way to respond, usually becomes part of a creative process through some of my favorite hobbies. Some of these hobbies include music, sailing, training dogs, and woodworking. All of these hobbies require working with my hands, which enables me to center my attention on who I am and what I am doing. The direct result of this focus creates the story of who I am and paints a picture of what I am. The products of these hobbies are pieces of the story I have to tell. When I work at any of these hobbies, I find myself using the time to focus on reflecting, remembering, and responding, after which time the writing in my journal becomes the marker of yet something more learned about myself. The final product includes the eagle and the chicken, the success and the failure, the past and the future.

Like everyone else, sometimes too many events pile up all at once and I find I need to disconnect and disappear for awhile. By using my process of reflect, remember, and respond, I am able to regain control of my environment, sort through and prioritize what is important to me, and respond appropriately so I do not feel threatened or frustrated. When these times occur, I find I am like a chicken running around without any real sense of purpose or direction. I can find myself and regain my inner peace by reflecting, remembering, and responding, while doing something simple like washing dishes, taking a bicycle ride with my wife, or going for a walk with my guide dog. Knowing when to and how to disconnect from my frustrations, my valleys and feelings of being a chicken, helps me sort through the many experiences leading to that moment of peace and finding the appropriate way to respond. It is through the images of reflect, remember, and respond, I find myself offering in prayer my need for the Lord to guide me through any difficulties so I might learn more about myself. Even if a particular fear or conflict appears to have no certain resolution, I can still find inner peace by offering in prayer my reflections, memories, and responses. Being able to identify my moments of conflict when the chicken is out of control through reflecting, remembering, and responding, has enabled me to let go of the conflict and move on with a better understanding of myself. So for me this process of prayer has helped my spiritual life grow, my faith increased, and my inner confidence become strong and secure in whom I am. I move closer to the middle space between chicken and eagle.

I like to use my images of reflect, remember, and respond, as part of my daily devotions. It gives me time to process what has been my journey, what I need to do for the day, and what things I might be looking for ahead. My time of reflection is looking back upon my experiences, the markers and stories of my journeys through life. Reflecting lifts out the significance of why these experiences are important to me. They tell me who I am. My reflection process functions both in good and bad experiences, realizing both eagle and chicken are equal halves to the same whole.

When I have identified the significant parts of my experiences for that particular moment, then I am ready to focus on the remembering. Remembering is the process of sifting through the what, when, where, why, and how of any given experience. Remembering the significant pieces to the experience begins to draw a parallel to the current events. Events are often similar but never the same. Remembering helps me to discern the little differences that make each experience unique and important. Drawing the similarities, the parallels, helps me to remember how I reacted. This gives me the foundation upon which to now stand when I make my newest and latest response.

Responding is using all of the available data available to any given moment's experience and seeking the appropriate path forward. The most classical example of this process is the memory and experience of touching a hot stove and learning not to repeat such action because of the pain felt when you get burned. Hopefully it takes only one time to learn this!

Most of us learn more by example and experience than by advice or explanation. A short poem has helped me to respond appropriately, realizing I learn so much more by experience and example rather than by advice or instruction. The verse reads:

"I would much rather see a sermon than hear one any day;

I would rather you walk with me than merely
point the way;
The eye is more the pupil than ever was the
ear;
Advice is often confusing, example always
clear."

(Author Unknown)

I had a life-changing experience that reminded me
just how much I am connected to the chicken side of my
fears and doubts. It also opened yet another door for me
to search within myself by reflecting, remembering, and
responding to the experience that somewhere, between
chicken and eagle, is this balance where I am and need
to be. While taking a required swimming test on a
camping trip with my family, I came close to drowning.
The experience frightened me, as it reminded me just
how fragile life is and how quickly it can be taken. I
discovered my ability to swim had suddenly changed
to an inability and was no longer something I could do
as well as before. It brought to my attention that I am
more vulnerable than sometimes I think I should be. I
am constantly changing, finding I am only as strong as
I am when I am at my weakest point.

I had some reservations about the swimming test
before I began, but had convinced myself I could do it

because I had done it many times before. I was aware of some new limitations, but managed as the eagle within me spoke, to convince the chicken part to ignore any of these signs. The winning argument within was if I wanted to sail during the week, I had to accomplish the swimming test. So it became no big deal to accomplish the required distances and time elapses to pass. The test included three elements; endurance, technique, and ability. Having been a swimmer for many years, I convinced myself there was no better time than the present to enter the water and accomplish the test. I began the test by swimming out to a floating raft about twenty yards from the dock. Arriving at the raft, I suddenly found myself very exhausted and fighting for oxygen to fill my hurting lungs. The reflect mode of my mind remembered "I don't float" and need to keep moving in the water to stay on the surface. Needing to finish this first leg of the test, I pushed off the raft and headed back towards shore and the dock.

About half way back to shore, I suddenly felt my body quit! I could not get my breath, my lungs screamed for oxygen, and my arms and legs just seem to thrash helplessly. Struggling wildly in the water and no longer moving forward, I rolled over onto my back to attempt to float, but I could feel my body sinking quickly, feet first. I rolled back over onto my stomach and gulped several quick breaths. I went under!

The first time I slipped beneath the surface, I was confident I could find the bottom, push off towards the shore with my feet and legs, and at least get into shallow water enough for me to stand. I had already admitted to myself I would fail the test. All I could think about at that moment was surviving, not panicking, and hoping I would find the beach in front of me. I never found the bottom of the lake.

I use to be a good swimmer. I have had training in swimming, training to be a lifeguard, and previous experiences of using swimming as a form of exercise and muscle conditioning. However, now attempting to fight my way back to the surface and beginning to realize I was in serious trouble, my previous swimming capabilities and experiences meant nothing! My head broke through the surface of the water and I once again flipped onto my back and attempted to float. I managed to gulp several breaths of air before I felt my body begin to slip downward, back towards the bottom of the lake. I cannot float, never have. When I stop moving I sink. And now my feet were becoming heavy anchors pulling me under. I managed to scream for help before my body went under for the second time.

I now experienced myself panicking and losing control. Fatigue was quickly overcoming my body and I could feel my arms and legs no longer wanting to function. Mentally, I fought with everything I knew I had and could find within to at least give me one more chance. I kept hoping I could find the bottom of the lake and I would either be able to stand and be safe or be able to push myself forward toward the nearby beach. My mind kept trying to convince me the beach was not far away and it should be just a matter of feet to be in the shallow waters where I could stand. Yet something felt like it was pulling me deeper into the water and farther away from the security I sought. I was afraid and scared of what would happen next. I was farther out than I had figured and I was in trouble. Physically my body had quit, leaving my mind to deal with what appeared to be the end. The chicken within me was giving up. I had to fight hard and desperately for the surface.

Something within me gave me one final push and when my head broke the surface, there were hands grabbing me and pulling me upward. My wife Sue, and the lifeguard Charla, were there to rescue! Working hard and fast, they got a flotation belt around me and headed for the beach. I was shaking with fear and having difficulty breathing because of hyperventilating. I was weak and useless, unable to help. I could feel a tremendous pressure closing in around me, making it hard for me to breathe.

We arrived in the shallow waters of the swimming area and I dropped my feet into the sand. Totally wasted from exhaustion, I collapsed in their arms and had to be lifted to a seat on the retaining wall along the beach. The seriousness of my experience was quickly taking hold and I was beginning to shake and cry with fear. Sue sat and held me, as I attempted to regain control of myself now that I was safely on dry land. It took me several long minutes of hard breathing to finally catch my breath and stop shaking from the fear. I was safe and lucky to still be alive. The tears increased as the reality of just how close to death I had been. My wife and father held me as I cried.

As I slowly recovered from my swimming experience, I began to use my "reflect, remember, and respond" model to help me process my journey. I am not afraid of death, just afraid of the process of dying. The more I live, the more I learn of what I can and cannot do. The more I learn about these limitations and boundaries, the better I am able to understand the space between eagle and chicken. I am always part of both within the same place. I cannot have the chicken without the eagle, nor the eagle without the chicken. It is important to remember both accomplishment and failure reside in partnership in order for us to understand and define what both are to us. Failure is success if something is learned. Reflecting, remembering, and responding is the process of failure becoming success, because we learn more and more about ourselves. That week of camp I got to sail, I just did it with a flotation device strapped to my body.

One of my greatest fears as a chicken is loneliness. I believe loneliness is the separation from other relationships. My fear of loneliness is an emptiness that overwhelms me and fills me with doubts, frustrations, and failures. The chicken within me confines me to a small, narrow reality that leaves me isolated and non-accepting of any change.

I believe we choose loneliness, it does not choose us. We choose to live in fear and frustration, failure and disappointment; it does not choose us. We choose to separate ourselves from relationships and place ourselves in isolation.

The time when I am the most chicken is when I choose to separate myself from other relationships. I find the pain of separation most severe because I isolate myself from those around me who care for me. Once caught in this isolation, I find myself extremely vulnerable to idleness and evil because it becomes an easy escape. Easy escapes are painful because it means that like a chicken, I am running away from something and not willing to face reality. Failure to face reality causes emotional pain. Emotional pain comes from within and is controlled by nobody else but myself. I have no one to blame but me. There is nothing else at fault but what I have done to myself in my isolation and separation from other relationships.

Whether we are chickens or eagles, we have to make choices. We can choose good over evil, life over death. We must come to an understanding of our choices and then decide which course and direction we will choose; good, evil, life, or death.

I believe many people become consumed by the isolation of evil, choosing to separate them from the love of God. They abandon their faith and become overwhelmed by doubts and fears. They quickly feel trapped and without choices and look for easy escapes. Often, this feeling of isolation leads to self-pity, playing the role of the victim and the chicken. I believe one who is filled with self-pity has abandoned all hope of self-confidence and is afraid to look for available choices. Failure to look for choices becomes the loss of hope within and opens the door for sin to take hold. I believe sin is the separation of self from the hope of God in our daily active lives. We have to choose to sin, to separate ourselves from our relationship with God, to allow evil to overcome. When a person begins to slide into the emotional state of depression and self-pity, it becomes easy to abandon faith and look for easy escapes. The escapes become painful feelings of isolation and loneliness leading to unfortunate, uncompromising situations.

When I have chosen to separate myself from the love of God, I have found myself in difficult, uncompromising positions. I have found my own choices force me into places where I discover I have fewer and fewer options. Soon the choices become so limiting it appears the only avenues are wrong paths that take me farther and farther away from my understandings of God's love. I have learned far too many times that once I have made a wrong decision, it becomes more difficult to make the right one.

If you consider it is easier to smile than frown, choosing good over evil is easier, if we allow our faith to guide our choices. Chickens do not like to risk anything. Eagles are aware there are risks involved with soaring. The chicken panics in the presence of pain. The eagle tries again regardless of the pain. If we are not willing to experience the pain of moving forward, then the evil of isolation catches us and becomes more painful.

It has been my experience, once pain has a grip on my ability to make choices, it becomes a vicious emotional cycle that is hard to change. Emotional pain of self-pity cannot be changed by any magical prescription or wand waving, but by deciding to and starting with making new choices. These choices are found in new understandings of self, based on experiences through reflecting, remembering, and responding. This process of reflecting, remembering, and responding, allows me the opportunity to explore the depth of the pain, discover the choices within, and respond in an appropriate manner as to move away from the self-pity and role as a victim.

Another way in which I have experienced the chicken side of me has been through the act of discrimination. Discrimination limits my participation in some activities. Discrimination occurs when someone or something else makes choices for me. Discrimination is painful, whether it involves handicaps and disabilities, race and nationalities, religious beliefs, sexual orientation, or difference of language. Discrimination is an emotional pain because it occurs when someone fails to understand or be understanding of someone else's situation. Discrimination becomes a fear, because the perceived sense of lost control causes a feeling of isolation and separation. The pain of discrimination causes the loss of communication, creates misunderstandings, and leads to a deeper and harder feeling of isolation.

It has been my experience when someone discriminates against me, both of us suffer. I experience an emotional pain from the act of discrimination that is difficult to overcome. My sense of trust in the relationship is damaged and the vulnerability of separation becomes threatening. I have to struggle to make the right choices to change the act of discrimination, so I can control my destination, not be controlled by the act itself. It is not easy and often quite painful.

The pain I suffer from a discriminating act is always different. Just when I think I have overcome the pain with a new understanding of myself, another situation of discrimination occurs, and the pain quickly returns. If I choose the easy escape, perhaps not deal with the discrimination, the pain becomes depression and frustration and grows within. If I struggle to reflect, remember, and respond, new understanding of self and situation eases the pain.

Disabilities and handicaps can be isolating and lonely. Disabilities and handicaps can be painful. Because disabilities are things we "cannot do" and handicaps are things we "do not want to do," we can experience two, sometimes immovable, forces pushing against each other. This too, is painful.

I know when I hurt, I can become very defensive. When someone hurts my feelings, I know many times I want to hurt them back. I want them to feel what I am feeling. Like chickens that go crazy and will attack their own at the sight of blood, when I am hurt I often feel the one who hurt me should also hurt. Through many and different life experiences, I have learned this is inappropriate behavior. By using my model of reflect, remember, and respond, I realize it is inappropriate behavior because it strengthens the wall that separates the relationship and causes more pain. This gives evil a greater opportunity to take over. When my pain threshold is breached, I become very angry. I feel isolated and out of control, usually losing my temper very quickly. I have had to learn through reflecting, remembering, and responding to seek out the right and good choices. Instead of hurting someone or something with an inappropriate behavior, I can strengthen the relationship with appropriate behavior.

I must work constantly on controlling my anger and responses when I am hurt. I have learned through the experience of my blindness there is always going to be the existence of pain because of discrimination. I have to constantly struggle with and learn from these experiences, because my blindness will never change. I struggle constantly not being able to see my family, drive a car whenever I desire, or read a book without adaptive equipment. When I feel the fangs of discrimination sinking their painful presence into my life, I need to remind myself I still have choices. I must learn to adapt and work through these moments of discrimination, seeking out the appropriate behavior so I can return to the creative tension that lies somewhere between the chicken and the eagle. To allow the discrimination to control me is to act inappropriately and stay a chicken. To over power the discrimination pushes me towards the outer limits of the eagle. Somewhere in between is where I must choose to be.

I believe that I, like everyone else, have been given the opportunity to respond appropriately. I have choices. I can choose good over evil. If I allow evil to overcome, I respond inappropriately and lose myself to separation and isolation. If I choose good because I am able to reflect, remember, and respond, I gain new understanding of self and discover yet another way to use my blindness creatively. I return to the middle space between chicken and the eagle.

As a chicken, I have experiences that bring me dangerously close to the dark, doubting side of my faith. I experience feelings of being isolated and alone, because I fear being different. My reality is *I am different!* I function differently, I respond differently, I have to think differently, because of the disabilities. I hate my fear of being different. If I allow this fear to control and make choices for me, I discover I abandon my belief in the Holy Spirit and my faith suffers greatly. I begin to doubt everything I do and isolate myself. I wrap myself in self-pity and no one wants to be around me. Quickly I find myself in uncompromising positions and caught in the midst of bad choices. It is within these moments I must struggle with my issues through reflecting, remembering, and responding, to allow my faith in the Holy Spirit to return to the middle space between the chicken and the eagle. The more I let this separation control me, the greater my depression and self-pity. Though I may be in great pain, I am always discovering I have choices; good choices and bad choices; appropriate choices and inappropriate choices. This is what gives me the inner strength to allow my faith in the Holy Spirit to move on.

The community of faith has always been my chicken-house source of strength and new understanding. I am my strongest in the company of other chickens, because we share those precious moments of vulnerability and weakness. My model of reflecting, remembering, and responding, has allowed me to tag my best experiences as those which have been within the community of faith. From the experience of losing my sight and becoming totally blind, to the experience of almost drowning, my worse moments have been my best moments because of the community of faith surrounding me. My family within the community of faith has always reminded me I do have choices and alternatives. Through this faith community, I continually learn everyone has fears and doubts, feelings of isolation and separation. Together as chickens, I have learn we can do much more than just one eagle, although it is also important to be an eagle and attempt things on our own. This is what keeps us in the creative, middle space between the chicken and the eagle.

I learned through my experiences how to depend upon my faith and, in many relationships, how to adapt to the adversities of life. There are always fears and doubts. I must make appropriate choices in order to move on and seek the middle space between chicken and eagle. When I felt I was failing and surrendering to the wrong choice of self-pity, it was my faith experiences that helped me understand myself and make the appropriate choices. Faith is not a constant, but an always-changing presence that grows no matter what the influence, which keeps it developing and moving.

It is my choice of appropriate behavior that has allowed my faith story to grow and become useful through the tools of my sense of humor. This humor has developed through the common thread experience with pain and suffering. The middle space between chicken and eagle is where my humor dwells. It has become a tool that enables me to make my failures successes, by looking and laughing at myself. I have no other person to blame for my choices but myself. I can choose to be humorous about my mistakes and offer my failures as gifts, just as easily as I can dump my pain and isolation behind me. I can make appropriate choices in bad situations and find myself growing, rather than making inappropriate choices and losing control to self-pity. It is my sense of humor that does not allow me to be my own victim, but to be the one searching for both the chicken and the eagle.

Because of my humor, I have become successful at adapting to the adversities of my life. I must make choices that are appropriate for me with an understanding there are certain boundaries in which I must function. When I extend myself beyond those limits, I am in pain. I suffer the consequences of my mistakes. When I am able to define the place or reason why I have strayed or gone beyond my limits, I learn by experience not to do it again. The eagle disappears and the chicken reappears. Failure becomes success, if something is learned.

When I began to discover the unique journey I was having between the chicken and the eagle, I started to journal my process of reflecting, remembering, and responding. As I expressed myself, the more I realized about myself. The more I realized, the more I understood about being an eagle or a chicken. As I understood the difference, the better I felt about myself. The better I felt about myself, the more others wanted to be around me and I began to understand this middle space between chicken and eagle. There are still moments and always will be moments of uncontrollable fears and doubts. The chicken is always dwelling somewhere close within.

Even when I soar like an eagle, there will be moments of hesitancy when the chicken appears. This is the creative middle space between the two; the chicken and the eagle that I seek.

Within these pages I have attempted to share with you some of the joy and pain I have experienced. I believe I am constantly discovering that God's will and purpose for me is to help others understand their pain and suffering that they might know the joy and celebration. I believe my model of reflecting, remembering, and responding can make our failures moments of success by learning from our choices. I believe my success is within my ability to adapt to the different adversities I encounter because of my faith in God, the humor in myself, and the constant search for the middle space between chicken and eagle. I believe this search is never alone, that the presence of the Holy Spirit is there with us as we experience success and failure. There are other chickens around us, other eagles, too. I believe everyone can do the same thing, adapt to their adversities by learning to reflect, remember, and respond to the appropriate choices.

I offer to you my story and my journey in searching for the middle space between chicken and eagle. Where this space exists for you is for you to discover. I have simply offered to you a possible tool to help you find your own middle space, or at least find the space where you want to exist. This is neither the complete story nor the total "do-it- yourself" type of tool. If all were told, there would be no end. Yet as I draw to the end of this part of my story, it is only the beginning. My own search continues. I offer to you the opportunity to reflect, remember, and respond. As you finish reading my story and begin your own story, begin to write your thoughts, feelings, and expressions of faith, which are your experiences. I believe if you begin such as I did, you will discover a unique statement of who you are and what you have to offer. I believe within that story, what you offer and share with others, comes the middle space between chicken and eagle.

Endings lead to new beginnings. In these past pages I have shared with you an insight of who I am and my faith journey. Following is my "statement of ministry," a document in process I share with others when seeking new opportunities for employment. I felt it was necessary and important to include it within the pages of this book; it is where I started on my own search for that creative middle space. I believe my life's journey is a ministry of connecting one relationship to another and attempting to understand the middle space I encounter.

"I believe in one unifying God who is made known to us through Jesus Christ, God's only Son, and sustained as a living presence in our daily lives by the Holy Spirit. We are the living essence of God's presence justified by our baptism into God's grace through our Lord and Savior Jesus Christ.

I believe that God is the everlasting presence of hope, the provider of grace, mercy, and love. I believe that God is a forgiving God who understands all mysteries of life of which we know very little yet are willing to trust in the One who has made us. I believe that God's mercy and love belong to all people regardless of their sins.

I believe that by our baptism we experience the ability to be Christ-like in our lives, seeking to establish peace, justice, and truth in all that we are and do. I believe that through Christ Jesus, his death on the cross, and his resurrection into glory that we, too, died in Christ so that we might be born anew into the presence of the Holy Spirit. It is in this act of salvation that we experience the fullest of life, the greatest potential of our gifts, and the purposes for which we have been given time on this earth. I believe that our entry into God's promised kingdom of eternal life, which has no end, is only possible through Christ Jesus.

I believe that as Christians we are on a spiritual journey that includes the sharing of our experiences and relationships with one another. I believe that it is in sharing of our experiences that we learn the fullness of life as witnessed through our many gifts. In sharing our gifts, we come to know that the Holy Spirit of God works in us and through us so that we might understand our own relationship with God and with each other.

I believe in you and me, that all people are brothers and sisters, who are called to proclaim the gospel to the entire world and resist the powers of evil. We are empowered by the inspired words of God as interpreted and written by those chosen people throughout time and recorded in the Bible. I believe that the Bible calls us to struggle with the issues of the day and to work with and through our communities that we may find new understandings of how God works in us and through us. I believe that by our baptism we have all been baptized into the ministry and need to minister to each other. We are called to be witnesses to the Bible through our daily prayers and by worshipping within our chosen spiritual community.

My journey as a Christian has taken me through many experiences which have allowed me to examine my faith in the love of my Christian family, the Church, and the larger world around me. It has allowed me the freedom to explore the many facets of God's purpose for my life and to share them with others so that they, too, may come to know God's will. Although there have been times when doubt and confusion have led me to disagree with and attempt to leave the Church, God's presence within has helped me understand the promise of love and I return. I believe that all of life meets its greatest satisfaction and fulfillment within the local Church community, the body of Christ interacting in relationship with each other.

Through the loss of my own physical vision I have been given a gift of insight which enables me to see beyond and within at the beauty found in the gifts of others. I believe that a Christ-centered community works in concert with each other through their gifts expressing God's will for a better community. I believe that I have exchanged my liability of being blind into an asset of guiding people to look at themselves. I believe that it is part of God's will that we use our disabilities and handicaps as teaching tools to better understand that all have a unique purpose within their life to share with others. The miracle of God's healing presence is to witness to the limits of our human situation and discover ways of adapting so that we might grow and become better people of God. As a minister of the gospel I see myself as a prophetic preacher, pastoral counselor, spiritual director, role model, and friend to all. As a prophetic preacher, I am called to blend the Biblical stories and their interpretations with the contemporary issues of the community I serve. The Bible enables us to accept the cost and joy of discipleship by addressing these issues through moments of teaching using the experiences of our relationships as God given tools. I believe that my preaching must enable each listener to weigh the implications of our actions and responses and then struggle with their own questions of faith, which calls us to risk everything for God's sake. I believe that through my gift of preaching that all are called to the Christ-centered community and to bind in covenant; faithful people of all ages, tongues, and races. I believe this is the covenant given to us as shared with Moses and has withstood the test of all times.

As a pastoral counselor I believe I am called to serve anyone who reaches out in need regardless of their perceived place in life. I am called to help people understand their experiences of pain, grief, joy, and celebration. I feel that it is my responsibility to guide them into a Christ-centered lifestyle as their friend and confidante. As a Pastor I am called to help counsel others to seek Jesus Christ as their Lord and Savior and as one who will never fail them in their relationship of faithfulness.

As a spiritual director I believe it is my responsibility to help others develop their personal relationship with Christ. I believe that it is important to use the tools of the Bible and my own experiences to demonstrate how life becomes enriched and rewarding through the practice of daily prayers and regular worship participation. I feel that I am called to assist people in their spiritual journeys to witness to their experiences with the Lord Jesus Christ. I feel that it is important to help them share their faith stories in dialogue with others, which makes us all better individuals in the Christ-centered community.

As an experiencing theologian I believe that as a role model I must constantly seek to bring the Bible to life, to help give it new meaning, and fuller understanding for daily living. I believe that it is my responsibility to ask the interpretive, analytic, imaginative, and responsive questions of our faith as they pertain to the living Christian community. As a role model I believe it is my responsibility to seek practical applications of faith as it is experienced in our daily lives. As an "experi-theologian" I believe it is my calling to assist people in interpreting and understanding their everyday experiences of faith and then witnessing these stories within the presence of the worshipping community.

I believe in you and me and that by our baptism we are called to minister to each other. I believe that each one of us, whether young or old, healthy or disabled, rich or poor, has a gift from God to teach and to learn from each other. I believe that we can together walk through our journey with Christ until we come to the day when we shall experience the fulfillment of God's promise of eternal life and everlasting peace in that kingdom which has no end. I believe in you and me as the embodiment of God's will to make this world a better place to live. I believe in you and me, in balloons and puppy dogs, in children and grandparents, in joy and in sorrow, in life and in death, in yesterday, today and tomorrow!"

I trust and pray, as you search for the middle space between your chicken and eagle, you will grow. As you grow, I hope you will share. As you share, I trust you will find that creative space between chicken and eagle where many of us are and want to exist. And so, until then, when then is now, now is when, when then is now... I think I will go and sail a sailboat and pray for your safe journey "From Eagle to Chicken and Back."

LaVergne, TN USA
01 October 2009
159575LV00001B/4/P